50 YEARS OF BASKETBALL

PRENTICE-HALL INTERNATIONAL, INC., *London*
PRENTICE-HALL OF AUSTRALIA, PTY. LTD., *Sydney*
PRENTICE-HALL OF CANADA, LTD., *Toronto*
PRENTICE-HALL OF INDIA PRIVATE LTD., *New Delhi*
PRENTICE-HALL OF JAPAN, INC., *Tokyo*

50 YEARS OF BASKETBALL

JOE LAPCHICK

PRENTICE-HALL, INC., Englewood Cliffs, N.J.

© 1968 by
PRENTICE-HALL, INC.
Englewood Cliffs, N.J.

Current printing (last digit):

10 9 8 7 6 5 4 3 2 1

Library of Congress Catalog Card Number: 68–31767
Printed in the United States of America

to

The Original New York Celtics

"my teammates"

to whom I am ever grateful for teaching me how to play the game

and to

the players of St. John's University

and

The New York Knickerbockers

who helped me carry out the Celtic principles in my teaching

FOREWORD

Nat Holman

Joe Lapchick has been widely praised as a coach who knew what he wanted and knew how to get things done. He ran a tight ship! He knew when to be patient and when to be impatient; when to be tough and when to be gentle; when to be corny and when to be direct. His "down-to-earthness," his fairness, his sympathetic understanding of his player's problems, the charm that he wore not as an occasional cloak but as his everyday garment—these things made him the ideal coach for all seasons.

In 1966, as a well earned climax to a magnificent career, Joe was elected to basketball's Hall of Fame, to take his place among the great luminaries of the sport. His name is now enshrined among the immortals. Around the firesides and in the gymnasiums across the country, now and in the future, wherever basketball talent is recognized and class extolled, his name and his achievements will be recalled by countless generations unborn. No greater epic could have been written into the pages of basketball history.

My personal reason for holding him in high esteem is that I believe the mark of greatness in this man is the fact that despite the position he has achieved in the game of basketball, he never lost the humility which characterized him from his earliest days with the Original Celtics.

Down through the years he put so much into bringing his goals to reality—talent, toil, time. Star as a player of the World Champions Original Celtics, Coach of St. John's University and the New York Knicker-bockers, lecturer at basketball clinics, Hall of Famer—these are some of the high points over the years, all tangible matters of record. Then, too, there are high points which are unlisted in record books. He was a "winner of boys" in the best meaning of the term, as well as "winner of games," all within the spirit of the rules of fair play.

In all sports, some men have a magnetism which sets them apart from their fellows. Such a man is Joe. To friends, basketball fans, coaches, players, officials, writers, he has made the long trip victoriously with whistles blowing, cameras clicking, and the presses rolling. We have climbed the hill together in this great American game, and as we come to the end of these experiences they melt into a mosaic of beauty like the rays of the sun and the clouds of a beautiful sunset. In retrospect and prospect . . .

Milestones of old memories
Along sweet friendship way,
Oh, how they brighten up the past
And cheer the coming day.

INTRODUCTION

Clair Bee

Joe Lapchick was born on April 12, 1900, in Yonkers, New York. He began to play basketball in 1912 with amateur teams in his hometown and was active in the sport during every season of the next fifty years and more as player or coach until his retirement from St. John's University in 1965.

Joe's father was born in 1877 in Prague, Czechoslovakia. He came to America when he was twelve years old and held a succession of jobs as coal miner, hat finisher, trolley motorman, and eventually policeman. Joe's mother was born in 1883 in Haverstraw, N. Y. His parents were married in 1899, and Joe was the first born. Two brothers and four sisters followed—Ed, Bill, Anne, Emily, Frances, and Florence. The family lived in a part of Yonkers called the "Hollow," where all Slavic families settled. Times were hard, and the Lapchick family had to struggle to make ends meet.

Finishing grammar school in 1915, Joe immediately began looking for work to help with the family expenses. His first job was with the Ward Leonard Electric Company in Bronxville. His earnings were small, but he added to the total by working as a caddie on weekends. One of the first golfers Joe met was Fred Merkle, who earned lasting fame for failing to touch second base in a play which cost the New York Giants a National League pennant. Among other baseball stars for whom Joe caddied was the great pitcher, Christy Mathewson.

Joe carried clubs for Grantland Rice, the beloved sportswriter, and for many golfing greats, including Jim Ray, Harry Vardon, and Francis

Ouimet. From the theatrical world he packed bags for Al Jolson, Douglas Fairbanks, Sr., and Sam Harris.

Joe's first sports interests were baseball and golf. Caddying had left its mark, and the deeds of the men for whom he caddied fired his imagination. His height soon attracted the attention of basketball enthusiasts, however, and they interested him in the amateur hoop game. Pushing 6–3, Joe was taller and stronger than his teammates, and it was natural that he should be the "big man" and play center. When he found that he could earn "as much as three dollars" for playing in a single game of basketball, he became aware of the financial possibilities of the game. (Three dollars was a lot of money in those days.)

The name and fame of the Big Kid from Yonkers spread, and he was in great demand. It was not unusual for Joe to play with four different teams in four different leagues. Joe could not play in all the games, of course, but he solved that problem by playing for the team which paid the highest dollar. The big kid now became aware of his potential as a basketball star. He was tall, he could run, and he was improving with every game he played.

Frequently he was hired by teams to play against the Celtics, even though he did not play with a particular team more than the one game. It was a frightening but inspiring experience for the tall, ungainly kid. The Celtics were the greatest team in the world, and Joe was called upon to face Horse Haggerty, the Shamrock's formidable big man. Haggerty stood 6–4 and weighed 240 pounds. And, in Horse's book, there were no gates of mercy for anyone!

For days after a game against Horse, the ribs and arms of his opponents bore mute but vivid testimony to his strength and ruthlessness. Joe always came in second in these meetings with Haggerty, but they strengthened his resolve to reach the top. Now he realized that height and speed were not enough; he could never really be great until he overcame the awkwardness that had accompanied his growth in height. There were no coaches in those days, so Joe became his own taskmaster. After work and every night when he was not playing, he would practice footwork—starts, stops, sprints, change-of-direction, and pivoting. He made slow but steady progress.

Then, in 1923, the Celtics asked him to join up with them. Joe was overjoyed by his incredible good fortune; jubilant, walking on air. He came down to earth with a bang in his very first game as a "Shamrock." He was a newcomer, the youngest Celtic, and therefore the target of criticsm.

Joe realized this was part of his Celtic training. Basketball was more than a game to these hardbitten pros. It was a religion! The abuse was hard to take, but there were compensations—good pay, fun, excitement, travel, the priceless privilege of rubbing shoulders with the greatest basketball players in the world, and the opportunity to join them in their grim dedication to the game they loved.

Joe's basketball education continued relentlessly. During meals, after the games, traveling (the Celtics always traveled first class, usually by Pullman); wherever it might be, the Celtics talked about one thing and one thing only—basketball!

It was inevitable that Joe should be imbued with the same physical fortitude, mental toughness and savage pride which gripped every man who wore a "Shamrock" shirt. Soon Joe was a star in his own right and talking the Celtic language. It was the Celtics against the world and Joe loved it.

The Celtics were so good that they ran away with every league in which they played. The league moguls had to do something, so they broke up the Celtics. However, three Shamrocks playing together were still too good for any league they entered. They won three more championships and the league was in trouble once more. When the depression arrived, the Celtics reorganized, became a road touring team, and were truly the original ambassadors of the sport. They played college and independent teams, anyone, anyplace where they could earn a dollar. Traveling in 7-passenger sedans, they played in church basements and skating rinks, on YMCA courts, in armories and in high schools, often facing antagonistic fans and hometown officials. And they won them all, or practically all.

Joe was married to Elizabeth Sarubbi in 1931, with Nat Holman as his best man. In 1946, Joe and Nat reversed roles. Joe became best man when Nat was married.

In 1936, Joe was offered the coaching position at St. John's University. He accepted the appointment and enjoyed great success in college ranks. This first tenure at the Vincentian Fathers school is known as the "Tourney Era." Joe's 1943 and 1944 squads won the National Invitational Tournament. In the eleven years between 1936 and 1947, the St. John's Indians were invited to the NIT, oldest of the postseason tournaments, seven times.

In 1946, Max Kase (sports editor of the New York *Journal* at that time) and a number of arena operators organized a new league on a national basis with Mr. Maurice Podoloff as the first president. At the end of the first year it was apparent that the venture would be successful, and Ned Irish, then Vice-President of Madison Square Garden and later President, offered the Knickerbocker coaching job to Joe.

Joe accepted and entered into ten of the most hectic coaching years of his life. The "win" pressure, travel problems, long hours, the need for a good "big" man, and the long schedule all added up to the possibility of a physical breakdown. Joe was ready to quit when, in 1956, he was again offered the St. John's job. He was glad to accept.

During his nine years as Knickerbocker pilot, Joe's teams never missed the playoffs, and he directed the Knicks to the final round of basketball's professional world series three times. Joe holds the honor of being the only professional coach who never had a losing season.

Joe's 1954 Knickerbocker team could have been termed the "Team of Coaches." Eight members of the team became coaches after their playing careers ended—Vince Boryla, Knickerbockers; Carl Braun, Knickerbockers; Harry Gallatin, St. Louis Hawks and Knickerbockers; Dick McGuire, Detroit Pistons and Knickerbockers; Fred Shaus, Los Angeles; Jim Baechtold, Eastern Kentucky; Al McGuire, Marquette University; and William H. van Breda Kolff, Princeton University.

The nine years leading up to Joe's retirement in 1965 were undoubtedly the most enjoyable of his life. St. John's had a fine new gymnasium, and Joe was respected by everyone, administration and students. The "win" pressure, the travel, and the long schedule were relegated to the past, and Joe could now enjoy the good life. Good life it was! He was home every night and in daily touch with his old pals and the sportswriters to whom he had endeared himself through the years.

His St. John's teams were winning and kept right on winning right up to 1965 when the Redmen repeated their 1959 feat of winning the Holiday Festival and the NIT championship to present Joe with Madison Square Garden's second "grand slam." St. John's had won back-to-back NIT titles in 1943 and 1944 and had also won in 1959. The 1965 championship established Joe as the only coach to win the NIT title four times.

In 1966, Joe was elected to the Naismith Hall of Fame at Springfield College. This was his second induction into the Hall of Fame. His first was as a member of the Original Celtics team and the second as a professional player of all times.

Joe treasures the memory of his basketball accomplishments, but the old pro's greatest pride and joy is his family. Mrs. Lapchick, "Bobbie," has stood beside him through all the successes, ups-and-downs, trials, tribulations, and heartbreaks of coaching, a devoted and understanding wife and partner.

Joe, Jr., was graduated from the United States Military Academy and served five years as a bomber pilot. Resigning from the service after his term of duty, young Joe attended the University of New Hampshire and received his M.A. He then won a fellowship to Harvard and earned his doctorate in administrative education. He is now superintendent of schools in Aspen, Colorado.

Barbara Jane won a scholarship to Barnard and was graduated summa cum laude. She is married to Dr. Ray Brown, and they are now living in

Uganda, East Africa. There, Barbara Jane is a national leader in the showing of African art and was chiefly responsible for the development of that country's national art gallery.

Richard, the youngest child, is majoring in political science at St. John's University and is on the dean's list.

Basketball has been Joe's life and his life has been basketball. His concepts of the way the game should be played, his basketball philosophies, principles, and teaching methods are contained in the pages of this book. The Celtic influence is always in the background. With guts and supreme confidence in one another, the Celtics wore their "Shamrocks" proudly and placed a fierce premium on their deeds.

Joe never lost his loyalty to his Celtic teammates, and he carried their desire and spirit into his coaching. Any reader, young or old, basketball player, coach, or fan will find this book filled with straight-from-the-shoulder Celtic basketball—the kind of basketball Joe and his Celtic teammates played and loved.

Clair Bee

CONTENTS

PART TWO

PART THREE

PART FOUR

LEGEND

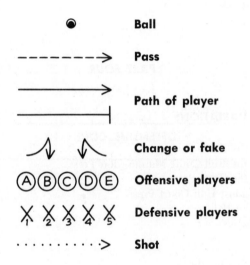

Symbol	Meaning
●	Ball
- - - - - - ->	Pass
——————>	Path of player
———————⊣	
⋏ ⋏	Change or fake
Ⓐ Ⓑ Ⓒ Ⓓ Ⓔ	Offensive players
X X X X X 1 2 3 4 5	Defensive players
· · · · · · · ·>	Shot

CHARTS

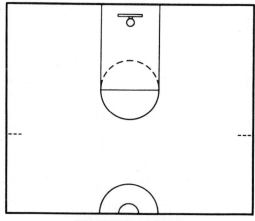

OFFENSIVE COURT

DEFENSIVE COURT

PART ONE

CHAPTER 1

GROWING UP
WITH THE GAME

H ALF A CENTURY is a long time and a man's memory often tricks him. Yet, when almost every minute and every incident of every day of those fifty years has been engaged in some manner with the thing to which the man has dedicated his life, he develops a time sequence which brings everything associated with it into sharp focus.

So it is with my fifty years of basketball. And, whether consciously or unconsciously, almost everything that I have seen or experienced in the game is as clear today as it was the day it happened. I have watched basketball struggle out of barns, church basements, and skating rinks where a "crowd" of a hundred spectators was a SRO affair, to modern stadiums built expressly for the game with comfortable seating to accommodate up to 20,000 spectators.

The terms "net game" and "cage game" developed from band-box courts which were enclosed with fish nets or chicken wire. There were no backboards, the baskets extended through the nets and the courts were so poorly lighted you could scarcely see the rings. Most of the courts were used for dancing before the game, between the halves, and after the game was over. They were so highly waxed that dancers often fell down even while holding on to their partners. Basketball players risked a broken leg whenever they tried to run.

Some courts were so small that local rules often restricted players to one bounce or dribble. Then he was required to shoot or pass the ball. In public school courts the backboards were flush with the wall. Kids in those days would actually run up the wall and lay the ball in the basket to protect themselves from their opponents.

It must be realized that basketball in the 20's was a young sport and not accepted by sportswriters. Basketball players wore short pants, and that made it a soft game in the eyes of the writers. This was also true of tennis. Basketball was slow to attract attention because playing conditions were ridiculous. In many halls the floors were never cleaned, and splinters of rare size would find their way into your rump.

Potbellied stoves were part of this type of court. The baskets were fastened flush against the walls. In Brooklyn, the city of churches, there was always a court of some sort. The problem was that there would be half a dozen pillars on the playing court, which would be used as a post to run your man into. This was the source of the name "post" play.

Present-day players can't possibly imagine the thickness of smoke in those halls. Everybody smoked, and if they did not like you, they would flick the butts right at you as you were charging in for a score. Players in this era had enough stitches in their faces and arms for a tailor to sew a suit of clothes. However, injured or not, if you didn't play, you didn't get paid. It was as simple as that.

Today's courts are brilliantly lighted, with gleaming floors, and there is plenty of running space all around the court and under and behind the 4' by 6' glass backboards. Practically all arenas are air-conditioned, and the spectators and fans are located far enough away from the courts to protect players from cigarette butts. Present-day arenas are policed, and even if they were not, the spirit of sportsmanship today is such that, instead of abusing players, the hometown fans are quick to appreciate and applaud visitors' good play.

When I think of backboards, I remember the first game I saw in the NBA. I was scouting for the Knicks, and the opposing teams were the Boston Celtics and the Chicago Stags. Just before concluding the pregame warmups at the Boston Arena, Chuck Connors went up for a lay-up and grabbed the rim of the hoop. *Crash!* The glass backboard shattered into hundreds of pieces.

What an opening for the late and gracious Walter Brown, President of the Boston Arena. It took two hours to get a replacement from the Boston Gardens. Chuck Connors played first base for the Brooklyn Dodgers and went on to even higher things than ten-foot basketball rims.

He became the "Rifleman" in the long and successful series in television and has starred in many other film and television vehicles.

The ball was oversized and lopsided and blackened by dirt and old age. The big, bulky pumpkin was laced and one end of the leather thong always protruded. The rubber inflation valve was pushed down and laced over, but a lump was always present and had such influence on the flight of the ball that it led to the shift of the ball so lace and valve were centered between the hands of the players to assure a straight flight on a pass or a shot. To this day, the influence of this shifting remains in the game although the valve and the leather lace have long since departed.

Today's basketball is highly polished, properly dimpled, clean looking, and so small that almost any player can "palm" it. In the 20's you didn't use a bounce pass because there was too much bounce or, in some instances, no bounce at all. The old bladder covered by leather caused us all kinds of trouble, but it gave us some laughs too. There was usually just one ball for the game. You waited until the home team finished their warmup and then, maybe, you would get to use the ball for a few minutes.

A player in those days wore padded pants, knee guards, and sometimes elbow guards. A sweater was worn for the warmup. Deck or tennis shoes were used and were of such poor quality that they often wore through during the course of one game. Uniforms were nondescript and the colors faded into a streaky, sweat-stained imitation of a foggy rainbow.

Today's uniforms are practically hand tailored and beautifully colored. Shoes are made especially for basketball, constructed for comfort as well as for quick starts and stops on any kind of a floor.

Coaching, organization, discipline, and regular practices are routine today. But in the early days they were fairly loose. The "coach" was either the oldest man on the club or the club owner, who kept his office in his inside coat pocket. Just before the start of the game the club owner would stick his head in the dressing room and say, "This is no baloney, you guys. You gotta win!" Then he would slam the door for emphasis and go out to "count the house."

Thinking back to the scarcity of basketballs for practices and games, I remember an incident that occurred in the NBA. Maurice Podoloff, N.B.A. president, was helping New Haven, Connecticut, promote a game between the Philadelphia Warriors and the Knickerbockers. About an hour before game time someone came to me and said, "Joe, there are no basketballs in the building."

I sought out Mr. Podoloff to give him this important information. When I caught up with him, I said, "Mr. Podoloff—"

That was as far as I got. "Please, Joe," he said, "not *now*. I'm very, very busy."

I thought to myself: "What fun if I obey him—I'll do it!" And I did.

About thirty minutes later Mr. Podoloff came by and said, "Now, Joe, can I help you?"

I said, "No, Mr. Podoloff, but I think I can help you. There are no basketballs in the building."

Prexy Podoloff's pivot was the best I ever saw as he hustled toward the telephone.

We played on 40′ by 60′ courts mostly on dance halls where the execution of the "Varsity Drag" and the "Charleston" required a floor so slippery you practically had to skate in order to move. Of course, the fellow guarding you had to do likewise. In these halls the people danced before the game, between the halves, and after the game until the old, familiar number "There Is No Place Like Home" sent them away.

Such things as out-of-bounds plays were impossible because you played so close to the bleachers or chairs which were jammed up against the courts that there was no room to take the ball out of bounds. Besides, you risked a hat pin in the leg (the ladies *could* get demonstrative) or a kick in the pants every time you ventured close to the side or end lines.

Playing floors and equipment were bad in the old days, but that was only the beginning. As soon as the ten players and the official were inside the net or cage, all hell broke loose. Once the official tossed the ball up between the centers, he was chiefly concerned with keeping out of the way and staying alive. There was only one referee, and he had about as much authority as an ant in a herd of elephants. There were no lines on most of the courts, and the ref would have to chalk out the center jump and free-throw areas. When you lined up for a jump, the poor guy would get a stiff neck trying to keep the wise guys from creeping over the chalk lines and erasing them with the toes of their shoes.

When you were fouled, it was a *real* one! With only one referee, the guy who did the fouling usually got away with it. So you belted him back. Fans say there is too much whistle-blowing today. Well, there was little or no whistle blowing by the officials in the old days and that was a lot worse. Even when the fouls *were* called, the fans would claim there was too much whistle-blowing.

Players used shoulders, elbows, and hips to block and practically tore their opponents' shirts and pants off when playing defense. Players were geared to almost any indignity as far as rough play was concerned, but the unforgivable act of those days was tripping. This was the lowest form of sportsmanship. When a player used this trick, the word went the rounds of the professional ranks, and the player was taken care of in two ways—first, physically, and then he was eased out of the game. To this day no real basketball player trips an opponent.

The roughhouse tactics didn't end with the players. Spectators invariably got into the act. Some of their tricks were ingenious: mirrors were used to reflect the lights into the eyes of shooters; lighted cigarettes and cigars were flicked through the nets; bottle tops were flipped at visitors. A common annoyance to visiting players in highly industrialized cities was the practice of some "fans" who would flip small stove bolts at the "out-of-towners."

After the cages and nets were abolished, the baskets were attached to backboards. The backboards were homemade with no padding on the uprights, which were placed right on the end lines—quite different from today, when they are located far back of the end lines. The hometown fans now had a new way to support their teams and made a regular practice of shaking the boards to deflect the visitors' shots.

I remember a game played in northern Michigan (I think it was Bay City). Nat Holman was dribbling the ball up court when a guy left his seat, rushed up behind Nat, and really brought one up from the floor. His fist landed on the side of Nat's head—"clunk!" Instead of being put out of the building or arrested, as he would be today, the fellow became the town "hero."

The referee was subject to terrific abuse from everyone—spectators and players. He wore a white shirt, and after many of the games it would be covered with blood. Most officials came prepared to fight their way out of the net and often needed police protection to get out of the building and escape from irate fans. Some of them were seriously injured. Chuck Solodare, one of the great officials of the game, once suffered a broken neck during a game and was hospitalized for nineteen weeks. Today, the rules and the growth of sportsmanship protect officials from such rough treatment.

When a referee gave the home team more than a fair advantage, the visiting team players would put on the "press." When the referee tossed the ball up at center, the forward and guard on the same side of the court would come head-on and right at the arbiter. When the two players met, the referee would be caught in the middle. After one such "press" the official usually got the message. The term "press" is now used to describe the pressing defense.

Referees had absolutely no backing and as a result were vilified by the players and the fans. Dick Meehan, one of the good referees of the era, tells of his first game in the New York State League this way: "I walked into the Troy Armory, dropped my bag, and looked at the dancers. A young man, a nice looking kid, said, 'Hello, who do you play with?' I said, 'I'm not a player. I'm the referee.' The young fellow said, 'Well———, you stink before you start.'"

That was the attitude of the era.

The offensive game was slow and deliberate, and a premium was placed on possession of the ball. A team ahead by a score of three or four points with five minutes to go was almost sure to win the game. The ball would be brought deep into the back court and held there for as much as five minutes. The result was low scores. Most of the games were won from the free-throw line.

The ability to draw fouls was important. Some players had perfected such acting ability that most officials would fall for the act when there was little more to it than a mere brush of the body. One man shot all the free-throws and was usually the high scorer for his team. A six- or eight-point man was indeed a star.

The only shots from the field were the "set" and the "lay-up." One player, usually known as the standing guard, seldom penetrated deeper than the center of the court. There was no coaching. Trial and error and advice from better players was the method used to improve.

The scores were always low, ranging from just a few points to such fantastic totals as 15 or 20 points. With the elimination of the center jump (1937–38) and the addition of the 10-second restraining line in the same year, plus the improvement of player skills, scores have shot higher and higher until today college and professional totals are soaring over 100 and often over 150 points per team. Wilt Chamberlain (Philadelphia 76'ers) once scored 100 points in a professional game.

The elimination of the center jump, the advent of the three-second and ten-second rules, the widening of the free-throw lane, and the bonus team shots which are awarded after team totals have reached a certain number have added further to the speed and excitement of the modern amateur game. In professional basketball the 24-second rule governing possession of the ball has practically eliminated foul trading. Other changes such as player positions on the free-throw lane, clarification of traveling, screening, and post blocking have made today's game the best of all time.

The new "bench" rules of 1965–66 governing the conduct of the coach and his players reminds me that I may have gotten out of the game at exactly the right time. My frequent trips to the water fountain and my "inadvertent" foot-contacts with the water bucket might be misconstrued by officials today. The new rule states that a coach may rise only to call a time out, talk with a substitute, or visit the scorer's table. Nothing was stated concerning standing at attention during the playing of the National Anthem. And, of course, no one on the bench may act in any way which may be construed as an attempt to influence an official.

The players have kept pace with the development of the game and have almost perfected their mastery of the skills. Today all players can dribble, pass, and shoot with amazing dexterity and accuracy. They have also grown taller. In early days, it was extremely unusual to see a player who was more than 6–2 in height. Many of today's high school centers are pushing the seven-foot mark, and 6–6 kids are no longer considered tall enough to play the pivot. They are restricted to corner and back court play.

Much of the credit for the development of today's players must go to school and college coaches. They have pursued perfection and the results have justified their dedication. The players were great in my day, but only a very few possessed the intricate skills which are performed with such nonchalance by today's youngsters. And that brings me to my own growth in the game.

I was born in Yonkers, New York, in 1900 and have always regarded the site of my birthplace as home. I attended Public School 20 and began to caddie when I was nine years old. When I was twelve I became water boy for a local baseball team. My first sports interests were, naturally, golf and baseball. Later I fooled around with basketball in the parks and on street corner lots whenever I could find someone to play against. Our basketball was a cap stuffed into an old discarded soccer ball. To score, you had to throw the "ball" on the roof of a shed. When we played in the streets, we used to circulate around the ice wagons and pass the ball under the bellies of the teams of horses to teammates. A score resulted when we could maneuver and toss the ball between the legs of the walking horses.

One day, around 1912, I met a man named Johnny Mears. He gave me a quick once over and asked me to play with the Trinity Midgets, a church team. That was the beginning. I was 6–3 and weighed 140 pounds and was probably the tallest "midget" in the world.

Naturally, as the tallest midget, I played center. In those days, most centers were used to get the tap, get the rebound, and then get out of the way. They were awkward and couldn't run. I could run fast in a straight line, but when it came to the footwork necessary for good basketball, I was sadly lacking. They called me a good floor man and I was—I was on the floor more than I was on my feet.

When I got through grade school, I looked for a job and found work in a factory at 15¢ per hour on a 10-hour basis per day. I played basketball at night and every weekend.

My first paying job as a basketball player came in 1915 when I caught on with the Bantams. We used to go to Beacon, Wappinger Falls, and Hudson, New York, and were paid $5 a game. Out of this we had to pay our transportation and meals. I netted the grand total of $15 the first year and $18 the second year.

When I first began to play basketball and long before I ever dreamed of being a good player, I became temperamental. When I made a bad play, I would explode in anger. I soon found that this affected my playing, and I worked at correcting the bad habit until I learned to control my emotional outbursts.

I hung out at Lou Gordon's sports store in Yonkers and listened to athletes who came into buy equipment and talk to Lou. I absorbed everything they said and was so intensely interested in their sports stories that Lou advised me to see Jimmy Lee at Hollywood Inn and try out for his team. Hollywood Inn was a privately conducted athletic club for businessmen, and Lou was the manager of the team. The players were recruited from the local high school stars, who had much more experience than I. To my great surprise, I made the team just the same.

Like all tall kids, I was extremely ungainly, and I soon realized I would never get anywhere in basketball unless I improved my coordination. I began a self-imposed training program on the streets and out of sight on the cinder roads back of the Alexander Smith carpet mills in the dark of night. I would run at full speed, stop suddenly, change direction, pivot, run backwards, and shadow box. Slowly but surely I began to improve.

Now, around 1917 and 1918, I began to play with other teams and was in considerable demand, chiefly because of my height. I had reached 6-5 and was considered exceptionally tall. A tall player was a rarity in those days. Since the ball was tossed up at the center of the court after every score, a tall player who could get the tap and the rebounds was vital to a team's success.

The Whirlwinds of New York City used me in some of their games, paying $7 per game. My expenses were practically nil, and since I was working as an apprentice machinist at $15 per week, I became affluent.

By 1919, I was getting $10 per game and was gaining some renown in basketball circles. I played with Holyoke in the Western Massachusetts League and Schenectady in the New York State League while they were still playing in a cage. Then the well-known Powers Brothers aggregation came to Yonkers, and I played against them. They liked my size and took me to New York to play *against* the Whirlwinds. Marty Friedman, Nat Holman, Chris Leonard, and Harry Riconda were on the Whirlwinds and insisted that I play with them. I was getting $3 per day on my job and $10 per game for playing basketball and could afford to take a day off from work now and then.

The Whirlwinds disbanded, but another team was formed and used the same name. This team played their games in the 168th Street Armory in New York and were considered big time. My experience with the Whirlwinds led to games against the Visitations in the Metropolitan League. Since their games were played on Sunday nights, when other teams were idle, I agreed to play with them. At this time I was playing in four leagues with four different teams at the same time.

My earnings increased by leaps and bounds. I played one manager against the other and sometimes got as much as $75 per game. Then I signed on with three other clubs—Schenectady in the New York State League, the Visitations in the Metropolitan League, and Mount Vernon in the Interborough League. Each team played two league games per week. Since I couldn't play in all the games, I bargained with the managers for every game. No manager could count on his starting team from one game to the next, but it was not considered illegal for a player to jump from one team to another for a game.

The standard rate of pay was a dollar a minute, but the rates were gradually increased until I got up to $90 or $100 a game no matter how many minutes I played. When there was a clash of dates I took the best offer. There was no income tax at that time, and I began to really live it up.

Dave Wassmer took me to Holyoke for a special game in the Western Massachusetts League, and I set a record by making 11 out of 11 free-throws. This really gave me a reputation. Now I was a full-fledged pro. The good players were well known, and they were all after the good high dollar. We would meet at the information booth in Grand Central Station on our way to games to talk basketball. The usual conversation would run something like this:

"How did you do last night?"

"Great! I got two and my man got one." (Not, did we win or lose.)

Some of the players we met in Grand Central Station were Benny Borgeman, Honey Russell, Elmer Ripley, Joe Brennan, and Roddy Cooney. All of these players later became college coaches. Others were Bucky Harris (baseball), Ray Kennedy, Dutch Dehnert, Dave Wassmer, Marty Friedman, Barney Sedran, and Eddie White.

We had no coaches, no trainers, and no dressing rooms. You brought your own towel, and it was also wise to bring along a pal to hold your money and valuables. The team manager was the coach and the travel agent. He knew nothing about the game except that the objective was to win.

We were all aware of the weakness of hometown timekeepers in stopping the clock when the home team forces were behind in the score, so the extra player always sat next to the timekeeper to make certain there were no manipulations of the clock in favor of the home team. (This type of sportsmanship was in operation in the infancy of the NBA. Mr. Maurice Podoloff, first commissioner of the league, cured that ill.)

John J. O'Brien formed the Metropolitan League in 1919. I played for Brooklyn in this league and was making so much money that I became a big shot. I bought a car and would park right in front of any hall in which we played, throw my bag up in the air, and escort the kid who caught it into the hall for free.

Understand, now, I'm talking about the amateur, semi-pro, and professional basketball I knew. When the American Basketball League was formed in the mid-1920's, we had more organization in professional basketball and began to attract more fans. College basketball was a minor sport at that time and did not hold much interest for spectators.

Even if there had been college-ball fans, there were no college gyms large enough to handle them, especially in the East. And the old pro leagues, even the American League, didn't last long. The bulk of basketball in the 1920's was played on the basis of a team holding its players together for a tour and visiting cities which hastily drew up teams to meet them. To get people to come to the games you had to add a dance. So you would play to a few hundred spectators who really came to dance.

Even in my days with the Celtics the crowds were not big, although I once played in a day-night doubleheader in Cleveland (1923) that drew 25,000 spectators. But that was one of the few times we played to big crowds. Today, and for the past few years, basketball has become the nation's biggest spectator sport.

In 1923, all my dreams and hopes reached a grand climax. I was asked to sign up with the Celtics. My heart was jumping so hard I could scarcely sign the contract. Now, I was really on cloud "9." For the next thirteen years I was part of the most renowned basketball team ever known. The Celtics were the biggest name in the history of the sport, and they lived the part. Their entire lives were wrapped up in basketball. They existed only to win games and to improve the game as well as their personal talents.

The Celtics were too good! In fact, they were so good that they broke up every league in which they played. Separation of the players didn't seem to do much good because even three of them on the same team was enough to make a shambles of any league race. When Pete Barry, Dutch Dehnert, and I were sent to the Cleveland Rosenblooms, our winning ways continued and eventually broke up that league.

When the Celtics were in a league, they also played exhibition and challenge games to the tune of more than 120 games a season. The Shamrocks appeared in every state east of the Rockies in all kinds of weather, on all kinds of courts, against any and all kinds of teams, and for peanuts—if they couldn't get dollars. The Celtics were the first and real "Ambassadors of Basketball."

In the late 20's the colleges began to realize that basketball was a big-time sport and began constructing buildings expressly for the game. Minnesota built a stadium which could seat 15,000 spectators; Iowa, 16,000; Washington, 12,000; Oregon, 10,000; Pennsylvania, 10,000, and West Virginia, 7,000.

College basketball lost its impetus a few years later because, in my opinion, the teams began to copy the Celtic style. Few college players were capable of playing the fast-passing, possession type of game the Celtics had developed, and the game lost its popularity.

An outstanding example of college adoption of the Celtic style of play was the St. John's "Wonder Five." This team was probably the best college five ever to use the Celtic system. Mac Kinsbrunner, Matty Begovich, Rip Gerson, Max Posnack and Allie Schuckman could control the ball at will. In one game they kept City College scoreless from the floor for 38 consecutive minutes. In another game the Wonder Five held Manhattan College scoreless from the field for the entire contest.

Little Rider College, Trenton, N. J., coached by Clair Bee at that time, was one of the few teams which extended the Wonder Team. In a home-and-home series, St. John's beat the Roughriders by a single point on a basket made at the gun and by five points on the Wonder Team's home court (Arcadia Hall) in Brooklyn. The style of play featured great passing, but it was uninteresting basketball as a steady diet.

Professional basketball faded because of the style of play. With the exception of the games between the Celtics and the "Rens," it was stagnant and uninteresting basketball. The pro players lost their pep, and new faces were slow to appear. Even when new and faster players appeared, they were frozen out by the oldtimers who liked the possession game because it preserved their legs and their tenures in the game. Few good players came from the colleges, and there was no real coaching. Because owners knew little about the game, the players ran the teams. A pro team would play in a town one night for a high fee and in a neighboring town the next night for a lower fee.

In addition to the uninteresting style of play there were several other contributing factors. The pros looked at the game in terms of dollars while the colleges concentrated on techniques of play and the talents of the players. And, unfortunately, the depression came along at this inopportune time (1930–36) to apply the clincher.

Finally, in the mid-thirties, I decided to call it quits. It was at this time that I accepted the head coaching job at St. John's University. Even after accepting the job, I was fearful that I would flop as a coach. I had never played for a coach, and I had never gone to high school or college. I was what was known as a sandlot basketball player, scuffling around with pickup and amateur and pro teams and finally reaching the top with the Celtics.

When I first began playing basketball, it was every kid for himself and the best man won out. The closest thing to a coach I had ever known was the owners of the teams or the players. The players really ran the teams. They decided whether or not they wanted to add a new member, and if they took him in they were the ones who told him how to play and what to do.

The Celtics had no coach, but they had great leaders—Johnny Beckman, Dutch Dehnert, and Nat Holman. They were the best teachers a player could possibly find. They taught me everything I knew. We played together as a team and talked over plays and techniques between games hours at a time. Later we would work out the plays on the courts. When a fellow made a mistake, the rest of the Celtics hollered at him and chewed him out until he got it right. No floor instructions, just hints.

Father Rebholz, moderator of athletics at St. John's, felt sure I could handle the coaching assignment and, to make the offer still more attractive from a financial point of view, added the baseball coaching job. During the years between 1936 and 1947 my St. John's teams won 181 games and lost but 54 for an over-all winning percentage of 77. St. John's also won NIT titles in 1943 and 1944.

Interest in basketball in the East was fading, but college teams in the West were employing fast-break basketball and filling the field-houses. Soon the Eastern teams began to use the "new" type of basketball. This different and improved game brought the fans back, and the popularity of the sport returned.

In 1934, Ned Irish rented Madison Square Garden and began to promote college games. He brought teams from all sections of the country, and basketball got its big impetus toward the big time.

In 1946, Ned Irish of Madison Square Garden and Walter Brown of the Boston Arena got together and organized the first really big-time professional league on a national basis. In 1947, Ned Irish offered me the coaching job at the Garden (Knickerbockers) and I accepted. I had kept up with the changes and developments of the professional game as well as the college game, and now I had confidence. After all, I had played professional ball for eighteen years and had coached college basketball successfully for eleven years. During the next nine years, as coach of the Knickerbockers, I saw professional basketball emerge as a big-time sport on a national basis.

Today professional basketball is definitely established. The game is played under college rules for the most part but with a few minor dif-

I just signed with the New York Knickerbockers, as the highest paid coach of the time.

Coach Joe Lapchick shouting instructions during a game in Madison Square Garden. (UPI Photo)

As coach of the New York Knickerbockers.

Coach Joe Lapchick with the Knickerbocker team which won three Eastern Division Titles in the NBA. (During Joe's tenure with the Knickerbockers his teams were never out of the play-offs.) Left to right: Connie
Simmons, Harry Gallatin, Vince Boryla, Carl Braun, Dick McGuire and
Coach Joe Lapchick. (Four of these players, Harry Gallatin, Vince
Boryla, Carl Braun and Dick McGuire became coaches of the Knickerbockers after their playing careers came to an end.)

ferences—48-minute games, the 24-second rule, and the elimination of
the zone defense. The arenas are the best in the country, playing rules
are uniform, officiating is constantly improving, colleges are turning out
hundreds of great prospects, and the teams are coached by experienced
coaches.

The style of play is exciting, and the fast break, coupled with the
deadly one-hand jump shot, makes the game interesting to watch. No two
plays are ever alike. The game is a demanding one; a professional basketball player runs 1/10th of a mile per minute. This, times 48 minutes, gives
you an idea of how tough today's pro game really is and how much it
requires of a player. The sudden starts, stops, changes of direction, jumping, and running in as many as a hundred or more games a season with
occasional streaks of 11 games in 13 days, suggests that professional
basketball is the toughest and most demanding physical game in existence.

In 1956, after nine years of coaching the Knickerbockers, I returned to St. John's. It was a welcome change from the demanding rigors of professional coaching. My Redmen teams were good too. In 1959 and again in 1965, St. John's captured both the Holiday Festival and the NIT titles. It was St. John's fourth NIT champsionship. I was retired from the university in 1965, but I am looking forward eagerly to the continued growth of basketball on all levels. I intend to continue my interest in the game and will keep abreast of changes and developments as they occur because this is the sport I love.

More people watch basketball today than any other sport. Attendance studies show that close to 150 million persons view basketball games each season in the United States alone. There are approximately 25 million additional hoop spectators in foreign countries, making a total attendance figure somewhere in the vicinity of 175 million. These figures do not include fans who watch semi-pro, church, industrial league, girls' college intramurals, and club games. Further, thousands of players on all levels play the game, some of them the year round.

Basketball has been my life, and I wouldn't exchange one minute of all the ups, downs, thrills, shocks, anger, disappointments, embarrassments, successes, and failures for anything in the world. The wonderful memories are compensation enough for a lifetime of dedication.

CHAPTER 2

THE
ORIGINAL CELTICS

THE ORIGINAL CELTICS were professional basketball's greatest team from 1917 to 1937, and the players have become living legends in their own times. I have often been asked how the Celtics would have stacked up against the modern professional teams and especially against the Boston Celtics and Philadelphia 76'ers of recent years. There are, of course, several important points to be considered.

First, and most important—height. At 6–5, I was considered a giant in the old days. Today I would be just a small corner man from the point of view of height and weight. Six-five players today are often capable of back court operation.

Then, too, there are the rules. Control of the tap was vital in the old days because a center toss-up followed every score. At 6–5, I wouldn't have a ghost of a chance against the twenty or more centers who are between 6–8 and 7–2 in today's NBA. However, if three Celtic players in their prime, such as Johnny Beckman, Nat Holman, and Dutch Dehnert were playing today, they would be just as great as they were in their own day. Beckman, Holman, and Dehnert were so great that they could play in any era.

Pete Barry helped form the Original Celtics in 1914 as a neighborhood team—The Hudson Guild. In 1916 they represented the Community House Club in New York City. Turning professional in 1918, they became a great drawing card. Jim and Tom Furey were the managers. Then Tex Rickard organized a team to play in Madison Square Garden that was known as the Whirlwinds. This team was managed by John Murray, who later became one of the greatest of officials. Nat Holman, Barney Sedran, Chris Leonard, Marty Friedman, and Harry Riconda made up the starting five with Ray Kennedy as the first substitute.

In 1921, the Celtics met the Whirlwinds for the "World Championship." The Whirlwinds won the first game by a score of 40–27. The Celtics won the second by 26–24. Then the Furey brothers, who were promoting a team under their family name, hired Holman and Leonard. That broke up the rivalry—the Celtics were on top of the basketball world to stay.

The players of the first Original Celtics team were Hart, the McCormick brothers, Goggin, Mally, Calhoun, Witte, and Barry. Five years later, when the Celtics started their great march to glory, only Witte and Barry were on hand.

Jim Furey made the first step to organize professional basketball in the winter of 1922–23. He hired the Seventy-First Regiment Armory in Manhattan for Sunday nights and signed the Original Celtics to contracts which stipulated that they play exclusively for his team. The Celtics signed the contracts and were guaranteed straight salaries. The Celtic players at that time were Pete Barry, Dutch Dehnert, Horse Haggerty, Johnny Beckman, Joe Trippe, and Ernie Reich. The team was coached by a veteran of the 1914 group, John Witte. Later Nat Holman, Chris Leonard, Davey Banks, Carl Husta, Nat Hickey, and I joined them.

A few years later the Celtics joined the Eastern League and won the championship. Then they hit the road and won 194 out of 205 games. They were a tremendous attraction, playing before thousands of spectators throughout the country and a capacity crowd (10,000) in the old Madison Square Garden.

There were two Celtic teams, with players from the first team merging with newcomers so gradually that it was hardly noticeable. The first included Ernie Reich, Haggerty, Barry, Beckman, Dehnert, Holman, Witte, and Leonard. Banks and I later teamed up with Barry, Beckman, Dehnert, and Holman to form the second team. The last-named players kept the Celtics going until the American League split them up in the late 20's. Even then, Nat Holman, Dutch Dehnert, Pete Barry, Davey Banks, and I kept the name and the fame and the Celtic tradition alive by reorganizing the team and adding Nat Hickey and Carl Husta.

The Celtics were different from today's great professional teams chiefly because of a tenacious defensive philosophy. Each player's sole purpose when he clasped hands with his matched opponent was to hold him scoreless. Their short-passing game and limited shooting meant a possession game. All they needed to be assured of victory was a lead of two or three points at any stage of the game.

I was asked to play with the fabulous team at the beginning of the 1922–23 season. With my heart beating wildly against my well exposed ribs, I quickly signed the contract. Now I was with the best.

The roof fell in during the very first game. I quickly found that I was only a beginner in the type of game the Celtics played. I was frustrated because of my ineptness, and the resulting anger which shot through me every time I made a mistake was no help. I had been bred to the theory of individualism, whereas the Celtics were devoted to team effort.

After many heartbreaking errors I finally mastered my personal mental and game weaknesses and eventually earned a place as a full-fledged Celtic. Even so, Celtic acceptance meant little. A mistake by any player drew an angry torrent of brutal criticism from the others, but rookies kept their mouths shut and listened. The Celtics had no time for alibis, excuses, or explanations. The big asset was *guts,* and the only objective was to *win* basketball games.

Those were rough days and rough going but I loved it. You carried your own uniform (always in need of laundering) from game to game, night after night, with or without sleep and with no relief from aches and pains—except for Beckman's legendary remedies which were cure-alls for anything from a stomach ache to a broken arm: Absorbine, Jr.

There was no training season. You got in shape by playing. If you complained about anything, you were gutless. One thing you quickly learned—to keep your fingernails trimmed and check your opponent's hands to make sure his nails were cut.

The offense was a "situation" offense much the same as I used with the Knickerbockers and at St. John's University. It was a free-wheeling, fast-passing pressure offense by the greatest ball-handling team I ever saw. But there was no "showboating." Every pass and every move had a purpose, and the technique broke the backs of practically every team we met.

Defensively, you played your own man and no one else. He was your responsibility—you took care of him or else. There was no "float" or "sag." You were completely on your own.

It was an honor to follow in the shoes of Horse Haggerty, a real legend. Horse came originally from the Reading, Pennsylvania, area but he played a lot around Springfield, Massachusetts. He was great!

Holman came out of New York's East Side and was gifted in all phases of the game. A pass-master and an artist at feinting and faking, he was a wizard at drawing fouls. Nat possessed a great outside, line-drive shot. He came to the Celtics from the New York Whirlwinds. During his playing days he studied at Savage Institute and got a degree in physical education. Later, and while still playing, he coached at CCNY. After a few years he was named an assistant professor and became nationally known as an authority on basketball. Holman averaged ten points a game as a player, often half the points the Celtics scored in winning a game.

Dutch Dehnert, the greatest post or pivot player in the country, then or now, was as solid as a rock, fast, enthusiastic, and loved the passing game. Not only did he invent the pivot play, but he was the fastest, most deceptive player from the pivot position in the history of the game.

Pete Barry, the originator of the Celtics, was older than most of us and the smartest. He was a master strategist, a team man, and a "bear" on the boards.

Johnny Beckman was a fighter, a leader, a great scorer, and a perfect back court operator. He ranked with Holman as a scorer, and with the ball he was a Houdini.

Nat Hickey was a good scorer, a hard cutter, and deceptively fast. He could really keep the ball hopping.

Davey Banks was a lightning bolt of speed and a dead shot. No one man could stay with Davey. No bigger than an average eighth-grader, he made any player who opposed him look like a beginner.

The owners who sponsored the teams we usually played, were, for the most part, shoestring operators with their offices in the pockets of their coats. If the money wasn't in the "house," you didn't get paid. Three thousand spectators was considered a sellout crowd and was usually the result of a "big" promotion. Eight to nine hundred was the usual draw.

Some promoters would simply gather the receipts and disappear before half-time. One such promoter in Louisville brought the Celtics and George Halas' Chicago team to play in the Kentucky city. He also booked an artist named Chaliapin in the theatre. This promoter put on a good promotion and hovered around the boxoffice until the game started. Then he evaporated with all the money. You felt mighty silly when that happened.

Owners seldom had regular lineups because, with the various leagues in operation, there were conflicting dates. Players bargained for the best pay, and that's where they would play. If they were good (and most of them were) they were always forgiven by the owners and other teams.

It was different with the Celtics. With them you had no problem when it came to regular work. You were *too* busy; more often than not, you would travel every day, play every night five days weekly, and then have double-headers to contend with on Saturdays and Sundays.

The first *real* big league came into existence in 1924 and folded in 1930. George Marshall owned the Washington franchise; George Halas owned Chicago; Max Rosenbloom owned Cleveland; Jim Donovan owned the Celtics; the Fort Wayne Chamber of Commerce owned Fort Wayne; Jules Aronson owned the Philadelphia Warriors, with Eddie Gottlieb serving as coach, and Rochester was owned by Johnny Murphy. Joe Carr was the president of the league.

There were frequent franchise failures, but replacements were quickly formed. Some of these were Brooklyn, Paterson, Toledo, Baltimore, and Camden. In 1927 the league voted the Celtics out as a team and awarded

The Original Celtics during their Playing Days—1923. Left to right: Johnny Beckman, Nat Holman, Pete Barry, Dutch Dehnert, Al Leonard (deceased), Joe Lapchick.

Holman and Banks to the New York Hakoahs; Pete Barry and Dehnert to Rochester; John Beckman to Baltimore, and me to Cleveland. Not one penny was involved in the league distribution of all this great player talent. The breakup of his team put Jim Donovan out of business, and we were forced to join the teams to which we had been assigned. It was a great blow to the Celtics.

Barry and Dehnert could not come to terms with Rochester, but they did get contracts with Cleveland. With the three of us in the Cleveland lineup, we were off to the races again. In addition to the league games, we played against independents anywhere and everywhere. All the players were doing well financially (I was earning $1,500 per month) but the league was losing money.

Wherever we played we were acclaimed by the sportswriters as the

The Original Celtics today: Johnny Beckman, Nat Holman, Pete Barry, Dutch Dehnert, Joe Lapchick. This was the induction picture for election to Hall of Fame (1963).

..COMING TO B'NAI BRITH DINNER TO SPORTS HISTORY MAKERS OF THE CENTURY.

Congratulations

The Original Celtics.

"Ambassadors of Basketball." A couple of excerpts from the Knoxville Journal may illustrate the point. This one was dated January 7, 1933:

> The Cleveland Rosenbloom-Celtics weird court magicians, headed by the one and only Joe Lapchick, elongated center, will be odds-on favorites to beat Tennessee's young cagesters. Those fans who have seen the professional champions in action before know just what to expect. There will be uncanny passes, startling maneuvers, deadly goal tossing, comedy, and all the other qualities that make the pro performers the great players they are.
>
> As is always the case, it will undoubtedly be Lapchick who will give the fans the most laughs. He can do more tricks with the basketball than a monkey can with the proverbial peanut. Palming the ball, wrapping his slim arms around it, and the like, is just a part of his repertoire.
>
> The gum-chewing nonchalance of the Celtics when they execute their trick shots will cause fans to stand aghast. Dutch Dehnert is the hub of the Celtics' famous 'wheel' play. Davey Banks had his arm in a cast in the last game but he played just the same.

You will have to excuse the personal reference, but I am sure you will appreciate the story. We never tried to humiliate an opponent. The teams who bowed gracefully, we treated nice and held the score close.

Great players today "palm the ball" with ease. But it was not easy with the oversized "pumpkin" of Celtic days.

Those who challenged us and were a bit antagonistic—well, we showed them who was boss. One thing I must say here: we had great respect for teams who fought back and gave all they had in their effort to win.

In league play, we were winning consistently, and finally the team owners got together again. "Hell!" one of them said. "We're right back where we were before we broke up Jim Donovan's Celtics."

They called another meeting, and Cleveland was forced to release Nat Hickey to George Halas' Chicago team. The move helped a little, but Cleveland still won the pennant for the next two years, and the league folded for good early in the 1929–30 season. When the league gave up the ghost, the crowds dropped off, and the Celtics again "hit the road."

In 1931 the depression came. Hickey, Dehnert, Barry, Banks, and I formed a road version of the Celtics and barnstormed. We had an old Pierce Arrow that we bought for $125, and we played for $125 per night with an option of 60 per cent of the gate. It sounded good, but we traveled light (usually the five of us with another player when we could find one) and we had to trust the promoters, scorers, timekeepers, ticket sellers, and gatemen.

There was one person we knew we could trust—the game official. If he didn't call 'em right, he got the treatment. The center jump followed every score in those days, and most of the "homers" learned fast just how really big Dehnert, Barry, and Hickey were when they came in for the tap. Their charge was made with such reckless abandon that even I feared for my own safety. The official didn't have a chance and usually landed twenty feet away or (worse) was caught between two angry bulls and hung up between them after their mad rush like a matador's cape on a berserk bull's horns. Officials working Celtic games never made the mistake more than once.

One way or another we held the Celtics together, and although we suffered a bit physically, we kept on winning. Our victory percentage was as high as ever. Around this time, Lou O'Neill, sports editor of the Long Island Star–Journal, started promoting us, and we played under different sponsors in practically every town in the East. We would play one half under pro rules and the other observing AAU or college regulations. It was a hard and demanding life, but the actual playing was far from being as grueling as it is today in professional basketball.

We never beat a team badly. I could usually control the tap, and this helped us control the game. If we were playing a weak team, we would be more concerned that the fans got their money's worth by a ball-handling exhibition and would manage to beat most teams by only three to five points.

The one thing that always impressed the Celtics was the number of yellow school buses we would see around the building in which we were

The Boston Celtics: Top row: Herlihy, Dehnert, Lapchick; bottom row: Birch, Banks and Hickey.

This was at the height of the financial depression—a complete touring team with 7 passenger Pierce Arrow. Left to right: Dehnert, Lapchick, Banks, Barry, Hickey and Herlihy.

to play. Coaches would bring their high school teams hundreds of miles to see us move the ball with that rhythmic free-wheeling that is championship ball at its best. When high school and college players were present, it was like a shot of adrenalin to us. We knew why they came, and we said: "Let's really turn it on tonight."

We had fun too. Once Dutch Dehnert was ailing and remained in bed while the rest of us went out for something to eat. When we came back, one of the gang asked Dutch how he felt.

"Lousy," was the reply.

"Want something for your cold?"

"Sure."

The questioner reached into the bag (Becky's medicine chest) and handed Dutch a small bottle. Dutch took a deep swig and threw the bottle across the room. His bellow of pain could be heard for 20 blocks. Dutch had swallowed half a bottle of Sloan's liniment.

There was a player in Indiana named Homer Stonebreaker. Our best guard was Chris Leonard, known as the "Dog" or the "Leech" because he played his opponent so tight from one end of the court to the other. Stonebreaker shot underhand from a distance of up to fifty feet, and he was always ready to let it fly. Leonard let him shoot from the latter distance unmolested. After all, who can shoot from 50 feet underhand and hit?

But this guy was really good. He could make them from out there. As a result, the Indiana Omars beat the Celtics. Stonebreaker got the staggering total of 12 points.

There is something about being a champion. Some call it pride that makes the real athlete and dynasties such as the Yankees, the Boston Celtics, and, of course, the New York Original Celtics. In my opinion, it is a great deal more than just pride. It is a swelling up inside you, a quiet fierceness. Your body can ache and you can be mentally exhausted, but the champion has a "reserve" to draw upon.

Champions may get old, but they have a way of showing the challenger who is boss. The champ walks with kings. And so it was when the Celtics played the Omars the next time, in Cleveland, Chris shut Stonebreaker out cold, and the Celtics went on to an impressive win. Just winning was not enough that particular night.

When the Celtics toured the South in the late 20's and 30's, they played mostly college teams. One night we were playing Mercer College in Macon, Georgia. As we were readying ourselves for a shower, there was a knock on the door.

"Come in," someone yelled.

A fine looking young man opened the door. He stared at us and seemed almost apologetic when he said, "My name is W. L. Stribling. I sure enjoyed the game."

Now it was our turn to stare. Young Stribling, as he was billed, was known as the fightingest heavyweight in the land at that time and was headline news. Every day his name was in the papers, because in just three weeks he was scheduled to fight Max Schmeling for the heavyweight championship of the world. We invited him in, of course, and he told us he had played high school basketball in Macon and loved the game. We told him we were playing Georgia Tech in Atlanta the next night and would suit him up if he was interested.

We were just kidding, but to our amazement he said, "Really? I would like that."

Our public relations man sent word to Atlanta that Young Stribling would play with the Celtics the next night. What happened was crazy. The crowd surrounded the arena for two solid blocks. You couldn't even get through to enter the building. More surprising was the fact that Young Stribling played for twenty minutes after being out of the game for several years. He was good too. Too bad he could not have continued being a member of the team. We would have had our most profitable year plus a good player and a nice guy.

In the early 30's there were two fine players from Egg Harbor, N. J., who made the Kingston club in the New York State League. This was the league where you played on a court completely enclosed by a net. The ball was always in play, and there was no backboard.

The two players were brothers, Carl and Mickey Husta. They would come to the Kingston Armory and help Frank Morgenwenk (manager and owner) draw the court lines and set up the chairs; then go home for a bite to eat, return, and play the game. Then they would hustle to the showers, rush upstairs, and join the orchestra for the rest of the evening. Carl was a drummer and Mickey played the cornet. For all this they were paid $75 per month plus room and board. And they were happy. The next year they got the "good-player" scale, a dollar a minute.

One time our control over the game failed us. We were playing Lou Gehrig's All-Stars. Lou was the "Pride of the Yankees" and was touring with a basketball team in the off season. It was a very poor team.

Lou came into our dressing room before the game to say hello. After the greeting and just before leaving he said, "Please don't rub it in tonight."

We assured Lou it was not our custom to rub it in. That night, with five minutes to go, Lou's team had a three point lead. We took a time out and said, "Let's go!" However, there was no urgency in our attitude because we knew we could win it when and how we pleased.

Well, it was one of those nights when things did not fall into place, and Lou Gehrig's team beat us by two points. From that time on, we won the game first and then let our opponents cut through for some points.

Before I close this chapter about the Celtics I would like to stress that I am not writing off the oldtimers as poor basketball players. No one can say that the players of my day could not play today's fast game, because they were never required to play under present-day conditions. After they had retired, the changes and progress came. Perhaps the oldtimers *could* play today's game, but we'll never know for sure. One thing we *do* know —they left their mark on the game and gave it the impetus for future growth.

You may be thinking, at this point, that Lapchick says the Original Celtics were nothing. Well, I didn't say that, and I never will. The Celtics played the game the way everyone played it in the 20's, but they did it in the grand way. They played basketball with a zest and enjoyment that I have rarely seen again over the years. I doubt if any other team got as much fun out of the game as we did.

"Make the ball work," we said. "Get the ball moving and hit a green shirt."

We would aim for the shirt, not the Celtic in it, and he'd be there on the move. We made the ball sing until a man got loose for a lay-up and then we would hit him for the score. We looked like a million, and we felt like a million! We were the first team, I believe, to use set plays, although most of them were simple things off the center tap. If we had to, we could "sit on the ball" for minutes on end.

We played basketball before constant and powerful attacks were originated, and we played well. Whether or not we could have played with the modern boys—well, let me put it this way: we played our game in our time and we were the best. Each Celtic was great then, and I feel that, as individuals, they would be great today. As a team, however, we would be too small for the modern professional game.

One thing is for sure! After the season is over, the pro player of any era has a feeling of something being missing everywhere he goes. He leaves the house to go down town and he wonders why he has such an empty feeling. Then it dawns on him—the *bag!* For six months he has carried his little uniform bag everywhere until it has become a part of him. At the end of the season, when it has been put away for another year or perhaps forever, he misses it as if it were a part of his arm.

The post-World-War-I era was a stagnant period for basketball. There was no thinking, planning, or striving for progress. The important rules changes that led to player improvement, intelligent coaching, and development of the game came along in the middle and late 30's. Now,

Here I am backed up by the great Celtic players who left their mark on the game in the early years.

thirty years later, basketball is an even tougher game to play. Greater individual playing skill is demanded, along with far more technical and strategic team play.

The Celtic name was kept going after the mid-thirties by one or two of the original players plus Bobby McDermott, Polly Burch, and a number of younger performers. They played under the banner of Kate Smith and her manager, Ted Collins, in the Hippodrome in New York City for a couple of years. Then the venture petered out, and the Original Celtics became a legend.

The golden years of my life were highlighted by my playing days with the Celtics. Year in and year out we were the champs. When I think of the team name, I always remember that we weren't perhaps as Celtic as we should have been. Pete Barry was the only Irishman.

It didn't really matter. The two Germans, Johnny Beckman and Dutch Dehnert—the two Jews, Nat Holman and Davey Banks—and the Bohemian, Joe Lapchick, played like Irishmen anyway!

One night after a game in Chattanooga, Tennessee, a man who was "feeling no pain" kept breaking into our dressing room. "Shure," he would say each time before he was ushered out, " 'tis grand to see a Shamrock, it is."

The last time, Pete Barry decided to help him along. Nat Holman was introduced as "O'Shaughnessy," Dutch Dehnert as "Callahan," and I was "O'Toole."

31

The Irishman was delighted. "And the champions, too!" he managed to say.

I guess we were, at that.

The Celtics were responsible for the big development of basketball in the early years, and they left a mark which will always be a part of the game. It is fitting to end this brief discussion of the Celtics by remembering that the Celtic players were introduced into the Hall of Fame as a group. It was a wonderful tribute to all the Celtics who wore the Shamrock on the front of their playing shirts.

CHAPTER 3

THE COACH
–PHILOSOPHY

T HE MOST IMPRESSIONABLE years of a man's life are those of his youth. Because I had spent the better part of my youth as a player growing up with the game of basketball, it was natural that I should think in terms of players when I approached my first coaching position. Today, after many years as a basketball coach, my thinking remains unchanged. The players are the essence. The quality of their skills, the pooling of their abilities, and the sum total of their desire, courage, spirit, dedication, and love for the game determine the success of the team and the coach.

HANDLING PLAYERS

The handling of players is far more important than knowing all the mechanics of the game. One player will respond nobly when the coach "chews him out." Using the same approach with another player may break him like a twig.

Fans often ask me the difference between college coaching and professional coaching. In my experience I have found college coaching more attractive. In college coaching you drill and drill and meet twenty-six different opponents. In professional coaching you drill for six weeks and then play the rest of the teams in the league over and over again. With respect to the players, I have found the professionals just like college youngsters—great to work with.

Championship-winning coaches will be the first to acknowledge that players make the coach. That premise is undoubtedly the chief reason why I have remained aloof from a stereotyped offense and far removed (indeed, almost antagonistic) to the use of any defense except man-to-man. Celtic players were free to attempt personal plays at any time, and I have always believed that my players should have the same freedom in making "situation" decisions.

During my entire career as a player, I never had the opportunity to come under the influence of a coach, as such. In fact, there *were* no coaches in professional basketball when I played. You learned basketball from experience and by watching, imitating, and listening to the great players of the time. It was a system of trial and error with the emphasis on not making the same mistake twice.

Most coaches I have met during my later years in the game played for outstanding high school and college mentors and carried on with the style of play they had been taught. Other coaches "adopted" the methods

March 19, 1965. Coach Joe Lapchick in action in Madison Square Garden in semi-final game against Army. The Redmen won by a score of 67 to 60 to qualify for the finals against Villanova. They were victorious against Villanova to complete St. John's second grand slam and also win the National Invitational Tournament for the fourth time. (Wide World Photos)

of successful "name" coaches and attempted to apply these methods to their own coaching. To my way of thinking, this is a mistake. I feel that a coach should remain in character and apply the type of offense and defense with which he is most familiar. The abilities of the players available are, of course, the determining factors in determining the style of play to be adopted.

The only coaches I knew much about when I accepted my first coaching assignment (St. John's University, 1936) were Nat Holman and Clair Bee. I had, of course, played with Nat when we were Celtic teammates. Since he had coached at CCNY while playing with the Celtics, he was the first man to whom I turned. Nat gave me a lot of fine advice and help.

I was not personally acquainted with Clair Bee, but he was setting some great records with his LIU Blackbirds at that time, and I decided to have a talk with him. Clair and I soon became friends and have remained close ever since.

During our conversation, Clair asked how the players addressed me. "They call me Joe," I said.

He shook his head and said, "That's no good. They should call you Mister Lapchick, or, preferably, Coach."

I never forgot that little bit of advice. To me, respect is an important part of discipline that always goes hand-in-hand with coaching success. During my first year of coaching, a player intensely interested in something might unthinkingly call me Joe. I would smile and say, "Sure, Mister 'X'—you're absolutely right." The player always got the point.

COACHING FROM EXPERIENCE

Clair then helped me draw up some practice programs, and just before we parted he said something which, at the time, passed right over my head.

"Joe," he said, "I am embarrassed that you should come to me for suggestions. Why, when I first started to coach, I used to drive several hundred miles to and from Cleveland just to watch you and your Celtic teammates play."

Later that statement came back to me, and I realized that I could best teach that which I had learned through personal experience. I had been playing basketball all my life, part of the time with the greatest team of all time. I knew Celtic basketball inside and out, and it had been good enough to beat anyone and everyone. What more did I need?

I carefully reviewed the fundamentals, team techniques, and game tactics I had learned the hard way as a Celtic and then adopted them as my coaching "book." Those Celtic principles of personal and team play have stood by me through nineteen years of coaching the St. John's Redmen and the New York Knickerbockers. They were good enough to win against the best opposition professional and college basketball could offer.

The Celtic game is as good as it ever was, and some of the best college teams in the country are using the style successfully today. Were it not for the 24-second rule (after obtaining possession a professional team in the NBA must shoot before the 24 seconds elapse) most of the pro teams would be using the Celtics' passing attack today.

St. John's University has always fielded great teams. Coincidentally, one of the greatest of the Redmen teams—the "Wonder Five," coached by Buck Freeman—used the Celtic style exclusively. In his nine seasons as head coach, Buck's teams won 103 games and lost only 31. My St. John's teams were consistently regular season winners and record tournament victors.

All of the St. John's winning successes are, in my opinion, due to the presence of great players at the University. Down through the years, and particularly in recent years, New York City high school coaches have turned out hundreds of well coached players, and St. John's was fortunate in getting its share of the talent.

PLAYER RELATIONSHIP CODE

Undoubtedly, my personal experiences when breaking in with the Celtics had a great influence on my coaching. At any rate, I developed a sort of player relationship code down through the years. Some of the parts are listed below:

1. Make a strong effort to help players develop high ideals, a moral sense of correct behavior, and the power to govern emotional control as a basketball player and as a gentleman. With this as a starter, fair play, appreciation of the rights of others, and general sportsmanship follow in natural sequence. As a player, I became considerably less effective if I became unreasonably angry with either my opponent or the referee.

2. Take an active interest in the academic standing and progress of every player. The chief objective in the player's life is a good education. Show him that you are interested in his life objectives and his desire for an education.

3. Guard the health and physical welfare of the players. Devote personal attention to injuries and see that treatment is prompt and

Player relationships should be kept at a distance but a warm concern
in their personal affairs should be shown.

continued regularly. Make sure that good equipment is issued to
every player and that he is given frequent medical checkups and
attention. (It is especially important that the players be checked
before the gut-ripping drills start.)

4. Keep players at a distance without building a wall of reserve. Express warm concern in matters pertaining to their personal affairs
where possible but show no favoritism.

5. Study and "know" every player. Make him feel that he "belongs"
and is important to the success of the team whether he is a starting
"star" or the last sub on the bench. Be reasonable and treat little
incidents with a sense of humor, but by all means praise generously
a job well done. Be a disciplinarian and a teacher, but keep in
mind that every player is different. Some players resent strong
criticism while others expect it and will respond to it. In this connection I have always made a practice of telling a player why I
took him out of a game unless it was merely for a rest.

6. Be friendly and industrious, take pride in your work, and permit
no disrespect. Be the boss, but work democratically with your

"Always tell a player why you took him out unless it was for a rest." Coach Joe Lapchick in private conversation with Mike Clair. Left to right: (after manager) Dan Mascia, Ken Wirrel (hidden by Dan Mascia), Bob Duer (Coach Lapchick and Mike Clair).

players. A pleasant but firm approach to the job will enable the coach to sell his coaching to his players.

7. Show that you expect players to take pride in their behavior and appearance by setting a personal example of cleanliness in speech, dress, and actions.

8. Develop a strong desire in your players to win. But be sure to stress that it is important to win with controlled joy and a degree of humility. Losing is never pleasant, but if something is learned, all is not lost. You can lose with dignity despite internal pain if you have played your best and acted like a gentleman.

9. Player discipline is a must, but it is far better to help a player overcome his faults than to make him turn in his uniform for an infraction. It is the coach's solemn duty to first try to save the boy, not because of his importance to the team, but for the good of the boy himself. However, this must never be done at the cost of loss of respect by the other members of the squad.

The respect of one player for another is as important as player respect for the coach. One of the funniest experiences I ever had while I was with the Knicks concerned Sweetwater Clifton and player respect.

We were in the club car coming home from a game with Indianapolis. Sweets sat across from me. I called him over and said, "Sweets, we bought you from the Globetrotters for a specific purpose. That purpose is to help Gallatin on the boards. You are not doing a good job. The other big guys of the league are pushing you out of the play."

Sweets said nothing, so I added, "Those guys are taking the butter off your bread, and you damn well better let them know you are in business too. If they push you around, shove them back."

I waited for a moment to see his reaction and then asked, "Can you fight?"

Sweets said, "Coach, I'm *terrible*."

"Terrible or not," I said, "I never saw a basketball fight where a guy really got hurt. So you go in swinging if you have to."

Sweets was still reluctant and told me that he wanted to make a good impression. My answer to that was, "Baloney! Athletics, like no other field of endeavor, counts only the man and his performance."

As the season went on, Sweets got somewhat better but still left much to be desired. The following fall we broke training camp and started our exhibition games. We were playing the Boston Celtics in Albany, N. Y., when suddenly—it happened!

Sweets was coming down off the board and got belted, but good! His opponent was 6–7 and well put together, so it was no mismatch since Sweets was 6–5. After Sweets had been belted, he called his opponent some uncomplimentary names and started down court. The big guy followed and said something, and Sweets stopped. They squared off. Believe me—never in my life have I seen a guy polished off so neatly and so quickly as Sweets' opponent. The Boston bench came charging out to join the fray, but the suddenness of Sweets' conquest was so emphatic and conclusive that you could smell the rubber burn on their shoes as they screeched to a halt a safe distance away from our Sweets.

Later I asked Sweets about his remark of the previous year when he had said he was terrible. He clarified that by saying, "What I meant, Coach, was—I'm *terrible* when I get mad."

Sweets carried a new respect from all the players in the league after that. One writer wanted to train him for the fight game. I never saw better hands in or out of the ring. Yet he was one of the most popular guys on the circuit. Fans really loved to see him handle the ball. So did I!

An Old Timers' Game took place in Boston a year or two later, and Sweets came in from Texas to play. Because the plane was late, Sweets appeared just as the teams were lining up for the second half. When he appeared on the floor, the crowd gave him a standing ovation. What a great tribute that was to Sweets, the man and the player!

OTHER COACHING DUTIES

The coach should always be the first to report for the practice session, and he should come prepared to work. He should be on his toes and remain alert until the practice session ends.

The job of the coach does not end with his practice sessions and games. He has so many other responsibilities that his time and his life are devoted to his work. He is a teacher and a leader in many of the school's activities, a friend to his players' families, a marked member of the community, a supporter of civic projects, the school's most sought after public relations figure, a publicity director, sports reporter, public speaker, equipment manager, and the target of blame for his team's losses. He is responsible for restraining his personal emotions as well as those of his players, managers, assistants, students, spectators, and fans. He must accept the responsibility for the behavior of *everyone* when his team appears in public places.

The coach must observe strict personal rules of behavior and demand the same from his players. He must be a real sportsman and teach his players to follow his example, accepting victories with modesty and losses with dignity. He should be enthusiastic, energetic, industrious, inspiring, and dedicated. He should have unquestioned personal courage and be ready to defend his players, his school, the game, and his profession at all times. And, he must be a supersalesman, eager to sell the game to anyone and everyone who is or might be interested. Printed schedules, daily releases, speeches, and personal appearances at student assemblies, faculty gatherings, visits to player families, the banquet circuit, awards dinners, and friendly greetings to students and fans on and off the campus are all part of his job as a salesman of the game of basketball.

In keeping with the previous paragraphs regarding good sportsmanship and control of emotions by players, students, fans, and coaches, the following statement which appeared on the back of the basketball programs at St. John's University is pertinent:

DUTIES OF A HOST

The impression visitors get of St. John's depends upon you, the student body. As the student body of the home school you have very definite responsibilities as a host. You must constantly strive to perform these duties:

1. Make your guests, including the visiting team and officials, feel at home and wish to return.

2. Conduct yourselves in such a manner that your visitors will not feel as though they have been treated unfairly or dealt with in an unsportsmanlike manner.

3. Remember that your team plays at least half of its games away

from home. You must extend every courtesy to your visitors that you would want your team to receive when it is away.

4. The officials assigned to our games are men of high standing in their community and give of their time to help the game of basketball grow. Yes, it is true that they receive a fee for their services, but men of their character will not subject themselves to ill treatment for the sake of a fee. Respect their opinion and judgment and realize that they have a difficult job to perform.

5. Your visiting opponents have been well coached and have practiced hard. Their efforts will reflect their coaching and their success is not luck or a gift of the official. Their skills should be appreciated and applauded. Recognize their ability and give credit where credit is due.

6. Silence is a sign of respect and good manners during an attempted free throw.

7. Booing is a sign of a poor sport. Direct your energy toward the encouragement of your own team rather than booing the opponents and officials.

THE PRESS AND PUBLICITY

There is nothing like a winning team to sell basketball. And there is nothing like a losing team which is willing to take losses without doing something about it to kill interest in the game. The best way for a coach to sell his sport is through the press.

In New York I have always had many wonderful friends in press, radio, and television circles and all modes of communications. Some of the happiest moments of my life in sports were spent with these wonderful friends. Naturally, I always made sure that the St. John's publicity departments provided them with plenty of material. And, when I was with the Knicks, it was the same.

I would like to say something about one of the greatest of all publicity men—Lester Scott. Lester was in charge of Madison Square Garden's basketball publicity and particularly that which concerned the Knickerbockers and the college teams which appeared in the Garden. He was a friend to everyone who loved the game, great or small. He died in 1965, but it will be many, many years before his memory fades away. He was a friend and pal to all coaches, writers, fans, and players.

Basketball, Lester Scott, Gene Leone, Mama Leone's Restaurant, my coaching and playing pals, Nat Holman, Clair Bee, Howard Cann, Honey Russell, and all the good guys who wrote about the sport are bound up in one big memory book as representative of the happiest days of my life. What times we had, and what great friends we were! Not many coaches have the opportunity to enjoy such a relationship. The Monday noon basketball "quarterback" luncheons were always a source of pleasure and enabled me to get many little "player stories" and other team publicity into the hands of the men who were interested in the sport.

PRINCIPLES AND PRACTICES

By this time I am sure the reader will have a pretty good idea of the kind of basketball to which my coaching has been dedicated. However, I will be a little more specific with respect to principles and practices at this point and go into the actual coaching in later chapters.

Practicing, playing, and coaching have always been fun for me, and I have always thrilled when my players enjoyed the workouts and games. All practices and games were approached seriously, but I have always believed in short, snappy practices where the players got a degree of fun and pleasure out of the drills and game preparations.

Naturally, fundamentals were given first billing during early season practices. However, when we neared the opening of the season, most of the time was devoted to perfecting our offensive and defensive play and to preparing our special game tactics and strategy. Once in the season, we relied on our scouting notes and made special game plans for each coming opponent.

A degree of freedom is necessary, in my opinion, during the practices, but that does not mean players may engage in horseplay. Preparing for games and winning them is the goal. That means hard work and concentration. But I have always felt that a player learned best when he was happy in the process.

OFFENSIVE AND DEFENSIVE TEAMPLAY

After the players have mastered the fundamentals, offensive and defensive teamplay is stressed, and the team is prepared for every possible situation that may be met. Today all sorts of offensive and defensive techniques and strategies are in use, and the team must be prepared for all of them.

Defensively, a team may face a fast-breaking, wide open type of game one night and be called upon to meet a team which plays a slow-down possessive game the next night. The team must be prepared to meet the "giant center" post and pivot attack; weaves and/or pattern attacks which operate with the under-basket area kept open; a stall attack; an entire-game press, or some form of the shuffle offense.

Offensively, a team may face a straight man-to-man defense similar to the one the Celtics used; an assigned and matched-man defense which incorporates sagging and floating; one of the zone defenses (perhaps as many as three different types during a single game); the switching defense, or combinations.

A word of warning. A coach who has been successful often goes to sleep and fails to keep up with the changes in the game. He is heading for disaster. Today the coach and the team must be ready for anything. However, I feel that too many coaches think and teach in terms of plays, pressing, and zone defenses to the extent that they are "two o'clock" wizards and "nine o'clock" failures. The reason: Not enough work on basic fundamentals—passing, shooting, dribbling, guarding, boxing-out, etc.

Another point. Once in a while a coach will pull his team out of a game because they have a big lead. We are supposed to be experts and confident of our team's ability to meet a rally, but it is best not to be too sure. On the other hand, a coach or a team should be careful not to humiliate an opponent. Let the other team walk off the court with dignity.

A brief description of my offensive team philosophy would include the following:

Free-lance with direction

1. The ball must move with the players in contrast to stereotype or pattern movement. Free-lance means that all offensive play is optional but that it had previous direction such as working off a post (high or low). Players pass and go away from the ball or pass and set inside screens for cutting through the lanes to the basket. Players cutting through always fishhook to the sidelines and out, leaving paths open for following cutters. Changes of direction and the give-and-go are used when the opportunities arise.

2. *"Make the ball sing."* This was a Celtic axiom. The ball would zip from one green shirt to another and could be compared to the flying keys of a typewriter. The faster the ball moves, the tougher for the defensive opponents to adjust. That was the offensive objective of the Celtics. Their constant cry, "Make the ball sing!" meant to treat it as a hot coal and get rid of it almost "before you got it!" (The more you move the ball, the more you move the defense; and the more you move the defense, the more you discover

their weaknesses.) This ball handling can be construed as doing some surgery on the defense.

3. *Fast break.* The fast getaway was used whenever the opportunity was present. A team must be fast-break conscious. The fast break was used whenever possible and meant that three lanes were in operation at full speed with the "quarterback" filling the middle lane and the first two men "out" filling the sideline lanes. The quarterback stopped on the free-throw line unless he could see daylight all the way to the basket. The wing (sideline) players cutting down the outside lanes swept on around and under the basket.

A brief description of my defensive team philosophy would be as follows:

1. *Match-ups with opponents.* The match-ups would be based on scouting information if available. Otherwise, match-ups were made according to size and positions at the start of the game. Adjustments were made when necessary.

2. Strictly man-to-man alignments using the switch when absolutely necessary.

3. Occasional use of a zone and the man-to-man or zone press.

After spending a good part of my life as a player, I felt it was almost too good to be true to end up as a college coach. College administrators

Coach Joe Lapchick receiving an honorary degree from St. John's University. Degree conferred by President Reverend Edward Burke, C.M. (St. John's University) Alumni Hall at the University 1965. (Thos. J. Ryan Photography)

and educators accepted me as one of their own; granted me the same respect, and treated me just as if I were a college graduate or a professor.

Basketball, like all sports, is a great equalizer. The administrators in our schools and colleges are gentlemen—thoughtful, considerate, sincere, dedicated to their lifework, and true sportsmen in every sense of the word.

WINNING AND LOSING

It is the coach's responsibility never to settle for "good enough." He is settling for mediocrity when he does so and is shortchanging his players. It is his duty to teach his players to be able to shake hands with disappointment and from disappointment to learn lasting lessons.

Losing a game is not the same as losing a season or a career. Just so long as you remember why you lost, you have paid the price for your mistakes, in a sense, but are now prepared to deal with your adversaries. The athlete or coach who so esteems his ability that he feels he is above advice is indeed headed for serious trouble.

On reflection, I made a fine decision in 1923 when I chose basketball and the Original Celtics as a career. It was the same year that Joe Deveney, golf pro at Grosse Isle Country Club near Detroit, offered me the assistant pro job. It was also the same year the Dodgers offered this underhand, cross-firing (but very wild) chucker a tryout. In view of later events, I chose well.

This chapter has been directed toward the coach, his basketball philosophy, and his dedication to the game. Perhaps the best way I can express my personal devotion to the game is through a little story that combines basketball with my family life.

Once, when I was with the Knicks, I was worried about an important road trip that was coming up. I was deep in thought as I packed my bag, and when I walked out of the house, I forgot to kiss Mrs. "L" goodbye. We won all three of the road games, and I didn't kiss her the rest of the year. When you have a good thing going, you should not disrupt it.

CHAPTER 4

THE PLAYER
–EVALUATION

T HE GREATEST DESIRE a high school or college athlete should have is to acquire an education. The second greatest desire should be to make any team for which he is a candidate. In my opinion, when a candidate reports for a team, he "comes to play." He comes prepared to work and to fight for a position.

In my book no player "comes to play" if he reports out of condition. There is so little time between the first day of practice and the first game that a coach should advise his players that he expects them to report "ready to go!"

Off-season conditioning by the player on his own can be invaluable in preparing players for the hard work incidental to pre-season practices. However, I want to make it clear that I do not believe in the use of weights in any form as conditioners for basketball. Basketball is a game in which supple muscles are required.

CONDITIONING

The coach can help his players by laying out a program such as the following one, to help them in self-conditioning:

1. *Feet and ankles.* All coaches have experienced problems with blisters and ankle injuries. Players should condition their feet by wearing sneakers in their off-season workouts, with two pairs of sox, applying some sort of skin toughener to help avoid blisters, and strengthening the ankles by stretching and lifting exercises.

2. *Stamina.* Wind sprints, stopping, starting, change-of-pace, changing direction, etc.

3. *Agility.* Special work in heavy bag punching, shadow boxing, and rope jumping.

4. *Leaping ability.* Wall and/or board tapping, spread-eagle leaping.

5. *Hands and wrists.* Squeezing paper or a rubber ball, executing finger push-ups, and exercising with a medicine ball to strengthen hands (fingers), forearms, and wrists.

6. *Speed.* Basketball is a game of speed. It differs from all other sports in the degree of dexterity required. The closest would probably be lacrosse, where the player must fake passes, use head and body feints, and perform the same stops, starts, pivots, change-of-pace and direction actions found in basketball.

   There is one *big* difference between basketball and lacrosse. The lacrosse player can run with the ball; the basketball player cannot.

   Basketball is the only game where the player must be able to catch and pass the ball on the dead run; get rid of it on a one-two step or maintain possession and proceed through use of a dribble. This requires a high degree of skill, and the greater the proficiency of the player, the more effective his offensive ability. Therefore, the player who does not possess natural speed must work toward developing this important asset through special running programs —with and without the ball. There is no longer a place in basketball for a slow man.

7. *Endurance.* Basketball "staying power" comes through work. The legs bear the brunt of the player's endurance power along with the capacity of the lungs to pump sufficient oxygen into the blood stream.

8. *Strength.* All-round strength of arms, legs, neck, back, and shoulders comes with special exercises. Working a little longer each day and a little harder when the muscles complain leads to improvement in speed, endurance, and strength.

I expect my players to report in condition because it is a step in making the team. If a player has to be goaded into getting into shape, he hasn't come to play. A little work on his own time covering the program listed above isn't much to ask of an athlete.

Personal, individual training was good enough to help me get rid of my clumsy, overgrown awkwardness and get in shape to play with the greatest team in the world. If it was good enough for a fellow like me, it is good enough for the modern athlete who has at his command all of the present-day advantages such as good food, leisure time, and fine equipment and facilities.

The reader may get the impression that I was not interested in conditioning and training my players. That is, of course, untrue. In our early practices, we picked up on each player's personal efforts and carried them into our regular workouts. It is important for players to realize that true conditioning starts at the point of fatigue.

Starting with players who were in good physical condition, we combined our conditioning with basketball drills and scrimmages run at full speed. No time-outs were permitted to allow our players to get their breath or take a rest. The coaches came to work, and we expected the players to come to play.

Checking the physical readiness of the candidate was the first important step in evaluating him. He possessed enough will or mental strength to report in condition—or he did not! It was just that simple. First impressions are important. When a player reports in good condition, I feel that he has desire, wants to play, and has been willing to "pay the price" by making the first step on his own. My estimate of this candidate immediately rises.

I would like to repeat that it is the responsibility of the coach to provide all candidates who will try out for his team with a program for off-season or pre-practice conditioning. A few notes mimeographed and mailed out to each player requires little time or expense.

STAYING IN SHAPE

Following closely behind conditioning comes training. Reporting in condition and staying in shape are two different things. A player must maintain his conditioning after he has reported for the team by watching his diet, sleep, and personal habits. The coach cannot possibly watch his players day and night. He *can* watch their weight and alertness in the workouts, and check their physical records with the trainer and physician.

Smoking and drinking are taboo. Many athletes continue to smoke and try to obtain a "pickup" by drinking beer. Few stop to think how much greater they might be if they possessed the moral strength to abstain from both. Naturally, the coach will take prompt action should evidence of dissipation become known.

MENTAL TOUGHNESS

Mental toughness is just as important as physical toughness. If a player goes all out when he is tired out, keeps trying for one more interception when he is sure his next step will be his last, makes that impossible but vital rebound leap when he doesn't have enough strength left in his legs to move, fights as if his very life depends on preventing his opponent from gaining possession of the ball—*he* possesses mental toughness.

This mental toughness depends on the intensity of feeling which grips an individual or a team during a particular period of time. Tremendous victories and unbelievable upsets have come about because of this intensity of feeling. Johnny Beckman, more than any other player I have ever known, possessed this great quality. Some players can bring intense feeling to a climax for a special effort, situation, or game. Becky had it all the time, whether the Celtics were facing a team of yokels or playing for the world championship. This intensity of feeling, coupled with his mental toughness, made Beckman the greatest player I have ever known.

In evaluating his players, the coach must place a great premium on mental toughness and the rare quality of "intensity of feeling." Even though inferior in some of the game skills, players possessing these

Coach Joe Lapchick with members of his team: Left to right: Bob Duer, Co-captain; Jerry Houston, Co-captain; Ken McIntyre; Coach Lapchick; Sonny Dove. (N. Y. Post Photo)

qualities will fight until they drop, give all they have and more right down to the wire, and will win the "big" games and the tournaments.

During all of my coaching days I have taught my players to be tough, to be in top condition, and to be able to go all out, all the time, all the way. I call this the "survival" approach to playing.

When I first joined the Celtics, Johnny Beckman was the leader. Johnny was a tough guy who doubled as trainer, doctor, holler guy, fighter, and team quarterback. Becky based all of his basketball teaching and playing on "guts."

During my early days with the team I once hurt my arm and asked Becky what I should do about it. "Do about it?" he shouted, glaring up at me with his mean fighter's eyes. "Since when does a basketball player run on his arms?"

Some time later I injured a blood vessel in my shoulder, but I didn't mention it to anyone. By now, I knew what Becky meant by "guts" and I knew that a Celtic *always* "came to play." The shoulder pained so badly that I could scarcely lift my arm, but I kept my mouth shut and played anyway. It was pure agony for several games until finally the blood vessel burst and the pain vanished. Now, however, my arm and shoulder turned completely black. Beckman caught sight of it while we were dressing that night and rushed over with his bottle of liniment.

"That looks bad," he said, pulling the cork out of the bottle. "You take it easy tonight."

"The hell with you," I said. "And get away from me with that poison! It doesn't hurt now! Besides, I can play."

Playing one night, traveling all the next day, and playing again *that* night was a regular menu. We played *every* night and traveled *every* day. No matter how tired or stiff or how we felt physically, injury be damned, we played! In fact, injuries were ignored chiefly because Becky always had plenty of his homemade liniment ready, and he derived a sort of malevolent joy in using it for any and all injuries, external or internal.

So it may be that I have been a little hard to convince that one of my college or pro players needed a rest. In my opinion, an athlete's body can become inured to bruises and aches and pains and will recuperate quickly if exposed to hard work and even more hard work. The player who can "take it" without a complaint and continue to put out with savage joy brings back memories of Johnny Beckman. Any player who reminds me of Becky moves right up to the top of the list. Somehow, he knew that circulation, not rest, was always the quickest cure for injuries.

That brings me to the emotional qualities a player may possess. These qualities have a tremendous bearing on the success of the individual player and the team. The will to succeed is the motivating force behind every player's performance. Determination, courage, aggressiveness, confidence, hustle, and fighting spirit are all important qualities, and the "complete" player possesses them all.

The quality of a player's offensive and defensive skills may be evaluated through the drills used. I have found that it is wise to try to base all drills on game situations. Further, the drills should follow as closely as possible the planned offense and defense. It should be kept in mind that not infrequently a player will look bad in executing a drill but will perform the skill perfectly in a game.

THE BIG MAN

The height problem cannot be avoided. The "big man" is here to stay. I am amazed at the number of exceptionally tall kids in high school, college, and pro basketball today. Not only am I amazed at the height of the players, but also by their dexterity, speed, and quickness. Twenty years ago there were only 10,000 persons in the United States six feet, six inches or over. Today there must be 50,000, and it seems as if they are all playing basketball.

When I first broke into basketball, I was considered a giant. Weighing 140 pounds and standing 6–5, I was a monster. In those early days, ball players were scarce and seldom moved around much. Later, as one of the few tall men in the game, I played with Holyoke as well as with Schenectady in the New York State League. The Original Celtics—Horse Haggerty, Dutch Dehnert, Chris Leonard, Pete Barry, Nat Holman, and Eddie Burke, with Johnny Witte as playing manager—represented Brooklyn in the old American League. Since I was the tallest man around, I was always being called upon to play against Haggerty.

Haggerty was 6–4 and weighed around 220 pounds. No one wanted to tangle with him, but I got many opportunities (if that is what the experience could be called to play against the "Horse"). It was the best thing that could have happened to me, because in addition to bruised ribs and black and blue arms I learned how to play the big-man game.

In the 1922–23 season, owner Jim Furey asked me to play with the Celtics, and at last I was safe from the aggressive action of this "bull" with the steel elbows. I had replaced Haggerty as the center of this great team. Now I was considered a "giant" and acknowledged as a full-fledged pro. I cite all the above only to give the reader a glimpse of the height situation forty years ago. Centers averaged 6–2, and I was considered a leviathan.

Today, especially in professional ball, I would be considered no more than average in height. Many backcourt players in professional basketball are 6–6 or more and are as fast, clever, and quick as some of the smaller players of my time. Checking the heights in the NBA last year, I found that more than 66 per cent of the entire roster of players stood 6–6 or better in height.

Over the years it has been firmly established that professional teams cannot win the championship unless a "giant" is a member of the club. The Mikans, Chamberlains, Russells, Bellamys, and Thurmonds guarantee their teams will always be in contention and generally in the championship brackets.

A high school survey made a year or two ago showed that the taller the team, the more games it won. Teams averaging over six feet in height won more than 80 per cent of their games. But that is just the beginning. Tall youngsters who soar 6–6 to 7–0 and more are becoming commonplace. To the everlasting credit of the high school and college coaches, basketball has given credibility, stature, and athletic dignity to the players, who only a short while ago were ridiculed as clumsy goons.

Colleges are keeping step, with entire teams averaging more than 6–6 in height and the tallest player over 6–10. A number of suggestions have been made and several innovations have been tried in an attempt to "stop" the big man in basketball. None have been feasible or adopted. So, in evaluating their players, all coaches must consider the value of the "big" man (or men) to their teams irrespective of any lack of what might be termed basketball finesse.

THE "COMPLETE" PLAYER

Observance of the rules and sportsmanship in playing basketball (or any other game) is the mark of the great player. Nat Holman, famous scoring ace of the Celtics, was the highest paid player of his era and could have been a temperamental star. But Nat was always a gentleman, despite the roughing-up and rugged defensive tactics employed by opponents assigned to "dog" him. As Horse Haggerty's successor to the title of the Celtics' big man, I was given the business under the basket in game after game. However, I have always believed in the sprit of fair play and seldom found it necessary to repay in kind and "dish it out."

Blend in desire with mental toughness, intensity of feeling, the proper emotional qualities, playing skills perfection, the spirit of fair play, teamplay, and height, and you have the "complete" player.

THREE OF THE GREAT ONES

The complete player comes along once in a blue moon. Regardless of the quality or amount of coaching, the fact remains that these rare individuals would have found their way to be stars entirely on their own. There have been a number of these superstars. Three who come to mind are Oscar Robertson, guard for the Cincinnati Royals; Bill Bradley, Princeton University's superstar of a few years ago, and Bob Cousy, court magician supreme, who brought fame to Holy Cross and the Boston Celtics.

Oscar Robertson is a must for discussion. Standing 6–5, he plays back court, center, front court, or any place you care to put him with equal ability and effectiveness. The "Big O" leads a clean life and has speed, strength, and endurance to burn. He possesses mental toughness, and anyone who has watched him play will attest to his intensity of feeling. He can run, shoot, dribble, score, lead the fast break, jump with the "big" men, rebound, quarterback a team, play defense, and break an opponent's heart with his consistency.

Oscar set many high school and college records (13 NCAA) and has been voted the NBA's most valuable player by the greatest margin on record. One such player means a championship team, because he not only delivers in his own right but he lifts his teammates to the heights with him.

The second player to come to mind is Bill Bradley. Like Robertson, he has the mental toughness, the intensity of feeling, the concentration, desire, and all the other qualities in plentiful measure. He is a great passer, team player, and shooter, as his school and college records testify.

At one time during his career at Princeton, Bradley converted 57 consecutive free throws, a record in college as well as in professional ranks. He has a great variety of shots, shoots accurately with either hand, and averaged over 30 points per game at Princeton in addition to setting all kinds of records for passing and assists.

Standing 6–5 in height, he has perfect coordination, can lead the fast break, and play any position up front or in the back court. He goes after loose balls, feeds teammates, welcomes the toughest defensive assignment, and, eventually, may be classified on a par with Robertson. He starred in the Olympics and is now continuing his basketball career as a New York Knickerbocker. Bradley is deeply religious and gives of himself to further the moral advancement of youth and religious beliefs whenever and wherever possible.

The third player is everybody's favorite and everybody's All-America superstar. Incomparable Bob Cousy could do anything with a basketball that anyone else could do, and he could do it better! He was the complete player with the added qualities of creativity and artistry. He led his college teammates to the national championship and was the leader who sparked the Boston Celtics to championship after championship in the National Basketball Association. He holds all kinds of records in scoring and assists. He made an impact on the professional game which will never be matched, because it was he who used his blazing color and unbelievable skills to launch professional basketball into the "big time."

Why have I brought these super-complete stars to your attention? Because they can be set up as ideals and examples of "complete" players to all team candidates; because they epitomize what is good and clean and decent and worthy of bringing to the attention of all the boys and men who play and coach and watch the great game of basketball.

While it is undoubtedly true that these stars were especially gifted and selected as athletic "naturals" long before they began to play basketball, it is also true that they were dedicated to perfection and worked long and diligently to bring their "hoop" talents to a high state of refinement. They are truly an inspiration and example for all the players who dream and hope that they may one day become "complete" players.

PART TWO

CHAPTER 5

PRACTICES
–CHECK LISTS

P RACTICING MEANT NOTHING to the professional basketball players of my day. The pros used the games to "play" themselves into condition. When I reported for my first practice session at St. John's University, I talked to the players for a few minutes and then told them to do the first thing which came to mind. "Practice shooting," I said.

As I stood watching them shoot, I debated the next move but came up with absolutely nothing. After a time it was obvious that the players expected a change in the action. So I told them to choose up for a scrimmage. It was a poor start as a college coach and it was a poor season. St. John's won no major games that year and lost all five of the games scheduled in Madison Square Garden.

During that first season, little by little, I made coaching progress— learned to coach the "hard way" just as I had learned to play the game as a rookie pro. Watching other college teams play, talking to coaches, listening to the coaches explain their styles of play at the Monday "quarterback" luncheons at Leone's Restaurant, reading coaching books and the writers' columns in the papers all helped. The big step came when, at the end of the season, I decided to attend the annual convention of the National Coaches Association in Chicago. There I rubbed shoulders with some of the great coaches of the game and *listened* during the lectures and the bull sessions.

When I returned from the convention, I was filled with ideas and the desire to be a better coach. I wanted to concentrate on basketball, and so I tried to resign from the baseball coaching assignment. However, Father Rebholz, the moderator of athletics to whom I owe so much, would not permit it. He expressed confidence in my ability to coach both sports, so I stuck with it. That summer, I made plans for the next season and developed a definite style of play by breaking down the Celtic offense and defense into parts which I could use in my practice programs.

The next season I put my Celtic system into use, and success as a coach began to come my way. During the next ten years that I coached the Redmen before taking over the Knickerbocker coaching position, St. John's had good basketball and baseball teams.

ORGANIZATION

Before discussing practice programs and the check lists, I feel that something should be said about organization. The athletic director, head coach, assistant coach, freshman coach, trainer, equipment supervisor, building caretaker, publicity director, and the student managers should be familiarized with all the details concerning practices and games. Although the burden of this organization falls on the shoulders of the director of athletics, it is up to the coach to see that all members of the staff do their part in promoting a successful season.

The school calendar and the game schedule are the guides to setting up practice programs. These are usually available before the first practice starts. Taking into consideration the school holidays and vacations, the coach can plan his entire season, including consideration of possible holiday and postseason tournament participation.

PRACTICE DRILLS

Starting with the premise that the players report in condition, the coach can maintain this vital asset through drills which are developed around the game situations. Calisthenics, unless tied in with basketball skills in some manner, are, to my way of thinking, valueless. Wind sprints can be combined with passing the ball; running backward can be tied in with defensive play where players are teamed up and the defensive player must maintain his position despite stops, starts, sudden sprints, drives, change of direction, etc., by his opponent. Footwork can be improved in this kind of a drill as well as condition.

I have found that running drills that exclude lateral movement eliminate blisters and shin splints and strengthen the ankles and legs. After a week or so, drills incorporating lateral movement can be initiated. Under this plan, players are less prone to injuries later in the season.

There will be practices, especially in the mid- and late-season, when nothing goes right. The players fumble the ball, miss shots, fail to box out, and perform all the skills sloppily. Although you know a day's rest will do them good, this is the time to appear angry and disgusted (not very difficult) and chase them off the court.

When they come back the next day, they will be raring to go, fearful you might chase them again.

MENTAL CONDITIONING

All coaches have witnessed and some have experienced a season where talent-loaded teams have fallen apart somewhere along the way. It will often be found that a combination of faults were responsible. The players began to believe their newspaper clippings, developed a lazy mental approach to practices and games, and failed to put out in both. As was to be expected, the first team composed of hungry players upset them. The first upset led to others and the potentially "great" team became an ordinary one.

Mental conditioning is just as important to the team's ultimate success as is physical conditioning. Mental toughness and intensity of feeling are absolutely necessary in developing a lasting will to win. It will not be necessary for the coach to develop these qualities in his players if he himself possesses them. They will shine through for all to see. Players always "know" their coach and are quick to follow his leadership.

CONFIDENCE IN THE COACH

With respect to the coach's style of play, it is vital that the players be "sold" on his system. Still, I do not feel it is necessary for a coach to attempt to sell himself. I do feel it is vital for him to remain in character, to be himself. Personal sacrifices of his time and efforts to equip the team with a sound offense and defense, plus special tactics and strategy to meet any kind of an offense or defense the opponents may utilize, will of themselves sell his style of play. Winning, naturally, is the big convincer.

The coach must keep his team mentally and physically conditioned before and during the season right up to the last second of the last game. The players must be disciplined to the extent that they *know* the offense, defense, special tactics, and strategies the coach has provided are the "greatest."

The Celtic style of play, taking into consideration the changes in the rules and the tactical innovations which have come along in the past few years, is a sound, championship-winning game. I have had no difficulty selling it to my players. In fact, I have found the disciplined free-wheeling style of play much to their liking.

GAME-SITUATION DRILLS

Drill work is necessary in the perfecting of individual and team skills and should be based on game situations. Starting with slow movements and analyzing when, where, and how the skills can be used, the action should be speeded up until the players can run them perfectly at game speed. The coach must demand alertness, accuracy and hustle in the drills and make corrections as the mistakes occur. It is well to remember that the work of the players in the practices will be reflected in their play in the games.

When working on situation plays, I feel it is important to use "slow-motion" action so that every feint, fake, screen, cut, pass, or shot and its importance to perfect execution of the "whole" play may be discussed.

Separating the squad into forwards (corner men), centers, and guards for group work is an effective way to teach position skills and responsibilities. Each player teaches the other. Rotating players so they work in the different positions will familiarize them with the requirements of each spot. A 6–10 center working with a 5–10 guard will bring out skills and moves which will benefit both.

A practice outline for each workout should be prepared before the coach steps out on the court. In my own coaching a standard time schedule and skeleton program was prepared and the general and particular work I felt necessary was inserted. After our fundamentals were perfected (are they ever?) and as the season progressed, the schedule was changed so that individual and team weaknesses that showed up in the previous game could be corrected.

SKELETON PRACTICE PROGRAM

2:50 P.M. to 3:30 P.M.

SHOOTING AND GROUP WORK

Players work on shots they use in their positions (particularly those in which they are weak). Group work includes "one-on-one" and "two-on-two" play in which shooting, passing, driving, and defense are stressed.

3:30 P.M. to 4:15 P.M.

DRILLS

Offensive:

Passing, jumping, dribbling, cutting, screening, outlet passes, fast break.

Defensive:

Guarding (sliding, over-the-top, switching, sagging, floating, boxing-out, rebounding).

4:15 P.M. to 5:30 P.M.

SCRIMMAGE

Half- and full-court work. Team offenses and defenses, the press, freezing the ball, situation plays.

GENERAL CHECK LIST

Game Administration
  Program
  Manager's duties
  Assistant Coach
  Scorers and Timekeepers
Dressing Room Procedure
  Previous to Game
  Between Halves
  After Game
Bench Arrangement and Deportment
  Seating
  Reporting
  Time-out Huddle
Game Rules
  Time-outs
  Personal Fouls
  Technical Fouls

OFFENSIVE PLAY CHECK LIST

Center Jump and Held-Ball Situations
  Signals
  Positions (Covering jumper's opponent)
  Controlling the Tap
  Stealing the Ball
Advancing the Ball
  Changing from defense to offense
  Slow Advance
  Fast Break
  Out-of-bounds
Free-throw Alignments
Number 1 Set Offense Formation (free-wheeling with high or low post)
Number 2 Set Offense Formation (free-wheeling with middle open)
All-Purpose Offense
Attacking Zone Defenses
Special Situation Offenses
  Out-of-Bounds

Own Goal
Opponent's Goal
Side of Court
One-on-One Plays
Two-on-Two Plays
One-Shot Plays
  Man-to-man Defense
  Zone Defense
Holding the Ball
  Playing out the Clock
  One Shot
Stall Offense
Semi-Freeze
Freezing the Ball
Meeting the Press
  Man-to-Man
  Zone
Sag and Float Plays
Meeting Man-to-Man Variations
  Screen-Switch
  Combinations

DEFENSIVE PLAY CHECK LIST

Center Jump and Held Ball Situations
  Defensive Alignments
  Stealing the Ball
Defensive Balance (Set Offense)
Changing from Offense to Defense
Stopping the Fast Break
Man-to-Man Defense
  Matching-up
  Use of Front-Slide-Switch
  Use of Screen-Switch
Boxing-Out
Rebounding
First Pass
Zone Defense *
Combination Defense
Box and One
The Press
  Man-to-Man Press
    Partial
    Three-Quarter Court

Half-Court
Full-Court
Zone Press
   Partial
   Three-Quarter Court
   Half-Court
   Full-Court
The Sag
The Float
Collapsing Defense
Special Situation Defenses
   Held Ball
   Out-of-Bounds
   Free Throws
   Big Man
   Stopping the Star

The above check lists overlap in certain parts, and few coaches will have time to thoroughly prepare their teams for every phase listed. However, they can prepare for eventualities by developing one or two all-purpose attacks and defenses.

All coaches should make sure that no part of their style of play, including tactics and strategies, will be overlooked in their practice programs. Drawing out a play on the sideline during an important game may be colorful and draw "oh's and ah's" from the fans and raves in the sports columns, but in my opinion it is a waste of important time simply because it has not been rehearsed and there is not enough time to plan it right. It is too late. To me, such action means the coach has not done a good job in his practice programs. The team should be ready for any possibility because it has been included in the coach's check list and has been practiced.

Practice programs should be geared to the team. A junior-senior team should work more on refinements whereas a sophomore-junior team should be trained to meet all situations. Multiple offenses and defenses can lead to *overcoaching*. The coach must consider his material in equipping them with the various offenses and defenses. Clair Bee, Hank Iba, Adolph Rupp, and John Wooden have won the big games and have stood in the winner's circle because their players were well versed in all phases of the game. Yet they relied on one basic offense and one basic defense, adding only necessary adjustments to meet special situations.

---

* In professional basketball (NBA) the zone is outlawed, and at St. John's University I rarely used it. However, when we were confronted with a tough pattern-type offense or when our personnel did not have the necessary mobility to cope with speedier opponents, we used the zone.

CHAPTER 6

OFFENSIVE SKILLS

BASKETBALL IS A SIMPLE GAME—on the surface. The chief objective is to put the ball through the basket more often than the opposition, and the modern "shooters" are so proficient in their execution of the various shots that they make shooting look easy. Many persons feel that shooting is about all there is to basketball. They fail to realize that the proficiency of the players represents years of practice and work and that shooting is the simplest part of the game.

The fundamentals of the sport have changed very little. With the exception of the jump shot, the techniques of the offensive skills are about the same as they were forty or fifty years ago. As far as team techniques are concerned, there is practically nothing new. The man-to-man press which many people consider a modern development was used the very first time Dr. James A. Naismith, the inventor of the game, threw out a soccer ball for a scrimmage (December 1891, American International School, Springfield, Mass.).

Despite the tumult and shouting which accompanies the scoring of a basket and the glory and renown gained by the high scorer, the fact remains that most of his success is due to the unselfish passing and screening support of his teammates. So, in discussing the offensive skills, I will start with the most important one of all—ball handling.

HANDLING THE BALL

"Make the ball sing," still rings in my ears. Handling the ball came first with the Celtics, and it still stands first in importance as the greatest skill in the game. Today all youngsters can shoot with deadly accuracy, but few are good passers or dribblers.

Catching the ball

Big hands are usually the mark of the good athlete. In basketball a big hand means length and flexibility of the fingers. The receiver must watch the ball until it comes in contact with his fingertips and thumbs. This does not mean that the player focuses his eyes on the ball to the exclusion of everything else. Peripheral vision should enable him to "see" everything in front of him and to his sides up to 180 degrees and still concentrate on watching the ball into his hands.

The receiver should move toward the ball at all times (unless cutting toward the basket) with his hands and arms held loosely and extended to meet it. The ball is caught in the fingertips, with the thumbs used for extra support. The hands and arms "give" with the contact, and the receiver must be sure that his palms do not touch the ball.

As soon as the ball comes into contact with the hands, it should be moved to a position where a pass, shot, or dribble can be initiated.

Fumbling

The major causes of fumbling are as follows:

Failure to meet the ball (step or run toward the passer).
Receiver did not watch it into his hands.
He fought the ball, tried to pass it before he received it.
Receiver was tired, off balance, possessed poor vision, or had weak hands.
The pass was too high, too low, or too far to the side. Or, the passer had given the receiver too much of a lead.

Making the pass

The responsibility for a good pass rests with the passer. First in importance is depth and peripheral vision so that he can see straight ahead and to the sides without turning his head. I have coached several great back-court players who possessed this asset, and their presence meant good teams.

The passer expects the receiver to meet the pass unless he is free and is cutting for the basket. Even so, the receiver should give the passer a target, extending a hand with the palm facing the passer. Keeping both hands on the ball and faking a pass to determine the defensive players' reactions aid in protecting the ball.

Blind passes (looking one direction and passing another) should not be permitted. These passes, along with cross-court passes, lead to interceptions. Behind-the-back passing is taboo. It is ineffective showboating.

The passer should not turn his head to look at the receiver. Feinting and faking with the ball will help disguise the direction of the pass and the receiver. Keeping both hands on the ball will often permit the passer to check his pass where a one-hand pass might result in an interception.

Players must be able to adapt the type of pass to the situation. There are times when the one-hand underhand (shuttle), back bounce, back flip, or jump pass may be necessary to "time" the play. However, few players are masters of all of these passes. The Celtics were probably the greatest "passing" team of all time, yet their repertory of passes was limited to the baseball, chest, and flip passes almost exclusively.

Timing requires intensive practice because of the speed at which passers and receivers travel. The position of the defensive opponent guarding the receiver will determine the type of pass to be used and the force with which the ball will be delivered.

The passes

No attempt will be made here to describe the execution of all the passes used in the game nor of those which I use in my coaching. However, the well equipped basketball player should be able to handle the following passes:

Two-hand passes
   Chest, bounce, overhead, and the flips (front, back, and side).
One-hand passes
   Baseball, bounce, chest, flips (forward, sideways, backward) and the "push." (The push-pass was a Celtic favorite. We were so adept in the use of this pass that the ball never came to rest in a player's hand—he met the ball and "pushed" it back to the original passer or to another teammate with a mere flip of the wrist.)

DRIBBLING THE BALL

Dribbling is the second most important skill in basic fundamentals. Although passing is the best way to control the ball and advance it for a score, present-day basketball, with its overshifting, individual pressure, sagging, floating, close coverage of teammates, and extensive use of the "press" as a strategic as well as a full-game defense, makes use of the dribble an extremely valuable offensive and defensive asset.

The dribble is made by pushing the ball against the floor with the fingertips. The first step should be long, and the player should maintain a low, crouched position with his head up and his eyes focused straight ahead. All players should be able to dribble with either hand.

Generally, the dribble may be employed as follows:

1. To advance the ball to the front court.
2. As a part of the fast break.
3. To time a play or to set a screen.
4. To score by means of a dribble-drive.
5. To escape from a dangerous situation.
6. To utilize a teammate's screen for a drive.
7. To protect the ball until teammates get free.
8. To initiate a personal give-and-go play.
9. To advance against the press.
10. To change direction or as a change of pace.
11. To penetrate an inner defense.
12. To draw sagging defensive players.

On drive-in plays the dribble should be kept at waist level. To escape from a dangerous situation or when freezing the ball, it should be kept at a height below the knee. When going around a defensive opponent, be sure to keep your body between him and the ball and dribble the ball in a sort of circle path rather than *at* the guard. (Right hand dribble when going to right and left hand dribble when going to the left.)

If the defensive opponent is stationary (one-on-one situation) the following moves are possible:

1. Dribble up, stop, shoot.
2. Dribble up, pivot, and continue on (left or right).
3. Dribble up fast, slow down (change of pace), pick up fast, and continue on in the same direction.
4. Dribble up fast in one direction, use the cross-over, change hands in controlling the ball, and drive in the opposite direction.

If the defensive opponent is approaching rapidly, advance slowly, then suddenly employ change of pace and the cross-over in changing direction, and drive on around him.

If there is one player who is more expert than others in the use of the dribble (usually a back-court player) he should have the responsibility of advancing and handling the ball when meeting the press. Not infrequently, such a player can meet the press almost singlehandedly. Further, when his team is leading in the score and going down the stretch toward the end of the game, this player is capable of drawing fouls, and in the one and one free-throw situation he may not only protect the lead but increase it. A good dribbler can dribble back toward midcourt to slow up the offense and/or realign for a balanced court.

FAKES AND FEINTS

Whenever I think of fakes and feints, I am reminded of an incident which happened in Brooklyn's Arcadia Hall. The Celtics were playing Chicago, and George Halas had discovered the tallest basketball player in the world, Clyde Shoun, who was 7–0. The first time I got the ball I feinted him out of position, and Shoun leaped so high in the air that his head hit the lights. Johnny Beckman rushed up to me and said, "Joe! Use your head! Don't feint him any more. We've got to finish this game and get our money. We need the pay!"

The ability to fake and feint is an important player skill, and guards and forwards must be expert in their use. Faking with the body and feinting with the eyes and head will often throw a defensive opponent off balance long enough to enable the offensive player to get a shot, pass, or drive away. Fakes and feints are tied in closely with footwork and driving and, for the purposes of this chapter, will be combined. The eyes and head can be used to disguise the approach of a pass when an opponent has his back to the ball.

Although fakes and feints can be used when a player is in motion, the great majority start when the player is alive (has not dribbled the ball) and is standing still. Here, it is important *not* to bounce the ball. Many players automatically bounce the ball when they first receive it (a playground habit) and this, of course, restricts their next play to a shot or a pass. This stupid bounce eliminates their opportunity to drive, and a smart defensive player will immediately advance and force the offensive player to pivot away or into a held ball situation.

The following "moves" combine body fakes, head and eye feints, and the drive. Their usage depends upon the defensive action of the opponent.

    a. Does he play tight, applying pressure in his defensive assignment?
    b. Does he lean to the left or the right?
    c. Does he sag or float away?
    d. Does he cross his feet on your moves?
    e. Does he leave his feet?
    f. Does he overshift in one direction or the other?
    g. Does he lunge for a fake pass?

The above action by the opponent determines the move which should be used to get a shot away, to make a pass, or to drive. (Right-handed player. Left foot is pivot foot.)

a. Long-short step and go. Take a long step forward, pause for a split second, continue with a short step, and drive.

b. Fake shot and go under. Raise ball as if to shoot, and when opponent advances to stop shot, use cross-over and go under for the drive.

c. Fake drive and shot. Take a medium length stride, fake with body to continue, step back, and go up for jump shot.

d. Rocker step and jump shot. Step directly toward opponent, bring foot back and slightly to rear of the other foot, rocking body forward and back simultaneously. Note reaction of opponent and drive to either side.

e. Fake drive and shot and go. Take a long step forward, come back quickly, fake shot, take long step, and drive.

f. Fake cross-over and drive. Take cross-over step, protect ball, return and drive in opposite direction with same foot, moving immediately into dribble and drive.

g. Fake drive, fake shot, and shoot. Fake drive with long forward step, bring foot back, fake shot, and then go right back up for shot.

The above fakes, feints, and drives may be varied in many ways, and the individual player should experiment with them until he develops a personal repertory. Some players will execute one or two of the moves

DIAGRAM 6.1 Fake Cross-Over and Drive. Player A fakes cross-over by advancing his right foot to the left. The right foot is drawn back, swung to right with a long step, immediately followed with a short step by same foot and into the drive.

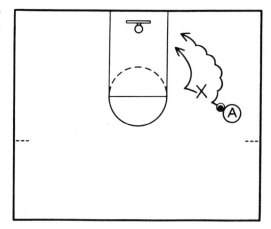

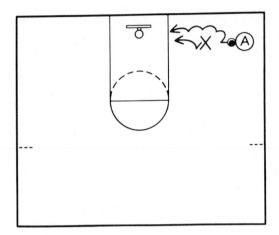

DIAGRAM 6.2 Fake Shot and Go Under. Player A fakes a shot, and when opponent shifts weight forward to stop the shot, A takes a long step with right foot and goes into drive.

to a higher degree of perfection than others. If they are found to be successful, these should be their stock in trade for use in a given situation (one-on-one).

FOOTWORK

The complete player is a master of the skills, starting with footwork. He has acquired the knack of body balance (keeping his body weight evenly divided on the balls of his feet), and he is fast, if not naturally, then because he gets the quick start and has worked on his footwork (running forward and backward, sprinting, changing at full speed, stopping suddenly, changing pace, leaping, turning, pivoting, cutting, driving, and screening) until he makes the moves automatically.

Every coach and most players are familiar with the techniques and execution of the above footwork and it is unnecessary to discuss all of them in detail in this book. The player who really wants to succeed in basketball will not need a coach to teach him footwork.

I lived in a tenement neighborhood where anyone who did the unusual was a nut. I would go out in the dark of night and practice all sorts of starts and stops, leg cross-overs, changes of direction, and other moves with my body tilted at such angles that I was sure at first I would fall down. But every night—or almost every night—I ran my crazy patterns so that, in the end, I had complete control of my legs. I was the first center who became more than a "get the tap, get the rebound, and get out of the way." I was a scorer.

I had never heard of a coach when, as a youngster and later as a budding professional, I realized the importance of footwork and began doing something about it. I spent hours and months after work, all alone and usually at night, in perfecting my footwork.

CUTTING

If a player understands what "move" means in basketball, he will find hundreds of cutting opportunities during a game. Cutting means that the player is sprinting for the basket because he got a "step" on his opponent by faking or feinting or because his opponent "took a peek." The cutter also uses teammates' screens and "picks" and takes advantage of every situation and play which permits him to cut to the basket providing his teammates are, or will be, in a position to get the ball to him.

Timing was mentioned in connection with passing, and it is just as important when cutting to the basket. Many players never realize this important point and will cut time after time and clutter up the area near the basket when teammates with the ball are not in position or ready to pass to them.

DIAGRAM 6.3 This diagram shows offensive player A using head and eye feints and a body and foot fake (to the left) before using teammate B's set screen or "pick" in cutting to the basket. Note that A is practically brushing B in his cut so the defensive opponent will not be able to maintain his guarding position. Note further that A has sped directly toward the basket on a straight line to make it difficult for B's opponent to switch efficiently. This sort of cutting technique can be initiated from any position in the front court.

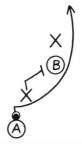

DRIVE

Drive requires that the first step be long and that the ball be quickly advanced ahead of the extended foot. When driving to the right, the player's left foot is the pivot foot. The dribbler lowers his left shoulder with his left arm and hand trailing loosely toward the floor. The right shoulder is carried higher than the left and the ball is dribbled close to the right side by the right hand.

Although it is possible for a player to use his right foot as the pivot foot when driving left, it is probably better for the right-handed player to use his left foot as the pivot foot irrespective of the side of the court from which he starts and whether he intends to drive right or left. The left-handed player will, naturally, use his right foot as the pivot foot.

SCREENING

Celtic players placed a high premium on their ability to do something without the ball. The various moves and cuts without the ball were un-named and no particular paths were required. The terminology was confined to one word: "Move!" One of the moves which was popular was to pass the ball to a teammate and cut away from him. This move or screen is still one of the best a player can make. (Pass and go away means to screen away from the ball.)

Today, screening is an important team offensive skill and, in one form or another, is used by all teams. Every player should be expert in the application of all types of screens. As a general rule, the screener should try to face the basket so he will be in a position to cut should he "see daylight" on a switch or defensive confusion on the part of opponents.

In setting a screen or in moving behind or in front of a teammate's opponent, the cutter must be sure to avoid charging or use of his arms, body, or legs to restrain the defensive player. Contact in such situations usually is the responsibility of the offensive player.

The term describing the screen is not important. It is the play which develops that counts. This statement is made because there is a wide variety of terms used to describe the various screens. A few of the more important screens are diagrammed in the following pages.

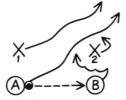

DIAGRAM 6.4 Inside Moving Screen. Player A passes ball to teammate B and cuts behind B's opponent. The screen may be fast, slow, or combined with a change-of-pace cut.

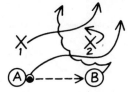

DIAGRAM 6.5 Outside Moving Screen. Player A passes ball to teammate B and cuts in front of B's opponent.

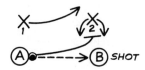

DIAGRAM 6.6 Outside "Set" Screen. Player A passes ball to teammate B and moves to a stop position between B and his opponent.

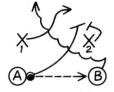

DIAGRAM 6.7 Inside "Set" Screen. Player A passes ball to teammate B and moves to a stop position back of B's opponent.

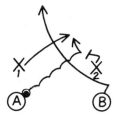

DIAGRAM 6.8 Inside Dribble Screen. Player A dribbles to a position between teammate B's opponent and the basket. (This is a set screen but A could continue on with his dribble if he desired.) B cuts as shown.

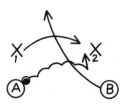

DIAGRAM 6.9 Outside Dribble Screen. Player A dribbles to a position between teammate B and his opponent. (This is a set screen but A could continue on with the dribble if he desired.) B cuts as shown.

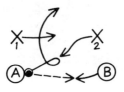

DIAGRAM 6.10 Roll Screen. Player A has passed the ball to teammate B and started to make a screen. However, contact seems imminent with B's opponent so A pivots to the back on his left foot and avoids a charging foul.

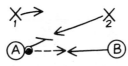

DIAGRAM 6.11 Screen Stop. Player A passes the ball to teammate B and starts to screen. He sees that contact with B's opponent is imminent and stops so that the opponent may pass by without interference.

DIAGRAM 6.12 Turnaround Play. A good forward-center play. Player A passes the ball to pivotman B, using a high toss in the air. The pivot man breaks out to the ball, leaps high in the air to catch the ball, lands on the floor, and immediately pivots toward the basket holding the ball overhead at arm's length.

Player A delays his cut until B has pivoted and then runs his opponent (X-1) into B (if possible). If B's opponent (X-2) switches to cover player A, pivot man B may shoot or dribble in to the basket. If pivot man B's opponent (X-2) does not switch, the ball is passed to A for a clear shot at the basket.

SHOOTING

The free throw is the most important shot in the game today. Box scores of many close high school, college, and professional games show that the losing team sank more baskets from the field but lost the game because their opponent was more accurate from the "line." Losing teams, in most cases, committed more fouls than the winners. The exception here was in games where one team was superior. Here, the percentage of conversions by the winners was higher, but they also committed a greater number of fouls. Seventy per cent is considered a good average for a college team from the line.

The one-and-one fouling rule has increased the value of the free throw, and many close games are determined in the closing minute or two by the accuracy of one team (player) from the line. The guard who is the best free thrower should do most of the ball handling.

Shooting averages for shots from the field have increased to such an extent that an outstanding scorer may average more than 30 points per game per season and boast of a 50 per cent shooting average. Many players possess the ability to score with a great variety of shots from all parts of the floor. Others, the vast majority, rely upon just three—lay-up, one hand "set," and the one-hand jumper. The shooting accuracy of players at all levels in the game is increasing by leaps and bounds. Not too many years ago 30 per cent was considered good; 40 per cent, unusual; 50 per cent, impossible.

Coaches need only teach correct techniques today. The players will do the rest. In fact, shooting has such an attraction that players would spend an entire workout taking pot shots at the basket if the coaches would let them. Most players practice shooting in their back yards, school playgrounds, and at odd times so that the coach can devote half of the shooting time scheduled for practices to perfecting the free-throw accuracy of his players. It will pay off. Many championships have been lost because the opponents knew whom to foul in the closing minutes of the game. Oddly enough, there is one great professional player who seldom averages 50 per cent of his free throws. He is constantly fouled.

So much has been written about shooting that it is unnecessary to detail techniques of all the shots. However, several principles will be discussed.

SHOOTING CHART

Areas for Various Shots

DIAGRAM 6.13

A. Jump shot, Pivot shot
B. Backboard shot
C. Jump shot, One-hand set, Two-hand set
D. Jump shot, One-hand set, Two-hand set
E. Two-hand set
F. "Hope" shots (last-second heroes)

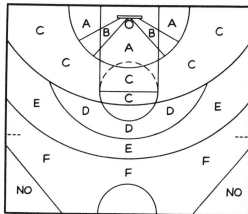

General shooting principles

The ball. The ball is held loosely in the fingertips, and the wrists must be flexible. It should be carried high and never lowered by the arms from the starting positions. The drop of the ball made by the wrists at the start of the shot is sufficient.

Eyes. As a general principle, the eyes are focused on an imaginary spot on the backboard for lay-up shots and bisect the rim on a line from the point where the shot is taken for the "clean" shots.

Shooting hand. Most players shoot from the "V" made by the thumb and the forefinger of the shooting hand for the one-hand shots. In the two-hand shots the ball is held with the thumbs, first two fingers, and the little finger. In the two-hand overhand shots the thumbs will usually be the last to leave the ball. In the underhand "sweeps" the first two fingers will be the last to leave the ball.

Fingers. The fingers control the ball on all shots.

Wrists. When the ball is released close to the basket, the wrist(s) is used almost exclusively.

Elbow. When some distance from the basket, the elbow is used to generate more force.

Knees. The knees should give a little on all shots. The greater the distance from the basket, the greater the knee bend and spring from the floor.

Feet. All shots are taken with the balls of the feet on the floor at the start of the shot.

Ankles. Spring is generated by the ankles. On jump shots the ankles play the most important part in getting the body into the air.

The arc of the shot. A medium arc is probably best for all shots. Some players use a high arc, but this requires a little more time for release and usually forces the body back, limiting to a small degree the amount of follow-through. Tall players usually employ a flatter arc because they leap so high in the air. When close to the basket, more and more professional giants are using the "stuff" shot to flip the ball down through the ring. (High school and college rules prohibit the "dunk.")

The spin. Many players exaggerate spin. Natural spin is best; fingertip control imparts a natural spin.

The snap. The distance from the basket governs the force that fingers, wrists, elbows, knees, and ankles give to the ball.

Use of the backboard. Expert shooters know the backboard angles as well as Willie Hoppe knew those which were necessary for accurate billiard shots. When coming in for a lay-up in area B, the degree of angle and the imaginary spot on the board on which the player will attempt to place the ball is important. Each player will learn these "spots" through experience. The corner of the painted rectangle on the backboard will be about right for the banking of the ball when a shot is taken from the rear of area B.

The closer the player gets to the basket, the lower the spot on the backboard (excluding underhand lay-ups). Placing the ball softly on the board is vital. Natural spin is best for all backboard shots. Excess spin is used by many players, and the result is that the ball actually whirls away from the spot and over the basket for the loss of a possible two points.

Tall pivot players determine their take-off point for a lay-up on their distance from the backboard. Many players' shots hit the basket support because they start their leap too late. This is particularly true of the inexperienced player.

Most pivot men use the backboard for their hook and the one-hand "push" as well as straight, step-away, reverse, and jump turn shots. Others restrict their scoring attempts from all parts of the A and B areas to exclusive use of the hook shot.

Tap-in or rebound shots. The tap-in is icing on the cake, not only for the player who scores the bucket but for his team. Some tall players are graced with a natural ability to estimate the direction, force, and height of the rebound and can time their leaps so perfectly that any rebound near them is a sure two points. Smaller players often possess the ability to cut in front of taller opponents and secure the ball. Not infrequently this is possible because their assigned opponents are not proficient in boxing-out or ignore them.

Whether the offensive rebounder should tap the ball back up, tip it out to a teammate, catch the ball and go back up for a shot, or throw it out to a teammate is a matter of player judgment.

Lay-up shot. The lay-up shot may be made with one or two hands. The one-hand shot may be attempted underhand but is usually restricted to overhand use. From the right side of the basket the ball is carried up as far as possible with two hands following a spring from the floor with the left foot. At the height of the leap the ball is transferred to the shooting hand (right) and laid gently against the backboard with the fingertips. From the left side of the basket the shot should be made with the left hand and the take-off should be from the right foot.

The two-hand underhand sweep lay-up was performed perfectly by

Dick McGuire, who played for me with the Knickerbockers. Dick would take off at the free-throw line and float through the air before releasing the ball with the two-hand underhand sweep.

If a player has constant trouble with lay-ups, he should check his "one-two" stride ("one" count on right foot, "two" count on left foot for right-hand shot and vice-versa for left-hand lay-up), his focus of eyes on the imaginary spot on the board, and the shortening or lengthening of his strides so he will leave the floor at the right spot before he goes up for the lay-up.

The one-hand set shot. Hank Luisetti was the first one-hand shooter to visit Madison Square Garden. He came in with a fine Stanford team and was the standout player in a game which saw the Indians upset the LIU Blackbirds and end their consecutive victory streak at 44 games.

The mechanics of the one-hand set, the one-hand free throw, and the jump shot are the same with the exception of the leap in the air for the jumper. In the one-hand set, the right-handed shooter should advance his right foot with his weight evenly balanced. The knees are slightly bent, and the ball is lifted with both hands to a position near the right shoulder with the elbow under the ball. The left hand pushes the ball back and falls away as the right hand is carried upward and out in a smooth, even follow-through to release the ball from the fingertips.

The one-hand jump shot. In 1945–46 Wyoming University came into the Garden with a kid named Kenny Sailors, who unveiled a new weapon —the jump shot. The shot was a sensation and has been basketball's chief scoring weapon ever since. Paul Arizin, former Villanova great, Philadelphia Warrior, and 76'ers star, became an outstanding shooter by using the jump shot almost exclusively during his career. Bill Sharmon, All-American from Southern California and later a star and back-court teammate of Bob Cousy, used the jump shot as *his* chief scoring shot from the field.

The one-hand jump shot is the most popular shot in the history of the game. It was developed on the West Coast and in the Middle West and is a combination of the running one-hander and the one-hand set. With the exception that the feet and shoulders should be squared to the basket before the take-off from the floor, the mechanics of the one-hand set shot apply to the one-hand jumper.

The jump should be as high as possible, and the elbow should be carried forward and out along the line of flight of the ball. Some players extend the ball over the head, but the great majority of the better shooters lift it over the shoulder. The arm must be fully extended and the fingers snapped forward at the last moment to provide spin and control to the ball.

Coming to a quick stop and at the same time "squaring" the shoulders to the basket both add to the shooter's accuracy. A few players employ a kick which flexes the lower legs backward, but the greater number of accurate shooters leap upward from the toes with their legs extending straight down toward the floor.

The great value of the jump shot lies in the deception which precedes the shot. The offensive player can drive toward the basket from any direction, and only he knows when he will attempt a jump shot. The defensive opponent may play the dribbler perfectly on the drive only to find that his attempt to force the dribbler away from the basket left him vulnerable to the jumper. The defensive player's concentration on correct dribble defense results in a delay, and this split-second pause permits the shooter to get the ball away without interference. With the development of the one-hand jump shot the entire concept of the game changed. For the first time, the offense surpassed the defense.

The jump shot changed the offensive game in the early 40's just as Dutch Dehnert, the Celtics' great passer, changed the game in 1926 with his pivot play. Now the jump shot was added to the push shot, and the low scores of 20 to 30 points per team were history. Incorporated with the elimination of the center jump following a score, the jump shot led the way to the high-scoring game of today, where total team points often soar into the hundreds.

In my opinion, the greatest fault in guarding against the jump shot is the effort made by defensive players to block the shot with a downward motion of the hand. This usually results in a foul and a two-shot free throw. "Hip" coaches now find it is wiser for their players to let the shooter get the shot away but to jump straight up as high as possible with arm fully extended above the head.

Leaping straight upward eliminates the forward charge, which usually carries the defensive player into the shooter, and forces the opponent to change the normal arc of his shot to an unfamiliar trajectory.

The team foul which results from a "sucker" defensive play adds to the player's foul total, limits his playing time, and increases the opponents' scoring opportunities. Such a foul often means victory or defeat in the closing moments of a close game.

The free throw. The free throw wins the games you want most to win—the close ones! There are three common free-throw types: the underhand, the one-hand set, and the two-hand set. In my opinion, players should be permitted to use the type they like best and with which they are most accurate and consistent.

Some players use the jump-shot from the free-throw line, but they are very much in the minority. (Hal Greer of the Philadelphia 76'ers uses the jump-shot in attempting his free throws and is quite effective in its use.)

The player attempting the free throw has ample time to get set and there is no point in hurrying the attempt. He should take his time and, if possible, obtain the ball from the official before he steps up to his shooting position on the "line."

Once on the line, he should relax completely, bounce the ball a few times if he feels it necessary (keeping his head up and looking at the rim of the basket), take a deep breath, and attempt the shot in an unhurried manner. If the player draws two shots, I prefer that he step back from the line and repeat his regular "ritual" before attempting the second shot. Successful free-throw shooting is a habit coupled with confidence.

The one-hand free throw. There was an era of the two-hand underhand free throw. Most coaches taught this shot because of the percentage edge. Today coaches permit their players to use their favorite shot and limit their shooting instructions to improving the technique.

The one-hand free throw is made with the same technique used in the one-hand set shot. Here, however, there is more time to prepare for the shot and the player can adjust his position on the line and pump (jiggle) the ball several times before the actual release.

The two-hand set shot. The two-hand set shot is the best long shot in the game, and it is too bad that it is disappearing from the sport. It is a good "distance" scoring weapon chiefly because the player has time to get set. The body is poised on the balls of the feet with the knees flexed. Practically all players take a slight leap from the floor. The height of the leap increases with the distance from the basket.

The ball should be held just below eye level with the elbows hugging the body. The arms should be fully extended at release of the ball and the hands should end up fairly close together. The ball is carried up and out and released with arms fully extended. The wrists turn inward and the snap of the fingers spins the ball toward the target.

Dolph Shayes, former NYU and Syracuse NBA player, used the two-hand set shot from an overhead position. Since he stood 6–7, it was impossible to stop Shayes' shot when he raised the ball above his head. In this overhead two-hand shot the ball is brought slightly over the head and released with an elbow snap made just before the release from the fingertips.

The Pivot Shots. Players who play in the "low" post position depend upon a number of shots which are taken with their backs to the basket. They should be versatile enough to shoot from this position on either side of the basket and have the ability to use either hand in their shooting. Practically all of the good "back-up" shooters I have known use the backboard, although some of the exceptionally tall professional players "stuff" the ball when they secure a facing position directly under the basket.

Hook shot. The pivot player's repertory should include the "hook," which is made from a standing or moving position. The hook, combined with a long stride or with a feint, fake, or dribble across the lane, is an effective scoring weapon. The ball is carried away from the body in the fully extended hand and, held in this position, is raised up and over the head, where it is released with a simultaneous snap of the wrist and fingertips.

Jump turn. The pivot player secures the ball in a back-up position close to the basket and leaps straight upward. Turning at the last instant, he releases the ball from the fingertips of his shooting hand when his arm reaches a fully extended position.

Jump push. This is a companion shot for the jump turn and is best used after a head feint or fake. The ball is carried up with two hands as if to shoot and the player looks up at the basket or backboard as he rises on the toes of his feet. Then, lowering his body and the ball, the player goes back up at full speed and releases the ball with the hand closest to the basket.

Underhand sweeps. These sweeps usually follow a fake. The shooter then turns quickly in toward the basket, lifts his head as if to take a hook shot, and then sweeps the ball up with both hands in an underhand sweep manner.

Cross-bank and buttonhook shots. These shots are made while the player is in motion and usually follow a feint or fake which causes the defensive player to leave his feet or at least lift his arms and body to stop the threatened shot. The shooter then steps or dribbles around and under the opponent and uses his outside hand to make the cross-bank shot.

The buttonhook is made with the inside hand as the player turns following a drive under the basket. Unless they are unusually tall, most players will bank the ball against the backboard following the turn.

Offensive Rebounding. There are two proven methods to employ when the defensive players do a good job of boxing-out. One is the roll off the body of the opponent at the point where he (defensive player) exerts the least pressure. If the defensive player has boxed-out the offensive player solidly (tail to belly) a side roll is necessary.

The second method is for the offensive players to cross as the defensive players start to box them out. This is a two-man offensive maneuver worked out in practice drills (see Chapter 8).

CHAPTER 7

DEFENSIVE SKILLS

THE DIFFERENCE between the mental approach of the Celtics and other professional players in the early days compared to that of the modern players is so marked that I feel it is worthy of comment. The Celtics were never concerned with scoring points. We knew we would get more than our share. Our main objective was to prevent the other fellow from making baskets.

Defensive basketball was the most important part of the game in the early years. Chris Leonard had the nickname "Dog" because he dogged anyone he played against from the first toss-up to the last second. The player who faced Chis knew he was going to have a tough night.

Perhaps the best illustration of the way we old-timers regarded defense would be to use Skeets Wright, of Jersey City, New Jersey, as an example. When Skeets walked out on the floor to shake hands with his opponent, he would grin and say, "I get two points and you get two, O.K.?"

The other guy would usually smile and nod. So, Skeets made sure he got his two first. Then, when they lined up for the center tap following the score, Skeets would glare at the other guy and say, "All right, I got mine. Let's see you get yours!" Moving purposefully between his opponent and the basket, Skeets would mutter, "Over my dead body!"

When his opponent scored, Skeets would go wild with rage. I remember once how his teammates, enjoying a comfortable lead in the game, plotted a little fun with Skeets. As the other team came down to the attack, a teammate called out, "Switch men, Skeets. I've got *your* man."

Skeets obediently switched and was horrified when his man got away from his teammate and scored. The next time the opponents came down the court with the ball, another teammate called out for Skeets to switch opponents. "I've got your man, Skeets," he yelled. "Take mine."

Skeets squared his jaw and nodded grimly. "Sure!" he called, "you go ahead and take him. *I've got him too!*"

Only a few players possess that type of fierce defensive pride. Sometimes, during the last years of my coaching, I have seen one of my players, presumably exhausted, dead on his feet and looking like the next step he took would be his last one while he was playing defense. Then, *we* got the ball and the result was astonishing indeed. The old love-light would glow in his eyes and he would become vibrant, alive, fresh as a daisy, and would dash madly toward our basket calling for the ball.

The Celtics brought the switch into basketball. Before the switch was developed by the Shamrocks, it was man against man on an intense personal basis. The big objective was to hold your opponent to fewer points than you got. The theory was, of course, that if every man did his part, your team had to win. I had never used the switch before I joined the Celtics and had quite a time mastering the skill well enough to suit the Shamrock players. They not only switched on a "block" play, but they always picked up the closest opponent. Heaven help you if a teammate's man scored on you.

On such adjustments are championship dynasties nurtured. You knew where you had to be *or go* all the time. At the moment of decision the champs make the right play. The New York Celtics and the Boston Celtics never defeated themselves when the marbles were down. Only the passing years and lack of good replacements eventually end athletic dynasties, yet the champions always have a reserve of pride and "know how" that enables them to win "one more big one."

The modern game of basketball is highly geared to telephone-number scoring, and, since all players like to see their names in the papers, they concentrate on the offensive skills of the game. However, defense is still a big factor, and it is up to the coach to sell his players on the importance of individual and *team defense.*

The "great" teams, the teams that win the championships, are those who play good defense. And the coaches of the great teams are dedicated to the teaching of defensive play. Their players are always well grounded in basic defensive fundamentals. That is the secret of *their* personal greatness, just as individual and team defense was the secret of the Celtic success.

Great baseball hitters often run into slumps when they cannot buy a hit, quarterbacks have days when they cannot generate an attack, and basketball players have nights when they swear the basket has a lid on it. But—if your defense is well disciplined, you still win in spite of a sputtering offense.

INDIVIDUAL AND TEAM DEFENSE

It is difficult to separate individual and team defense. The two are so closely interwoven that each would fall apart without the other. Mentally, the same qualities are required in both—pride, desire, determination, hustle, alertness, aggressiveness, and resourcefulness in applying continuous concentration.

Most players want to be "complete" players, but few have the guts required to stick with this exacting part of the game. Those who possess the intestinal fortitude to master and apply good defense are the players who win the big games despite the fact that their contributions are seldom recognized.

Starting with the assumption that the player wants to be a complete player and has disciplined himself to go the hard way in his defensive part of basketball, we can turn to the individual skills.

INDIVIDUAL SKILLS

I like to think of the defensive skills in terms of back-court players (guards), corner men (forwards), and pivot players (centers) because, in my opinion, it is a waste of drill time to teach *all* players *all* the position skills. There is a great difference in the skill needs of players in the different positions, particularly with respect to stance and defensive floor alignment.

After there has been a general approach to the fundamentals in the early part of the pre-season workouts, it is probably to the advantage of everyone—coach and players—to separate the candidates and stress the skills which apply to the different positions.

Stance

The boxer's stance, with one foot forward, is preferred because it provides greater coverage than the lateral (parallel) position. The feet are staggered so they are separated approximately the width of the shoulders, and the arm on the side of the forward foot is raised high and extended toward the opponent. The other arm is held wide to the side.

Balance

The weight is evenly distributed on the balls of the feet with the heels barely touching the floor. The knees are slightly bent, and the back should be straight, leaning forward a bit. The head should be up. When moving laterally to keep up with an opponent, the lifted arm may be dropped to the side.

Floor position

The old axiom of keeping between your opponent and the basket has been outmoded by overshifting, the pressure defense, playing between the opponent and the ball, and playing in front of opponents close to the basket (particularly the big man).

Sloughing-off

(Sagging and floating), shifting right or left, beating opponents to positions they prefer, protecting the baseline and switching, all violate the principle of "staying between the opponent and the basket."

When an opponent cuts or dribbles to his right most of the time, the good defensive player will overshift to hamper the other man's moves. However, at no time will the good defensive player turn his head to locate the position of the ball or check the action behind him.

Footwork

Position on the floor and whether or not the opponent possesses the ball governs the stance and the footwork of the defensive player. If the opponent is not in scoring distance, the stance can be adjusted to guard against cutting, passing, dribbling, and driving. Stance and body balance should enable the defensive player to maintain his position.

The shuffle (glide) should be used when possible. Crossing the feet and taking long back steps are to be discouraged, as is leaping in the air when faked. Moving both feet simultaneously in a quick, skipping fashion will enable the defensive player to "stay" with his opponent and prepare him to meet changes, stops, starts, pivots, and drives.

When an opponent drives against the forward foot, it should be swung quickly back by using the shuffle-skip and hop. The first step is back, and the body must be held ready to shuffle in the opposite direction should the opponent use a change or a cross-over.

If the opponent cuts to the back-foot side, the move is again a little shuffle and the hop with the feet remaining in the starting position. Should the opponent outmaneuver the defensive player, the cross-over step is used and the hands are raised in line with the cutter's eyes and the position of the ball. The defensive player must stay with his opponent so he will be in position to back up a teammate who switches to help out.

Vision

The defensive player should concentrate on his opponent, but peripheral vision should be used to see as much of the playing court as possible (position of the ball and opponent's teammates). Turning the head to follow the ball is dangerous; smart opponents will quickly spot the weakness and retaliate by cutting to the basket for a pass.

Opening the stance slightly and sagging or floating will enable the defensive player to watch the ball and his opponent without turning his head. The defensive player should watch his opponent's hips, but peripheral and depth vision should enable him to also see the ball and his opponent's teammates.

Use of hands

Quick hands are important in defensive play. The hand on the side of the advanced foot should be kept moving to distract the shooter or hamper his vision even if it is impossible to block his shots. When an opponent checks his dribble and comes to a stop, the proper use of hands will force the opponent to pivot away and may lead to an interception or a held ball. In this situation, teammates will, naturally, put pressure on their opponents and be poised for interception attempts.

Backtracking

The good defensive player backtracks when retreating from the front court to the back court. The ability to run backward will enable the defensive player to direct traffic, point out his own man, and help teammates locate their opponents and get into defensive positions.

A nonchalant retreat with back turned to opponents who are coming down court with the ball marks a lazy player. Retreating to a defensive position is the time to be alert and fire up teammates so opponents will not be able to score easy baskets.

Talking

Defensive players can help out in the general team defense by "talking it up." Warning teammates of impending screens and picks is an important team-defense fundamental. The terms should be short and pertinent: "Hands up!" "Watch the pick!" "Stay!" "I've got number 22, take 34!" "Switch!" "He's dead!" "Ball!" "Low post!" "High post!"

Defense screens

There is some discrepancy regarding terminology when screens are discussed, but for the purposes of this discussion "outside" screens will be considered as those set *behind* defensive players; "side" screens are those set on the sides of defensive players, and "inside" screens are those set between an offensive player and his defensive opponent. The following diagrams will illustrate the screens.

The basic defense *against* inside and outside screens is the "front" (over the top), the "slide," and the "switch."

In all situations involving screens and picks, the defensive player closest to the basket is responsible for calling the play. It is he who must make the first move in the switch. His move must be positive, and he must make a fast, aggressive switch. The player who is being screened

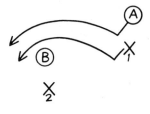

DIAGRAM 7.1   Front (Over the Top). As shown above, offensive player A has cut around his teammate (B) in an attempt to pick off defensive player X-1. However, the offensive cutter (A) left room enough for defensive player X-1 to "front" or stay with him and "go over the top."

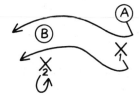

DIAGRAM 7.2   Slide. Again offensive player A cuts around his teammate (B). This time he cuts close so there is no daylight between A and B, so defensive player X-1, must "slide" between offensive player B and his defensive teammate X-2. (Defensive player X-2 has cooperated in this play by moving back a step to give X-1 room to slide through.) He has also helped X-1's momentum by giving him a shove toward his opponent's drive.

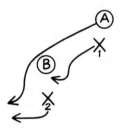

DIAGRAM 7.3 Switch. In this play, offensive player A moved more to his right and got an angle cutting path. Defensive player X-1 could not go over the top or slide through, and a switch was necessary. Defensive player X-2 called "Switch!" and picked up offensive player A while defensive teammate X-1 switched to cover offensive player B.

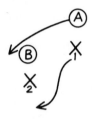

DIAGRAM 7.4 Going Behind. Defensive player X-1 goes "behind" his teammate X-2 in an attempt to cut off his opponent (A). This is a poor defensive move because offensive player A can stop, receive the ball, and take an uncontested shot. Most coaches feel this defensive move is inexcusable.

(blocked) must immediately take the responsibility of guarding his teammate's opponent.

On high post or pivot defensive plays where the ball is in the possession of the post or pivot man, the switch should be made only toward the ball. In defensing post splits, the defensive man guarding the post player often switches to the first cutter, whether the ball is passed or not. Most coaches prohibit this and permit a switch only when the ball is passed.

When the pivot opponent is close to the basket, most defensive players will play in front of him. A switch will occur in this situation only when the two defensive players collide. The rule—no contact, no switch!

In making any switch, the deep (back) defensive player should move quickly forward (jump-switch) and try to force the cutter to move laterally. Forcing the cutter to move laterally prevents him from turning the corner and getting off a good shot "facing" the basket.

Defensing the double-screen. When opposing a team which uses the double-screen, a three-man slide may be necessary. This type of defensive move should be practiced in advance. Scouting notes will determine the methods to be used. If the opponents make extensive use of the double-screen, a two-man zone, which the defensive player guarding the cutter joins when his opponent cuts off the double-screen, may be used.

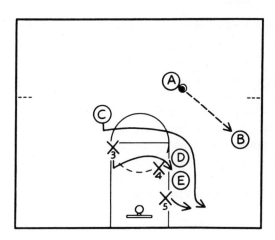

DIAGRAM 7.5 Double-screen Defense. Offensive players D and E have set a double-screen on the side of the free-throw lane. Usually, double-screen players leave no space for defensive players to cut between them. This makes it necessary for the defensive players X-4 and X-5 to slide as shown, X-5 switching to cover the cutter (C) and teammate X-4 to cover offensive player E. Defensive player X-3 will switch to offensive player D.

Defensive roll. The defensive roll is tied in with the switch. When a defensive player is forced into actual contact with an offensive post or pivot player, the roll (toward the basket) will help him recover from the pick and cover his teammate's opponent.

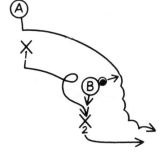

DIAGRAM 7.6 Offensive player A runs his opponent, defensive player X-1, into the pick set by offensive player B. Defensive player X-2 sees the play coming and calls "Switch!" and moves to drive the dribbler (A) away from the basket.

Defensive player X-1 hears the call "Switch!" and almost immediately makes contact or is driven so closely to opponent B that he must roll (toward the basket) in order to cover the pivot or post player when he turns toward the basket.

In all individual guarding practices the player should ask himself what move the opponent—passer, cutter, dribbler, post or pivot man, player with or without the ball—can make. This will reduce the possible moves to the minimum and the defensive player will be prepared for them.

Guarding the playmaker (quarterback)

This player is the key to the opponents' fast break and set attack. Practically all defenses now apply pressure, play the "point of the ball" tight. This pressure could very well be applied to the playmaker, whether he has the ball or not. If the ball can be kept away from the playmaker a good part of the time, it is a good step in the over-all team defense.

In guarding the playmaker, aggressive pressure with arms moving may restrict his passing or force him to make erratic passes. When this occurs, defensive teammates should, naturally, play potential receivers closely even to the extent of overshifting and risking "back door" moves. After the playmaker completes his pass, the defensive player should drop back and toward the direction in which the ball has been passed to lessen the quarterback's opportunity to set a screen.

Guarding the cutter

The defensive player should give the cutter room when he is deep in his back court. Without the ball he is not as dangerous as he is with the ball, so the defensive man can drop further away. If scouting notes or game play shows he favors one direction, overshift to that side and try to make him go the other way. If the cutter has the ball, he is dangerous. Then the defensive player must play up on him and be ready for the give-and-go. As soon as the cutter passes the ball, the defensive player should drop back quickly and turn his body so both the ball and the opponent may be kept in view.

It is important that the defensive player refuse to fall for the cutter's feints and fakes. Keeping his eyes on the cutter's hips, his weight evenly distributed, and his feet on the floor will help if it is necessary to move laterally. Should the opponent gain a step and appear likely to outrun him, it is permissible for the defensive player to use a half turn and utilize a running stride to keep up. And, when in doubt, he should take a half step backward so he can handle his opponent's moves a bit better.

Guarding the dribbler

If no scouting information is available, the defensive player should guard the dribbler straight away until he finds out in which direction the player dribbles best. Once determined that he favors a particular side, the defensive player can force him toward the other direction by overshifting. Give him room unless he is close to the basket and be sure to keep your weight back.

The hands must be kept low and the inside hand used to stab at the ball. The defensive player should never lunge at the dribbler or try to steal the ball. It is better to force the dribbler to go laterally. When the dribbler moves laterally, he will be forced to reverse in order to dribble toward the basket, and this provides the defensive player with an opportunity to knock the ball away. When a reverse is made, the guard should drop back a little and keep his center of gravity low so he can stay with the dribbler.

When the dribbler goes to his right against a defensive player whose left foot is advanced, the guard should drop his right foot far back and swing his left foot to the left with a double-shuffle of his feet. Again, the body should be kept low unless the dribbler swings toward the basket or stops and faces the goal.

Guarding the scorer

The scorer should be played so closely that it is difficult for him to get the ball. Most scorers have favorite areas in which they are dead shots. If the scouting notes reveal these areas, it is wise for the guard to keep him from reaching these spots, with or without the ball. The weight must be balanced and the extended hand held high and "on the ball" when the opponent is in possession.

When the "scorer" keeps the ball low while standing, faking, or dribbling, the defensive player should retreat a half-step. As soon as the scorer stops following a dribble or raises the ball when in a "facing" position, he should be played aggressively—forced to get rid of the ball or made to pivot away.

Guarding the man without the ball

The distance from the basket governs the space the defensive player can give his opponent. Generally, the defensive player should overplay toward the ball and make a determined effort to close the possible path of the ball to the opponent or his path to the ball. The opponent should be forced to work to get into position to receive the ball, especially when he is close to the basket. If he is some distance from the basket, it may be more important to sag or float away and help with the general team defense.

Sloughing

(Sagging and Floating). Sloughing-off is employed by practically all team defenses. When the ball is on the side of the court away from defensive players, they can "float" toward that side to jam up the basket area or help out with general team defense.

When the ball has been passed beyond them and close to the basket, the guards may "sag" back to jam up the middle. In this sag-off, the guards should avoid turning their heads. Shifting a bit off-line will enable them to see the action and still concentrate on their opponents.

Double-team traps

All pressure and pressing defenses utilize double-teaming. The double-team trap may be the result of a planned or an unrehearsed action by two players acting in unison to overwhelm an opponent. The object is to force bad passes, secure held-ball situations, or steal the ball. Usually the trap is a well-planned "team" action, used as part of the man-to-man or zone presses. In my opinion, double-teaming works best off the man-to-man defense, although a great many teams use it successfully as part of the zone press. At any rate, since it requires two or more players, it may be considered a team effort. It can be applied on the first pass from out-of-bounds; on the second pass; when the ball is advanced across the ten-second line; following a held-ball situation, or in opposing the opponent's big man.

In developing a "trap" the defensive players should stagger their advance so that the first man can force the opponent to change direction or pivot away. Then the second defensive player advances until he reaches a position close enough to his teammate to eliminate the possibility of the offensive player dribbling between them. Now the hands should be raised and the logical passing lanes closed.

The trap may be applied on a switch play; when opponents screen and cross in their back court; when the ball is passed to the pivot, especially when the big man is inclined to bring the ball down close to the floor; when a dribbler pivots away from an aggressive opponent, or following a defensive rebound. On all double-team plays the remaining teammates must cover the loose man by swinging their defense around so the man closest to the basket will be covered.

Beating opponent to position

Many players have favorite scoring positions on the sides of the court or under the basket. Scouting material or a diagnosis of the opponent's moves early in the game will often provide the necessary information. Playing the offensive player on the side and in front in certain areas will often force him away from his favorite scoring position.

Boxing-out

Each defensive player is expected to keep his opponent from getting position where he may retrieve the ball or score by means of a tap-in. As soon as a shot is taken, the defensive player should hesitate a second to determine where the player opposed will try to move. His path to the ball must be blocked; a cross-over step taken toward the path the opponent is taking to reach the ball may be necessary. Thereafter, by watching the opponent, the proper shifts to the right or to the left can be made to meet a change of direction.

Rebounding

In going up for the rebound, the defensive player's weight is carried low, the legs are spread, and the elbows and arms are extended slightly. There is usually some contact under the boards, and the defensive player must make sure he is not forced so far under the hoop that he cannot make the rebound. Players who can leap high often take off for the rebound only to see the ball sail over their hands. Boxing-out is not a one-man job. It is an integral part of team defense.

Against a high-scoring offensive rebounder it may be more effective to continue playing the opponent face-to-face. This may succeed in keeping him away from a good rebounding position. Here, of course, recovery of the ball is the responsibility of teammates. Defensive guards should drop away from their back-court opponents to a point near the free-throw line to take care of deep rebounds.

All five players should be expert in boxing-out and in "delaying" opponents until recovery is possible. Normally, the big men can control the area close to the basket, but if the back-court players (guards) are careless, the "overs" which rebound deep can beat a team well equipped with "inside" rebounders.

Blocking shots

Big men today have developed great skill in blocking not only opponents' shots but those made by their teammates' opponents. Bill Russell of the Boston Celtics is an expert in this department, as are Wilt Chamberlain (76'ers) and young Lew Alcindor of U.C.L.A.

When an opponent outmaneuvers a defensive player and drives for the basket, the only way to block the shot is to follow at full speed and try to stop the shot with the inside hand just as the shooter releases the ball. This requires timing and practice. Good hustle pays off here.

The save

Many centers are proficient in making "saves." This means that a teammate's opponent has escaped and is driving in to the basket for a sure score. Again—as in the block—alertness, good timing, and speed of foot and hands are required. This is a spectacular play and an important team defense asset.

Guarding the out-of-bounds opponent

The opponent out-of-bounds with the ball should usually be played in a position between him and the basket. The defensive player should turn sideways so he can see the ball and any play that develops on the court. It is well to keep in mind that the player out-of-bounds with the ball is often set up for scoring plays.

Free ball

Loose balls are important. The recovery of a teammate's fumble or that of an opponent means a possible four points. In close games the aggressive players who have the guts to go after the free ball are invaluable to team offensive and defensive play.

One-on-one defense

All teams have one-man plays, and the ability to meet the one-on-one situation is important. This is the ultimate in defensive play because the opponent has the ball and just one idea—to score. Body balance, footwork, and heart are important in shutting out the opponent.

Two on two

Two-on-two defense is similar to the one-on-one except now the defensive players will have the screens and picks to contend with. Front, slide, switch, talk, aggressive play and the use of the double-team moves are important here. Two-on-two offers wonderful training for offensive play as well as defensive work.

Pressure defense

Pressure defense is based on good body balance, footwork, alertness, and hustle. Practically all teams are using pressure today in one form or another, and coaches must drill their players in the ability to prevent opponents from getting clear to gain possession of the ball and in the tricks of double-teaming. It is important to impress on players that pressure means more interceptions but can also lead to unguarded scoring shots.

Interceptions

Interceptions result from bad plays by opponents. Careless passing (cross-court, soft looping tosses, blind passes, straight-away passes to pivot-men), fumbles, "traveling," and bad shots result from pressure defense. All defensive players should be alert to the opportunities which result from pressure.

Guarding the big man

Big men today are agile, fast, and great shooters. Many of them can play wing and corner positions, and a few can even play in the back court. Individually defensing the big man calls for playing him on the side toward the ball, in front, beating him to his position, and frequently playing him face-to-face on teammate's scoring attempts. Tip-in experts must be boxed-out, and if the big man is particularly adept at tip-ins, it may be necessary to assign teammates to rebound duty and let the player guarding the big man forget about the ball.

The defensive player should be so active that the opponent's feeders will find it difficult to get the ball to the big man. He should be played aggressively and strongly, and all passes to him should be contested. When the big man is clearly superior and one defensive player cannot handle him, it might be wise to get help from the forwards and guards through sloughing-off or even double-teaming. Use of a zone may be necessary. In this event it might be wise to remember that the One-Three-One was designed by Clair Bee for just this purpose—to hamper the scoring of the opponent's big man.

Helping out

This is a team effort. All players should be alert to helping teammates through talking, deflecting passes, playing the point of the ball aggressively, watching for bad passes, interception opportunities, batting at the ball when a dribbler passes close by, double-teaming, etc. However, the coach must be sure his players realize the importance of defensing their assigned opponents first and "helping out" second. It is silly for a defensive player to gamble for an interception or a "steal" and neglect his own opponent. Scores which result from such plays can be demoralizing, especially in the closing minutes of a game. Only when time is running out and the team is behind should players gamble (40 per cent to 60 per cent chance) on "steals."

CHAPTER **8**

DRILLS
—OFFENSE, DEFENSE

T HE PRACTICE COURT is the coach's classroom. I believe in
starting with the principle behind the skill or play and then,
through drills, applying the subject to game situations. Setting
up situations, analyzing them, and applying the skills according to player
positions can conserve valuable time. Drills should be a combination of
fun and work. When players begin to show fatigue or lack of interest,
the drill should be changed. As a player and coach, I have found that
the greatest players were the hardest workers. I believe in conditioning
my players through drills, and I have little faith in the "gimmick" conditioners which flood the basketball market.

Reflective teaching is excellent after the season starts. Looking back
over plays and games enables the coach and the players to review the
subject (skill or skills), analyze the effectiveness or weakness, and apply
remedies or improvements.

Opposing one player against another or groups of players against
other groups, requiring a number of passes to be executed in a given time,
and the use of problems such as methods of meeting the man-to-man
and zone presses are good ways of maintaining interest in drill practices.
Today all coaches use movies, illustrations, and examples in their teach-

ing. The method which gets results for the individual coach is the one he should continue to use.

In my early days as a Celtic I seemed to do everything wrong. All the veterans were yelling at me and bawling me out. I was always in the way. Then, one day, I got a big break. John Witte, the Celtic manager at that time, took me aside and taught me how to do things without the ball. The Celtics expected players not concerned with the particular action or play to help out by getting out of the way or to make a move which would set someone else up for a dash to the basket. This was the real offensive creed of the Celtics—"do something without the ball!"

The Celtics worked on this "creed" in every game. A jerk of the head or a shift of the eyes designated the move they expected a teammate to make, and he had better make it! The individual and team skills were taught and practiced during the games. Today, perfection in the skills is gained during workouts and then put into practice in the games.

MEDICAL EXAMS

Since I believe in hustle, hard work, and pushing the athlete just a little further each time in his pre-season work, I want to stress the importance of medical examinations. The school physician should be provided with forms which require a "complete" physical examination prior to the first workout. The authority of the physician is absolute in all matters pertaining to a player's physical fitness, injuries, and treatment. A thorough examination will discover and pinpoint abnormalities (heart disease, hypertension, diabetes, etc.) which would limit or exclude a candidate's eligibility to participate in the game.

The drills which I use are simple, just as the basic game of basketball is simple. I have tried to rely on a few favorite offensive and defensive drills to teach my game, the Celtic game. A team must be ready for the offensive and defensive variations, of course, but it is my belief that player instinct and lightning reaction to opponent's mistakes is the way the game should be played. This is the reason I have never attempted to teach a pattern game.

Because of my Celtic training (learning the skills by practicing them in the games), I never went too far in drill work. I think drills are great in books and excellent for clinics, but in practice I believe in my personal theory—no gimmicks and no theory, just plain logic and hard work applied to game situations.

The game has advanced, and coaching techniques have changed in recent years, but I still believe that 75 per cent of coaching is the handling of players. The remaining 25 per cent in my case has meant providing them with a free-wheeling offense and the hardnosed man-to-man defense developed by the Celtics.

Just knowing the X's and O's is not enough to win the big games. Nor are locker room tirades on the glory of the Alma Mater important. The rapport between coach and players which makes the team want to go through a wall to win is the answer, provided the players are fundamentally sound and the coach uses them in the right positions.

OFFENSIVE DRILLS

GENERAL CONDITIONING

Full-court running drills which tie in with game action can be used as general conditioners. In addition to fast-break practice drills, I particularly like the Three-Man Weave and the Five-Man "Up-and-Down-and-Up." These full-court running drills demand accurate and fast passing.

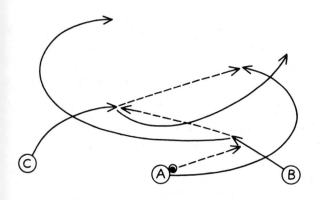

DIAGRAM 8.1   Three-man Weave. This drill is exercised at full speed up and down the court. Three players start under one basket, and the ball is passed from one player to the next as they proceed to the other end of the court and return. The ball does not touch the floor, but the players are permitted to attempt lay-up shots.

Player A passes the ball to teammate B and cuts behind him. Player B passes to teammate C and cuts behind him. This passing and cutting behind the receiver continues to the baseline at the other end of the court, where the players reverse direction and continue the drill back to the starting point.

DIAGRAM 8.2 Five-Man Up-and-Down-and-Up. This is a wonderful conditioning drill which contains many game skills. The ball may not touch the floor at any time, and all five players must handle it at least once. A successful attempt for a score must be made after all players have handled the ball. Players may not travel (run with the ball) and passes must be sharp and accurate.

After the basket is "made" the ball must be caught by a player before it hits the floor. Then, all players must reverse and start back "up-court," continue the passing and running, and end with a successful lay-up. Should the ball touch the floor, a player be omitted from the passing, a goal attempt missed, or traveling occur, the coach calls "and two." This means all teams must make perfect runs up and down the court. The words "and two" are used when the kids must muster up to perfection.

In the diagram, Player A starts the run by passing the ball to teammate B. Thereafter, the ball travels from B to C to D and back to teammate A. Player A passes to teammate E for the shot. Players B and D should be in best positions to take the ball out of the net and start the return back up court. Normally there will be several more passes than are shown in the diagram.

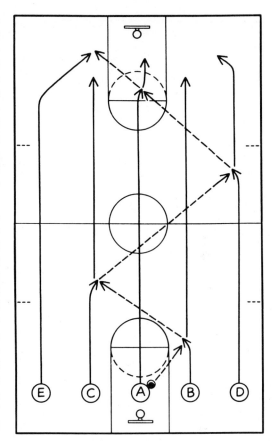

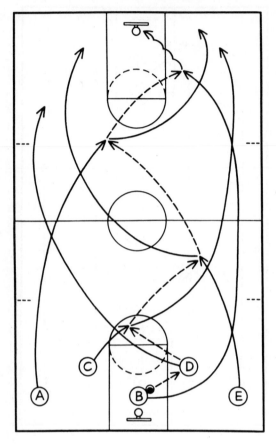

DIAGRAM 8.3 Two-Four-Six-Eight-and-Two. This is a conditioner and fast break drill with a premium placed on ball handling and cutting (go behind) and making lay-ups. The drill is increased to six and eight times until the players are in shape. When the "and two" is called by the coach, the players must not dribble, throw bad passes, miss lay-ups, or fail to cut behind the receiver of the pass. If they commit violations, the "and two" is repeated until the drill is executed perfectly.

The above drill was the most important factor in my training program. It had more virtues than ball handling, cutting, and the lay-up. During the "and two" I would invariably ask a player to show me a nice bounce pass or jump shot. If the player complied, I would yell "and two," much to the dismay of the four other players because both requests were violations in the drill. This made for continued thinking during the drill.

At the start of the season this drill is most exhausting as well as exacting. Untalented candidates usually find themselves lacking in the necessary skills and invariably fail to show up for practice the next day, thereby saving the coach the disagreeable task of cutting them from his squad.

DRIBBLING DRILLS

All players should be taught to use their left and right hands in mastering down-the-middle, sideline, and baseline drives. Each drive should include the feints and fakes which have been discussed. The defensive players (X's) should play the dribblers closely and make them work to get loose.

DIAGRAM 8.4 Dribble Drive (down the middle). Players A and B alternate in driving to the basket. The dribblers may drive to either side in attempting to go around their defensive opponents. Above, player A has faked right and dribbled to his left, keeping his right shoulder low and his right hand trailing to protect the ball. Player B faked left and dribbled right (left shoulder low) with his left hand trailing to protect the ball.

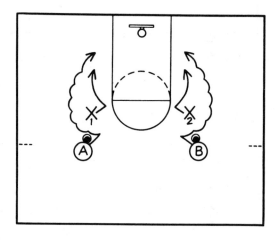

DIAGRAM 8.5 Fake and Sideline Drive. Passers (A and C) pass to teammates B and D who meet the ball. The dribblers use a shoulder fake as if to continue to the inside and then drive to the outside and along the sideline.

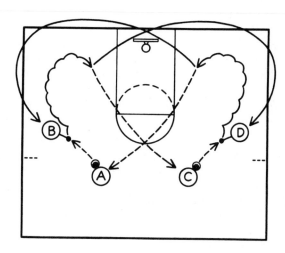

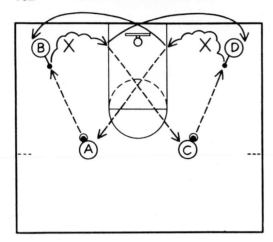

DIAGRAM 8.6 Fake and Baseline Drive. Passers (A and C)
pass to teammates B and D who
meet the ball. The dribblers use
fakes as if to continue on toward the basket and then change
and drive along the baseline.

GAME PLAY DRILLS

One-on-one. Continuous day-after-day practice in one-on-one offensive work is vital in combatting today's pressure defenses. Pressure defenses (man-to-man or zone types) are most effective when they cause
indecision on the part of the man with the ball. This provides defensive
players with time to set up in pressing situations. For this reason if no
other, intense work on one-on-one play is vital. Matching players in one-
on-one situations and teaching the fakes and drives which were discussed in Chapter 6 will prepare players for the emergency situations
encountered when facing pressing defenses.

Two-on-two. Here we run head-on into the use of give-and-go
screens and moves between guards, guards and forwards, guard-pivot,
and forward-pivot in two-man plays. Setting the players up in two-on-
two formations, then practicing the cut-and-drive plays and incorporating
screens and return passes will develop two-man plays which will be effective in game situations.

Basically, the moves are listed as: Pass and cut; pass and go behind
(outside screen); pass and go inside (inside screen); pass and go away;
pass and change direction. These moves are determined by the set-up
of the defensive players. Therefore, the plays are not run off in order but
in accordance to the positions of the defensive opponents. Good ball
handling and use of correct cutting paths are essential to the proper execution of these plays.

EXAMPLES OF CUT-AND-DRIVE PLAYS

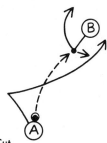
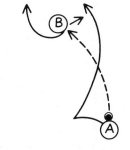

DIAGRAM 8.7   Two-Man Cut-and-Drive Plays.   Players A and B team up in cut-and-drive plays with the use of a "pick." Player A is the cutter or dribbler in each case, and teammate B handles the ball and sets the pick to trap A's opponent.

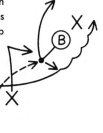
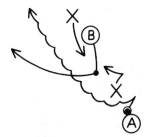

DIAGRAM 8.8   Pass and Cut. Player A passes to teammate B, follows his pass, then changes direction and cuts for the basket, ready to receive a pass from teammate B.

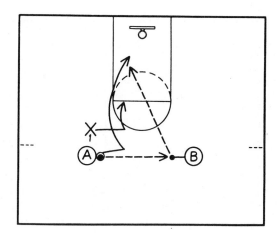

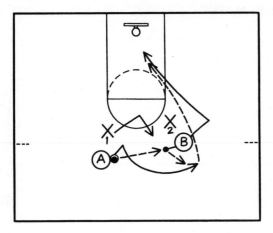

DIAGRAM 8.9 Pass and Go Behind. Player A passes to teammate B and cuts behind him to receive a hand-off. Player B returns the ball to teammate A and cuts for the basket ready to receive a pass from A.

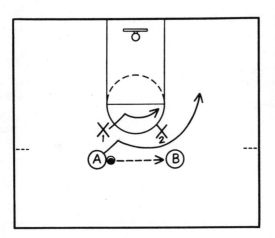

DIAGRAM 8.10 Pass and Screen Inside. Player A passes to teammate B, drives forward two or three steps, changes direction and cuts between B and opponent X-2. The screen may be made slowly or at full speed.

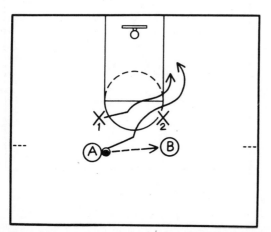

DIAGRAM 8.11 Pass and Screen Outside. Player A passes to teammate B and moves toward him as if to execute an inside screen. After two or three steps, player A changes direction and cuts behind teammate B's opponent (X-2). The screen may be made slowly or at full speed.

DIAGRAM 8.12 Pass, Follow Pass, and Reverse Direction. Player A passes to teammate B, cuts between B and opponent X-2, throws a hard stop, reverses direction and cuts toward the basket. If A can break free from his opponent (X-1), B will pass the ball to him.

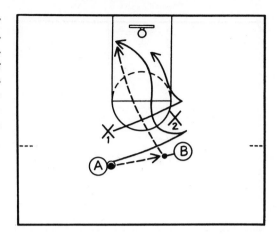

DIAGRAM 8.13 Pass, Follow Pass, and Cut Away. Player A passes to teammate B, follows pass two or three steps, reverses direction and cuts away from ball. This maneuver by A is designed to provide a screen for a teammate on the opposite side of the court. Should this teammate break free he will receive the ball from B.

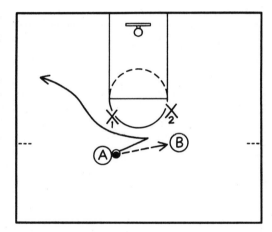

DIAGRAM 8.14 Dribble Off the Screener. Player passes the ball to teammate B and moves in front of opponent X-2. This screen is usually made slowly. Player B dribbles close behind A's screen and drives for the basket.

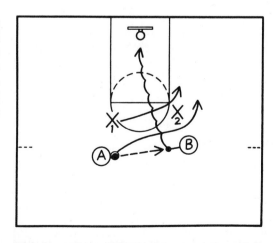

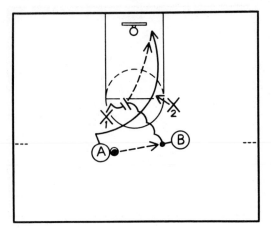

DIAGRAM 8.15 Dribble Block. Player A passes the ball to teammate B and fakes left. Player B dribbles to a position behind A's opponent (X-1) and sets a screen facing the basket. Player A now drives opponent X-1 into the screen and cuts for the basket. If he breaks free, B will pass the ball to him (preferably by means of a bounce pass).

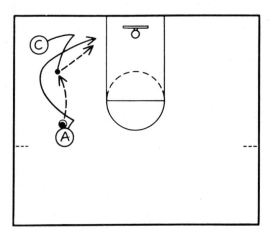

DIAGRAM 8.16 Guard Around. Player C cuts toward the basket, throws a stop and reverses to the position shown. As soon as C secures position, A passes the ball to him, fakes to the right and cuts to the left in a guard-around play. If A breaks free, C will pass the ball to him.

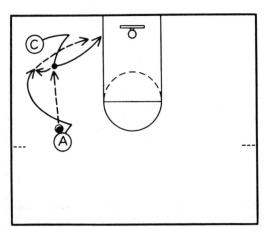

DIAGRAM 8.17 Over-Shoulder and Cut. Player C starts for the basket, throws a stop, and reverses as shown. Player A passes the ball to C, fakes right, and cuts left to a position behind C. Player C executes an over-the-shoulder pass and cuts for the basket. If C breaks free, A will pass the ball to him.

DIAGRAM 8.18 Guard-Forward Return Pass and Drive. Corner-man C breaks out to meet a pass from A. After passing the ball to C, player A cuts straight forward and then swerves to the outside. Teammate C returns the ball to A who now dribbles hard along the baseline and toward the basket.

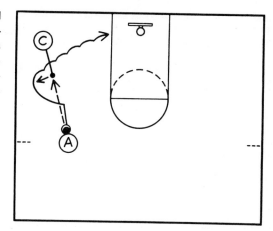

DIAGRAM 8.19 Baseline Clear-out. Player A fakes a pass to C who has advanced as if to meet the ball. Suddenly reversing, C drives hard along the baseline and toward the basket (back door play). If C breaks free A will pass the ball to him.

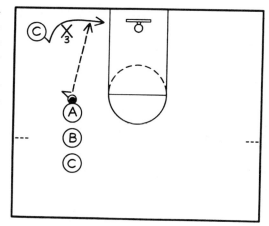

DIAGRAM 8.20 Three-Man Pass and Go Away. Player A passes the ball to C, changes direction and cuts away from the ball. Teammate B, on the side of the court away from the ball, fakes right and times his cut to take advantage of A's screen. If he breaks free, teammate C will pass the ball to him.

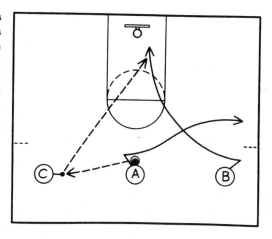

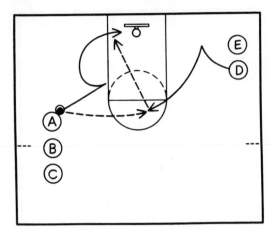

DIAGRAM 8.21 Forward-Guard Change of Direction. Player D cuts toward the basket, reverses and breaks to the free-throw line. Player A passes the ball to D and cuts toward the basket. Changing direction after a few steps, A circles to the left and along the baseline. If he breaks free, D will pass the ball to him.

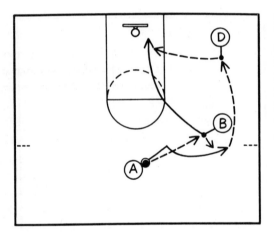

DIAGRAM 8.22 Guard-Forward Three-Man Play. Player A passes the ball to teammate B and follows his pass to a position behind B. Player B passes the ball back to A and cuts for the basket. A passes the ball forward to cornerman D. If B breaks free, D will pass the ball to him.

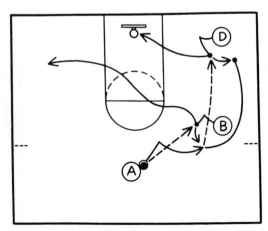

DIAGRAM 8.23 Guard-Forward Three-Man Give and Go Away. Player A passes the ball to B and follows the ball to a position behind B. Teammate B passes the ball back to A and cuts to the other side of the court. Player A now passes to cornerman D and cuts down the sideline to a position behind D. Teammate D returns the ball to A and cuts for the basket. If D breaks free A will pass the ball to him.

PIVOT MAN DRILLS

The big man has always been the focal point of my offense. He is expected to take part in the regular "skill" drills and, in addition, must be drilled in the game plays which enable him to blend in with the team offense.

Rope jumping, shadowboxing, push-ups, leaping, tapping the ball up against the backboard, and other coordination drills are important to his and the team's success. In the offensive team drills we always keep our pivot man moving—from the high post to the low post and from one side of the lane to the other. Much time is spent in teaching him to time his moves with the cuts, drives, and passes of his teammates.

Almost daily I would take my pivot man aside and throw the ball to him as hard as I could—passing it high, low, inside, and outside. Standing not more than 15 feet away, I would pepper him with the ball. My aim was to acquaint him with foot movements and use of his hands so he could handle bad as well as good passes.

After a time I would work with him on head and shoulder fakes, inside and outside rolls, and permit him to score with drives and other shots. Immediately after scoring he was required to retrieve the ball and make a fast pass to me and await the next command. I would say, "Low and inside; low and outside," etc., and he would meet the ball with his feet in position for the roll. This drill usually ran a "rapid fire" fifteen minutes.

DIAGRAM 8.24 Pivot Man Moves. Big man (C) here moves with the ball as it is passed by teammates A, B, D, E and F from one to another. He is taught to use stops, pivots, turns, quick starts, and fakes and feints in securing "position."

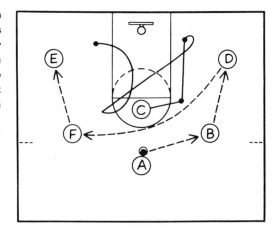

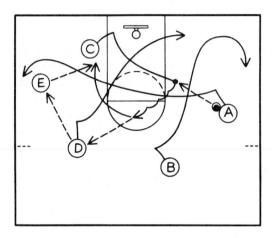

DIAGRAM 8.25 Pivot Man Breaking to Ball. In this diagram, pivot man C is being taught to break to the ball and work into plays. C receives the ball from A after breaking across the lane, dribbles to the high post, passes to teammate D, and cuts toward a low post position where he receives the ball from E.

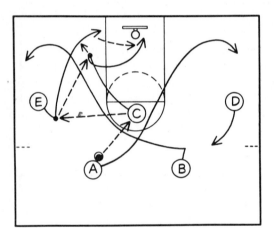

DIAGRAM 8.26 Pivot Man Scoring Move. From a high post, pivot man C handles the ball and then moves to a low post position. Receiving the ball, he waits for the cutter, makes the hand-off, and then swings away and toward the basket where he receives a return pass for the shot. This is a common play but must be drilled into the big man until his swing toward the basket becomes automatic.

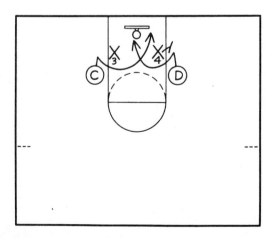

DIAGRAM 8.27 Offensive Rebound Drill. Defensive players X-3 and X-4 have secured good boxing-out positions on opponents C and D. Offensive player C puts pressure on the left side of defensive opponent X-3. Teammate D pressures the right side of X-4. Player C then cuts in front of X-4. Offensive teammate D cuts off C's tail to an inside position.

SHOOTING DRILLS

There are hundreds of shooting drills, and each coach will undoubtedly adopt those he feels are necessary in developing good shooters. However, there is a great difference between "practice" shooters and "game" scorers, so the drills should be based on competition and/or game conditions. The simple but effective drills follow.

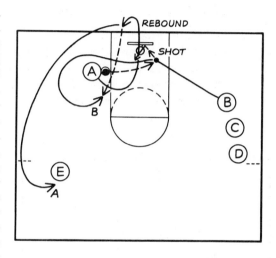

DIAGRAM 8.28 Pass, Shoot, Rebound Drill. This is a fast passing, cutting, and moving drill which requires perfect timing and accuracy. Player A has the ball on the left side of the basket. Player B starts the action by cutting for the basket at full speed.

Player A passes the ball to teammate B who attempts the lay-up. Player B then continues on around and replaces A. Player A follows his pass to B and makes the rebound. He immediately passes the ball back to the shooter (A) and takes his place in the line on the left side of the court.

The action continues until all of the players except the last are on the left side of the court. The last rebounder then moves to the right side of the court and the cutting, passing, and shooting continue from the left side.

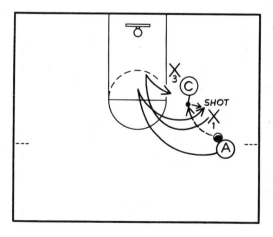

DIAGRAM 8.29 Screen-Pick and Jump Shot. Player A passes the ball to C on the high post and cuts down the lane as shown. Reversing direction, he cuts back close to the big man and receives a return pass for the jump shot.

FAST-BREAK DRILLS

1. *Rebounding.*
   Teach players to get position and pitch out correctly. (Two-on-two or three-on-three off the boards. Defense gets rebounds and passes to wings.)

2. *Passing and Cutting.*
   Three lines form at half-court and work pass-and-go-behind drill. Develops passing, cutting, and making lay-ups.

3. *Three-Man Fast Break.*
   Players form in three lines and pass the ball and break down court. Middle man stops at the free-throw line.
   Add the tandem defense versus the three-man fast break. Same as above except a trailer is used.

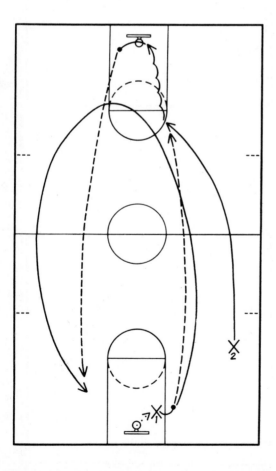

DIAGRAM 8.30 Rebound and Long Pass Drill. Player X-1 takes rebound and throws long pass (length of court) to teammate X-2, who dribbles in for the lay-up. Player X-1 follows down court, reverses at free-throw line, and dashes for other basket. Player X-2 makes his own rebound and throws ball to other end of court. Player X-1 makes the lay-up and the drill is continued (5 times).

4. *Five-Man Fast Break.*
  Three players rebound. Two players take wing positions. Coach tosses ball against backboard and rebounders start the drill. Add two defensive players at mid-court. They fall back into the tandem defense under basket.
  Add or use offensive trailer.

5. *Five-Man Fast Break with a Half-Court Scrimmage.*
  Five on five half-court scrimmage. Defensive players initiate a full-court fast break each time they steal the ball or secure a rebound. Teams reverse positions at other end of the court.

6. *Fast Break from Free-Throw Set-up.*
  Five on five in free-throw situation. Defensive players initiate fast break whether the free-throw is made or missed. Teams reverse positions at other end of court.

DIAGRAM 8.31 Three-Man Fast Break Drill. Player X-1 takes rebound, passes to teammate X-3, and cuts up court. Passing between X-1 and X-3 continues until X-1 reaches his own free-throw line at other end of court. Player X-1 fakes a return pass to teammate X-3 and then passes to teammate X-2 for the lay-up. The drill repeats three or four times with players exchanging positions after each basket.

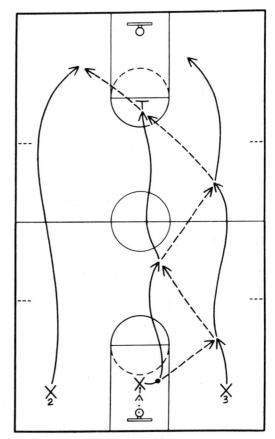

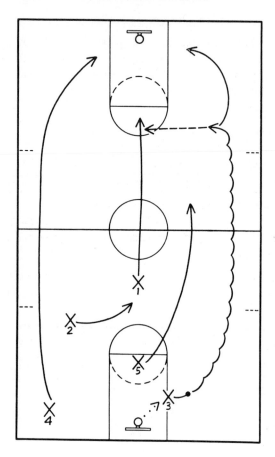

DIAGRAM 8.32 Rebound and Dribble Drill. This drill is used to teach the dribble when passing is impossible. Players X-2 and X-5 are presumed to be pressed, making a pass to either of them dangerous. Player X-3 now dribbles up right sideline to vicinity of free-throw line and hits teammate X-1 at the line. Player X-3 then continues on in to the basket. (These drills can be varied to meet all kinds of defensive situations and serve to strengthen fast-break attack as well as serving as conditioners. Five players can also be used.)

DEFENSIVE DRILLS

ONE-ON-ONE DEFENSIVE DRILLS

Celtic defense was played on a pure man-to-man, nose-to-nose basis, and I still believe that matching men one-on-one is the correct way to start the teaching of individual defense. Preliminary to starting drill work, the entire squad should be put through drills which include running backwards, lateral shuffling, and diagonal sliding.

Then, starting without a ball, players are paired up, and the offensive man uses the full length of the court in trying to break free from his defensive opponent. Later the offensive player is given a ball and, again using the full length of the court, attempts to get free from the defensive player. If the dribbler can get loose without committing a violation (traveling, double dribble, palming) he may attempt a shot.

Both players fight for the rebound. The player who comes up with the ball after the shot immediately drives back up the court with his matched opponent trying to hold him in check.

Other one-on-one drills include defensing the passer, defensing the cutter, defensing the dribbler, and defensing against two offensive players under the basket. These are situation plays that the coach can set up at different points on the court and check the mistakes. It is slow, tedious work but must be done.

TWO-ON-TWO DEFENSIVE DRILLS

This is the next step in teaching individual defense. Here overshifting, floating, beating opponent to favorite spot, two-timing dribbler, over-the-top, slide and switch without ball, and switching on the ball can be covered by pairing men and following the same procedure used in one-on-one defense. After the Two-on-Two drills have been mastered, Three-on-Three, defensing the post and pivot, and rebounding may be continued.

ONE-ON-ONE DRILL PRINCIPLES

A. *Basic Stance.* One foot ahead of the other with not too much spread. Do not lunge forward. Do not slap or swipe at the ball unless you think you really have it.

B. *Against Drive.* First step is backward (with both feet) slant. Protect the baseline. Force opponent into the pack. As opponent approaches basket, close the gap. You may draw a charge penalty. Watch for him to "change" off the dribble.

C. *Hands.* One up and one down. Neither hand extended too far. Slap *up* rather than down. On a shot do not slap down but rather go straight up, forcing the shooter to extend his shot.

D. *After all Shots.* Make sure to check opponent: (*a*) After he or one of his teammates shoots, and (*b*) Make sure there is no second shot.

E. *Use the Three Areas.* Practice defense in middle and on each side of court.

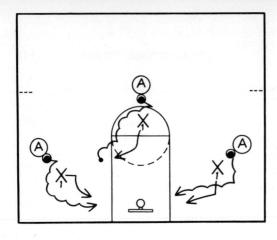

DIAGRAM 8.33 One-on-One Defense. Defensive player X-1 defenses offensive player A from various spots on the court. Here the baseline drive, the jump shot, and the change-direction dribble are contested.

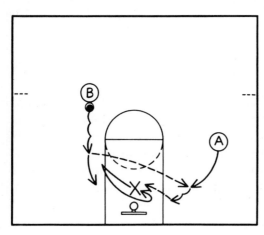

DIAGRAM 8.34 Two-on-One Defense. Defensive player X is defending his team's basket against two offensive opponents. He must fake his moves always to cover the man with the ball and force a pass but keep his balance so that he can retreat to cover the pass. All players (particularly back-court men) should be drilled on this defensive play.

DIAGRAM 8.35 Floating and Overplay (pressure) Drills. On the left side of the defensive court, defensive player X-2 has "floated" away and back toward the defensive basket in such manner that he can watch his opponent and the ball without turning his head. This is a simple maneuver that should be drilled into the players so that "head hunters" can be eliminated.

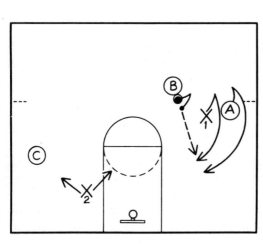

On the right side of the defensive court, defensive player X-1 is overplaying his opponent (A). This is fairly safe since his opponent is beyond the high percentage area. Defensive player X-1 is expecting the "backdoor" maneuver by A and cuts between him and the ball for the interception.

DIAGRAM 8.36 Beating Opponent to "Spot." Defensive player X-3 anticipates opponent C's break to his favorite position on the "line" and beats him to it.

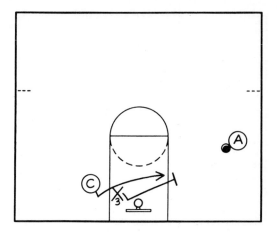

DIAGRAM 8.37 Defensive "Pinch" on Dribbler. Defensive player X-1 plays man with the ball closely and forces him to dribble to the outside. Teammate X-2 plays his opponent closely and times his move so pinch can be applied effectively. This requires considerable practice. Defensive player X-2 must advance on opponent A with arms moving to prevent a pass.

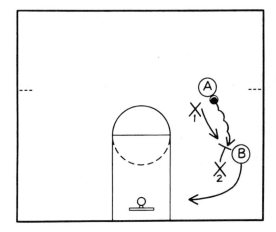

DIAGRAM 8.38 Fighting Over the Top. Aided by teammate X-2, who calls "Stay," player X-1 sticks with his offensive opponent and makes the "over-the-top" defensive play.

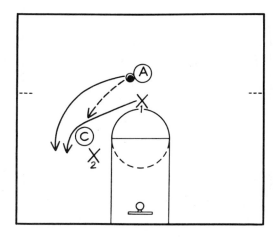

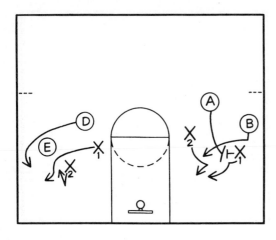

DIAGRAM 8.39 Slide and Switch Plays. Defensive players must talk so that the proper defensive move may be made. In the above drills, defensive player X-1 on the left side of the defensive court "slides" in his move to keep up with his opponent. Defensive teammate X-2 aids X-1 by moving back slightly to give X-1 room to slide through.

On the right side of the defensive court, offensive player A has set a screen beside his teammate's opponent (X-1). Defensive player X-2 sees the screen and must call the switch. He switches to cover opponent B while X-1 will defense opponent A.

The above defensive plays are a few of the many screen situations where only correct defensive moves will save a score. The moves must be drilled over and over until they become automatic. In all cases the player closest to the defensive basket is assigned the responsibility of calling the play.

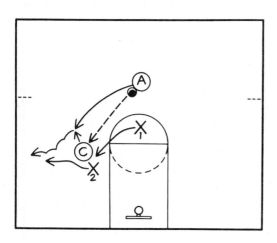

DIAGRAM 8.40 Switching to the Ball. On a tight screen, defensive player X-2 must call the switch and defense opponent A. Defensive player X-1 must pick up offensive player C.

DIAGRAM 8.41 Post and Pivot Defensive Drill. Defensive player X-1 forces opponent A to go left (X-1's right) in cutting over the top. By overshifting a bit to his left, X-1 may encourage A to pass to the high post and cut left. This is another "over-the-top" move. Defensive player X-2 can help teammate X-1 by calling "stay" and moving back in case contact should occur, in which case he would quickly change the call to "switch" and shift to guard opponent A.

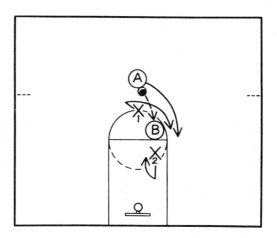

DIAGRAM 8.42 Three-Man Defense Drill. Defensive players X-1, X-2, and X-4 must fight their way through screens and over the top. This three-man defensive drill against an offensive three-man weave is an excellent way to improve over-the-top, sliding, and switching moves. (Stay and switch are "must" terms in this drill.)

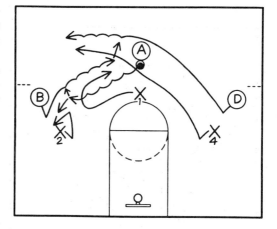

DIAGRAM 8.43 Defensing the High and Low Posts. On the right side of the court, defensive player X-3 is playing in front of the low post opponent C. Teammate X-1 must play his opponent (point of the ball) closely.

On the left side of the court, defensive player X-5 is moving "with the ball" in an attempt to keep between the ball and the low post player E.

In the center of the court, at the free-throw line, defensive player X-6 is defending his high post opponent and trying to stop the dribble and prevent a jump shot.

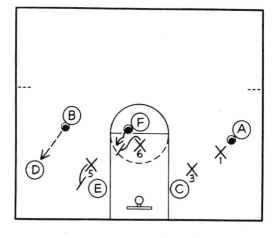

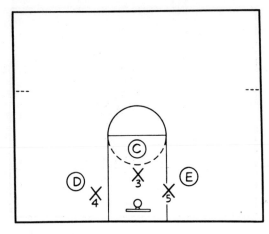

DIAGRAM 8.44 Rebounding Drill. Three-on-Three Rebounding Drill. Defensive players X-3, X-4, and X-5 work at boxing out opponents C, D, and E. The coach may stand behind the defensive players and signal the moves which C, D, and E make to secure inside positions on the defensive players.

A ball may be added to the drill and an actual shot taken by another player. Again the opponent (offensive) will try to outmaneuver the defensive player in securing position and gaining possession of the ball.

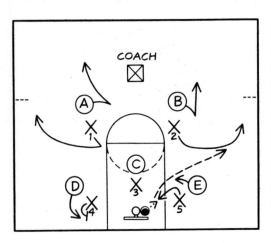

DIAGRAM 8.45 Defensive Rebounding and Pitchout. Five offensive players take positions, and the coach takes a shot at the basket. Defensive players X-1, X-2, X-3, X-4, and X-5 box out. Players X-3, X-4, and X-5 recover the ball, and pitch out to a teammate (X-1 or X-2). Above, rebounder X-5 secured the ball and fired it out to teammate X-2, who cut to the sideline to receive the ball.

PART THREE

CHAPTER 9

TEAM DEVELOPMENT —PERSONNEL

TEAM DEVELOPMENT is more than a matter of choosing the best players and providing them with an offense and a defense. The development of class, pride, spirit, loyalty, and desire to win are influenced by many facets which, at first glance, would seem to be unimportant in building a team. Yet all play a vital part.

PERSONAL APPEARANCE

The class of a team reflects upon the coach. The coach should set the example by his dress and actions. If the players wear coats and ties, it reflects upon the coach; if they dress sloppily, it also reflects upon the coach. Players appearing on the court and playing in a game with their shirttails hanging out are still another reflection upon the coach. Sloppiness begets sloppiness.

Whether for practice or game, the players should report clean shaven and with their hair trimmed neatly. And, when they run out on the court, their shirts should be tucked in properly and kept that way. All my players, college or professional, were clean shaven, dressed in suits, wore clean shirts and ties, and behaved like gentlemen whether they traveled across town or across the country. They represented more than themselves; they were the ambassadors of the institution they represented.

When I first started out in basketball, the team I was playing with had no uniforms. We used undershirts and pants, but there was no lettering across the shirts. My father was working in a hat factory at the time. When he arrived home one evening, he brought some felt along. The possibilities were obvious, but I said nothing until the next morning after my father had gone to work. Then I asked my mother to cut the felt into letters and sew the team name on my shirt as well as on the shirts of my teammates.

My mother washed the suits, sewed the letters on them, and hung them on a line on the back porch. The year was 1912, but to this day I can vividly remember those shirts. In the fashion of the times, the name— TRINITY MIDGETS—ran diagonally from the right arm pit to the left hip of the shirts.

That evening I was sitting on the porch admiring the uniforms when my father came home from work. He stopped in his tracks and surveyed the uniforms in amazement. "What in the world are those things for?" he asked, pointing toward the uniforms.

"Basketball, Pop," I said proudly. "We wear them when we play the games."

"You mean you're going to wear one of those outfits out in public? Out where people can see you in them?" he asked incredulously. Today, all teams wear colorful and serviceable uniforms. Good players take pride in their appearance, and it is the coach's responsibility to see that they are equipped with attractive playing and warmup suits. The coach should also make sure his players are well shod. Basketball is a game of speed afoot, and a sprained ankle or a mess of blisters can ruin a season. Thinking about shoes reminds me of a story concerning an important Celtic game.

As the reader knows by this time, the Celtics were pioneers in every sense of the word, living from day to day and from game to game. One time, we were scheduled to play the Rens, one of the greatest Negro teams of all times. The Rens played in the Renaissance Casino in Harlem and were almost unbeatable on the beautiful dance floor. There was a keen spirit of rivalry between the Rens and the Celtics, and both teams always tried to be at full strength for the contests.

On the day of the game, Dutch Dehnert's mother was taken ill, and the master of the pivot play had to rush home. It was a disastrous blow, not only because Dutch was the key player in our offense, but because it left us with only four players. Then someone thought of Johnny Beckman. Becky was 39 years old, and had been out of the game for two or three years, but we knew how fiercely he revered the reputation of the Celtics. He had been our captain and long time leader and, like the rest of us, felt that the Celtics had been the greatest thing in his life.

Our manager, John Witte, managed to locate Becky somewhere in New Jersey a couple of hours before game time and told him about our predicament. Without the slightest hesitation, Becky said he would be on hand. However, in his haste to get to the game on time, he forgot his shoes. There was only one pair of extra shoes between the players of both teams, and that pair belonged to big Cappy Ricks, the great Negro ball handler.

Cappy's "two-step" shoes were three or four sizes too large for Becky, but he put them on. Then Becky proceeded to play the entire game and emerge with feet that were blistered raw. Despite that, he was the high scorer—and the Celtics won the game! Becky was a great player and a vicious competitor.

I remember another Celtic game against the Rens at Renaissance Casino. A shot was taken and the ball bounced off the ring. I followed up and tried to tap the ball back up on the board and in. I missed the tap and was about to try again when someone gave me a terrific push in the back.

I landed up in the crowd with what felt like a broken back. It took me a few seconds to recover. Then I rushed back on the floor, angry, boiling for a fight and looking for the guy who pushed me.

"Hold it, Joe!" Pete Barry said, pulling me aside. "I did it! You were shooting at the wrong basket." I am sure that the players whom I coached in later years would give their right arm to see that great play reenacted.

The Celtics were proud of their team and its record and they couldn't stand defeat. When we lost a game (seldom, indeed) the dressing room resembled a den of starved wolves. The desire to win was uppermost in every player's thoughts. Defeat sent the Celtics back to their dressing room after the game raging mad. Recriminations, accusations, and even physical action resulted.

The Celtics believed in playing the best teams in the country, and I carried that same philosophy into my coaching. You do yourself and the team an injustice by playing "patsies." There is no fun in beating a weak opponent. It is far better to revel in victory over a tough foe or bask in the fact that you gave the champ a heck of a game. Playing tough teams prepares your team to have "what it takes" when it is necessary to win the "big" one.

RELATIONSHIP WITH OFFICIALS

I wanted my players to understand that they came to play and not to officiate. Today's officials are highly trained individuals who love the game as much as the players do. Most of them *were* players. Officials study the rules and the rule changes, attend officiating clinics, take examinations, work under expert supervision, and make the calls "as they see them."

It is true that I tried to help officials work the games from the bench once in a while, but they never did seem to need me. No person is perfect and no official is perfect. Players must understand that they too are far from perfect. True sportsmanship on the part of a coach is demonstrated when he goes to the officials' dressing room after losing the game and compliments the officials who worked a tough game well.

In a fast-moving game such as basketball, the speed of the players, the angle of vision, the screening between the officials and the play, and the lightning rapidity of action sometimes causes the official to make a bad call. When an official errs, I feel that it is the responsibility of the coach to do the talking or questioning—not the task of the player or players.

It is necessary sometimes, too. You can imagine my feelings one night when I was coaching the Knickerbockers. We had won our way to the finals of the NBA and were playing the Minneapolis Lakers (Mikan, Pollard, Mikkelson, Harrison, and the fabulous little man, Slater Martin) in Minneapolis for the championship. Al McGuire took a shot, but neither of the two officials saw the ball go through the hoop for two points which would have won the game for the Knicks.

The officials gave Al two shots but *not* the basket. And, would you believe it, Al missed both free throws!

You can be sure I talked to the officials that night!

In the old days the pros used to circle officials and tell them the facts of life. I was no exception. Yet two of the officials (great ones, too) that I used to abuse in practically every game, Dave Walsh and John Murray, were the very ones who recommended me for my first coaching job at St. John's University.

One night the Celtics were playing in Nashville, Tennessee. I felt that the official was making some bad calls, so I decided to give him a little talk. This was the usual procedure in those days, because some of the hometown officials needed educating. I really let this one have it. Then I turned away and walked back to the bench.

The official followed me and said softly, "I was looking forward to meeting you tonight, Joe. I am sorry now that I was called upon to officiate this game because you have ruined an image. Now that I have met you, I see you for what you are—an animal."

I went back to the dressing room after the game and, instead of changing immediately into my street clothes, sat there and thought about the official and what he had said. Then I decided to look him up and apologize. I found him in the official's dressing room. I learned something about officials and their feelings that night and have never forgotten it. He knew how to tell me off.

At this point I would like to emphasize to young coaches the importance of "growing up" in their relations with officials and the necessity of understanding the arbiters' responsibilities. Most coaching neophytes are so inspired with the desire to win and are so anxious to prove their loyalty to their players and schools that they permit their emotions to take charge when they feel the official has made a mistake. Sometimes the outbreak is completely out of character, an act, and recognized as such by everyone, including the players.

The old axiom of "counting to ten" before acting (or, as was my habit, going to the water bucket) should be changed to "counting to a hundred" to acquire time to gain control of the emotions. Leaping up from the bench on every adverse call and exploding violently with yells and waving arms attracts attention, all right, but it doesn't help the "cause."

"No more trips to the water bucket!" Coach Joe Lapchick sips a drink of water and watches his players return to the floor after the half-time intermission. (N. Y. Post Photo)

Calmness accompanied by intelligent action and speech will gain the respect of everyone, indicate maturity, carry much more weight, and stamp the young coach as a "comer" in the eyes of officials, players, school administrators, fans, rival coaches, and sportswriters. Think it over!

Some of the young coaches who matured early in their coaching careers and whom I have observed were Lou Carnesecca, who succeeded me as head coach at St. John's; Bob Knight, West Point (U.S.M.A.); Al McGuire, Marquette; Tates Locke, Miami (Ohio); Fred Taylor, Ohio State; John Bennington, Michigan State; Bob Foster, Rutgers; Bob Greenwood, Penn; Ken Rosemond, U. of Georgia; Jack Kraft, Villanova; Joe Mullaney, Providence; Jack Donahue, Holy Cross; Roy Rubin, L.I.U.; Jack McMahon, St. Louis (NBA); and Red Manning, Duquesne.

RELATIONSHIP WITH PLAYERS

The coach's players are entitled to his loyalty, not only with respect to their basketball life but in their personal life. A player will sometimes bring his personal problems to the coach in preference to anyone else, including his parents. This is the big opportunity for the coach to be the man he is expected to be.

Most of the opportunities I have had to help young men have been tied in with my college and professional coaching. Toward the end of the 1946-47 season I had signed to coach the New York Knickerbockers the following year. One of my college players, Harry Boykoff, a 6–9 center, was a senior and I was looking forward to adding him to the Knickerbocker roster. In order to better acquaint myself with the Knickerbocker players, I journeyed to Cleveland to watch them play in the Basketball Association of America playoffs.

While I was there, a businessman from Toledo approached me and said that he would like to sign Boykoff for his team, an entry in the National Basketball League. Not only would he give Boykoff a salary of $10,000 (exceptional in those days) but he promised to see that the boy got a good job in an insurance company. Despite the fact that Boykoff could have helped the Knickerbockers, the opportunity was so great that I advised Harry to sign the contract. He did so and developed a good business in that city. Today he resides in Memphis, Tennessee.

EXPLOITING PLAYER TALENT

When it comes to building a style of play, I feel that the players are the essence and that changes in the system should be made when necessary to get the most out of the material at hand. The coach should teach the plays he knows will work and shy away from those which are pleasing to the eye but of little or no game usefulness. Above all, a coach should not adopt a style of play just because a famous coach achieved success with it. The problem must be solved with consideration for the talent on hand, and the coach should not be afraid to change his style of play until it meets his players' capabilities.

If the players possess speed, the fast break must be considered. If they are slow, forget the running game. If the players are weak, take the air out of the ball and hide it in your offense. If the players are poor "outside" shooters, the coach must resort to ball control and possibly add some sort of pattern to their play. If the players lack defensive agility, then it might be wise to set up a type of defense which would not place them at a disadvantage—a zone, the switching defense, sloughing-off, etc.

I recall my dismay at the start of one season when I found that my players could not handle the free-wheeling offense. I realized that we would get killed if we continued the way we were going. After thinking it over, and notwithstanding the fact that we opened our season the following week, I decided to change the offense. I put in a four-man weave with a high post to start. Then I eliminated the "first-shot" idea some of my players possessed. If a player persisted in forcing his shots, I moved over a little on the bench so he would have a good seat from which to watch the game.

From the four-man weave we were able to get a reverse, a clearout followed by a change of direction, or the simple give-and-go. Offense wasn't all the story. We had to make some defensive adjustments. We tried the switching defense, presses, overplay, and experimented with a zone. Finally we came up with a combination which suited us just right. At the beginning of the season it looked like we would lose every game by 50 points. We didn't! In fact, we had a better than average year.

BUILDING AROUND THE BIG MAN

Because height has always been an important offensive and defensive factor, I like to start team development with a big man. If he can't shoot, I use him as a high post for hand-offs and blocking. If he can score under the basket, I try to blend him into a general attack which will free him for low post shots. If he is a good outside shooter, I utilize him around the free-throw circle and restrict him to facing shots.

Defensively, the big man is vital. If he cannot contain the opponent's center, then I try to give him help—sloughing-off by teammates, application of some sort of press to keep the opponent's big man away from his scoring area, etc. There have been several championship college teams who lacked the exceptionally tall man (UCLA in 1963-64 and 1964-65 seasons) but the great majority featured a big man or men.

In professional ranks the big man is the key to everything. Without Russell, Boston was just another NBA team. With Russell, Boston fashioned a record which made the professional fans forget the feats of the Minneapolis Lakers.

I think the following ditty, set to the tune of "The Man I Love" and written by Len Koppett, then of the Herald Tribune, for one of the Madison Square Garden programs just about describes how I feel about the value of the big man in basketball.

LAPCHICK'S LAMENT

By LEN KOPPETT, *Herald Tribune*

(To the tune of "The Man I Love")

Some day he'll come along,
The man I seek,
Six feet ten inches tall,
In stocking feet.
He'll score and feed and run
From end to end
Of every court.

Fatigue won't bother him,
He'll never tire
Defensively his skill
You will admire.
He'll pivot, jump and leap,
And most of all
He won't be short.

Maybe I will see him Monday,
Maybe Tuesday, maybe yes—
Come to think, I'll see him Wednesday,
But,
He's playing for Minn-e-ap-ol-ess.

Some day he'll come along,
Not merely big—
But slick and smart and quick
(Ain't I a pig?)
Oh yes, one other thing, of course,
He'll play for just
The love of sport.

SELECTION OF PLAYERS

Now we come to the actual selection of the players. Naturally, the coach will be looking for players who are alert and want to play both ways—defensively as well as offensively. I go for the tall, lean type of player with thin legs who is strong and fast. In making selections, I prefer to select the best players irrespective of positions.

In my opinion, the squad should not exceed 12 to 14 players. Cutting is a task all coaches abhor, but it must be done. Scrimmages help the coach form his own ideas concerning the players' abilities, and he can support his selections by asking two of his players to choose sides, using two different players daily—two forwards, guards, or centers. The coach can take the choosers off to one side so the selections will be unknown to the other players, who are warming up. By this procedure, no player will know whether he was first or last in the choosing, but the coach, who might have already chosen his squad, may be in for some pleasant surprises as he stands beside the choosers and listens to the selections.

Once the selections have been made, the real work begins. Now it is important that the players be classified with respect to position duties according to the offensive and defensive style of play. The lists of duties which follow may help in classifying the players.

Duties of Back-court operators

1. Handle the ball, feed cutters, post, and corner men.
2. Set up screens and blocks.
3. Dribble. (Score or set up plays.)
4. Freeze the ball in final stages of game.
5. Balance the offense. Set up the defense.
6. Steal the ball (from big men underneath and from back-court opponents—dribblers and passers).
7. Play front part of zone (chasers).
8. Apply press entire game or in final stages.
9. Shoot (good set, drive, and jump shots).
10. Quarterback the team. (Take-charge guys.)

Duties of big men (post and corner players)

1. Rebound. Clear the boards.
2. Score. Possess good jump shot in close, pivot shots, sets, and drives from the corners.
3. Tap-in ability. (The easy basket.)
4. Score "garbage" shots—rebounds, loose balls, etc.
5. Pitch out—able to initiate fast break.

6. Pass off to cutters.
7. Deflect drive-in and jump shots.
8. Take small man inside and score.
9. Play both post positions as well as corners. (Pass off, block, and screen.)
10. Defense opponent's big man or men.

DEVELOPING THE TEAM

The coach is ready, at last, for the actual team development. As a start, five players by positions should be selected and worked as a team combination. These players are tested in different game situations until a smooth-working team is found. Then the alternates, the first line substitutes, should be selected and blended in (one at a time) with the starting five.

I always made sure that one of my starters was a sophomore. By getting his baptism early, he would be one of my experienced helpers in his junior and senior years.

That brings us to the style of play and the final step in developing the team. Individual playing talents and habits must be coordinated into the coach's offensive and defensive plans. Thereafter, team unity is achieved by practicing each part of the offense and defense piece by piece, so to speak, and gradually pulling them together until all the parts are in place. Then the team can function as a complete unit, each part synchronized into an efficient machine. By playing together over a continued period of time, each member of the team will instinctively know the reactions of teammates in a given situation.

The developments of the game have been so great that the coach should not find it necessary to make any changes and/or variations in his style of play. Basically, the game I knew as a Celtic—hard, nose-to-nose, match-up basketball, where pride and desire and determination are deeply imbedded in the spirit and souls of the players—is still good enough to win.

CHAPTER 10

TEAM OFFENSE
—BASIC

S PEAKING FRANKLY, I believe that basketball today is far better than it was years ago when I was an active player. I realize that most of us oldtimers like to dwell in the "way back when," days and I'm not trying to set myself up as an exception to the usual rule. Neither am I trying to criticize the early days of a sport to which I owe so much.

Basketball in the World War I era was a slow game and was not played with the offense in mind. However, today, basketball is a game of offense; it is a sport that, by its very nature, is geared to scoring. The team with the ball is always the team in command. In the old game the big question was "Can he play defense?" In the modern game the talent scouts ask "Can he go over?" The point here is, of course, can he shoot well? If the answer is affirmative, it means opponents can't sag off on him.

When I first set foot on a basketball court, there was little to learn in the way of offense. There *was* little offense. You had two shots, the set and the lay-up. If anyone had ever thought of a one-hand shot, he would have been branded as a dangerous radical.

With only these two shots, there was little progress made toward team play. Usually the best man did the outside shooting and, more often than not, he was the fellow who went in for the lay-up. As tall as I was, I didn't play the pivot on offense. A hook shot was unheard of; you didn't even attempt a shot with your back to the basket.

The result? Games would see both teams score a total of 30 points. A fellow like Elgin Baylor gets that many today without working up much of a sweat. When the endless arguments of past versus present are held, I've often heard the statement that a team from the old days could beat a team of today even with the 10-second rule in effect.

"The teams today wouldn't even touch the ball," they say. Well, I doubt that in view of the press and other innovations. Even if it is true, which team had it easier? The one that didn't have to cross midcourt in ten seconds or the one that had to watch the ball, the opposition, *and* the clock?

SIMPLICITY AS THE KEYNOTE

Simplicity is the keynote of an offense. In my opinion, too many hours are spent on "razzle-dazzle" offenses and defenses. I like my team to work the ball in as close as possible (without the use of the dribble) before risking a shot but have no objections against long-range shooting, provided the player is reasonably set. Even an occasional one-hand heave is not considered a crime, as long as it is thrown from a spot close to the basket. Some of the shots we don't even blink at today would have made the old masters shudder. The only demand is that the player shoot within his accuracy range.

St. John's star Jerry Houston attempts "unorthodox" shot. (It missed!) Players opposing Houston are Army's Dennis Shantz (on floor) and John Ritch. St. John's beat Army in this semifinal game of the National Invitational tournament (1965). (Wide World Photos)

There was a time when practically all forms of one-hand shooting were taboo, and a one-hand heave on the run was the quickest route to the bench. Today it is the so-called "unorthodox" shooter who always seems to give you the most trouble. A St. John's player, Bill Lloyd, an unorthodox shooter if ever there was one, drove many a St. John's opponent to the aspirin box during his playing days.

Lloyd used to drop into the pivot, cradle the ball on his wrist, step out, and shoot with a stiff-arm motion. He was absolute death with this hook-like shot, so much so that he still holds many of the individual scoring records in the metropolitan area and in the East. What made the shot really unique was the fact that he made it without looking at the basket!

The use of the dribble was not frowned on, but the Celtic attack was a passing attack, and I stand pat on its use. In our passing attack the player will always have the dribble left in case of trouble. All coaches equip their players with styles of play that work the ball close to the basket for the good shots. The attack may move along definite paths (patterns and weaves) or it may be constructed with freedom for individual action as the motif (free-wheeling).

SET STYLE VS. FREE-WHEELING ATTACK

There has always been some disagreement as to how specific a preconceived method of setting up scoring attempts should be. Many coaches will argue that a grooved attack discourages individual initiative and is too easily hamstrung by a well-planned defense. However, the staunchest advocate of systematic basketball cannot deny that a zone defense, for example, is anathema to any form of screen attack. Against a team that plays the ball rather than the man, the most beautifully timed set plays are not worth a straw.

On the other hand, there are many who believe in systematic coordination and play the game according to the prescribed formula of some system. They contend that a set mode of attack is essential in high-school basketball, that schoolboys have neither the basketball intelligence nor the experience to go 32 minutes on their own, that they need a well-organized offense calling for the movement of players to certain areas under certain situations and conditions, and that if the set offense does nothing else, it prevents their youngsters from becoming careless or wild in their playing.

Hence, the question as to which is the better system—the set style with plays or the style which depends on the players to create their own scoring opportunites—may hinge upon personnel. At St. John's we pinned our faith to a large extent on the resourcefulness of the players. We stressed fundamentals with particular emphasis on fast, accurate passing and fast breaks. Everyone moved and everyone was a potential scorer. One *must* in our offensive plans, however, was the pivot man. We used him in a high or low post position, depending on the opponent's defense.

Players such as Oscar Robertson, Bob Cousy, Dick McGuire, Maurice Stokes, and Elgin Baylor can create more plays by accident than many coaches can by design. This type of player is adapted to free-wheeling and would be badly hampered by a disciplined offense.

Set plays were not too important in our style of play, but we had and would use three or four standards and/or the shuffle for an offensive change-of-pace. We had certain formations which were set up in our front court in meeting the man-to-man defense (Weave, Figure 8, and the Two-Three) and our players were free to cope with situations as they developed. We did have preconceived plays for the held-ball and out-of-bounds situations.

Although we seldom met a zone defense, we were fully prepared for the eventuality. We used the One-Three-One formation as an all-purpose offense to meet the various zone and combination defenses. The One-Two-Two was also used when we met the variations (see Chapter 13).

The Celtic type of play was not new to the players who made up our teams at St. John's. The average boy in New York City starts playing at a tender age. By the time he arrives at college, he has had a diversified basketball education in playgrounds, community centers, church leagues, elementary schools, and high schools. He has learned his way around the court and has picked up most of the tricks of the trade.

New York City kids learn a free-wheeling type of play which is handed down from generation to generation. The city kids like the freedom that free-wheeling permits, and they have mastered all the skills which make the style effective. New York City coaches follow through with this kind of offensive basketball because, in most part, they grew up playing this type of ball.

The big job remaining for college coaches is to teach these city boys the importance of teamplay. Most of the big-town boys have gained their experience along personal lines and have spent most of their time competing on a one-on-one or, at the most, a two-on-two basis.

In our pre-season offensive practice sessions the players are drilled extensively on the quick pass and constant circulation. With these drills as a basis they soon get to know one another and learn all there is to know about each teammate's game.

Reference has been made to the formations we set up in our front court. These will be presented a little later in this chapter. In all these

Action in Holiday Festival championship game in Madison Square Garden. St. John's vs. Michigan. St. John's won by a score of 75–74. In the photo Michigan's Cazzie Russell charges into Redmen's Bob Duer (21). Shot missed. Left to right: Michigan's Cazzie Russell (shooting ball); St. John's players No. 21, Bob Duer; No. 55, Sonny Dove; No. 22, Ken McIntyre; No. 44, Bob McIntyre. Michigan's Bill Buntin, No. 22, is circling under basket. This was the start of St. John's second Madison Square Garden's Grand Slam. The Redmen completed the slam by winning the National Invitational championship in March of 1965 to give Coach Joe Lapchick his second "grand slam." (N. Y. News Photo)

formations the big man takes a prominent part. And that brings us to the birth of the pivot play.

THE PIVOT PLAY

The Celtics first went on a Southern trip during the 1925–26 season. Miami booked us for three games, all outdoors. The games were not a financial success. As we traveled north we played at Sebring, Tampa, and St. Petersburg. It was there that Jim Furey, the owner, left us to go to New York. Nat Holman joined him because his CCNY team had a big game coming up. That left just five players: Johnny Beckman, Dutch Dehnert, Benny Borgeman, Pete Barry, and me.

The next game was scheduled for Chattanooga, and we didn't have the slightest conception of the distance from St. Petersburg when we got on the train. We did know there was a $500 guarantee with a 40 per cent option clause. Taking seats in the Pullman sleeper-type seats, we started on our favorite topic, but even that got a little boring after 20 hours of travel. We were dead tired when the train pulled into Chattanooga the next afternoon at 5 P.M. and even more tired when we learned the game was to begin at 8 P.M. We were scheduled to play the Chattanooga Railities, a local industrial team composed of college stars that had made quite a name for itself. The auditorium was sold out.

The interesting part of this game was that the local sportswriter almost blew his stack when he saw five bedraggled players loping through an unorganized warmup. Teams at that time had only one ball each with which to warm up. We shot lazily, followed up, and made the lay-up.

The sportswriter charged the promoter and proclaimed that he had been made the victim of a fraud perpetrated by the local promoters, Tom Humphreys and Bill Redd. (Redd was the greatest player turned out in the South up to that time.) The promoters assured the writer that the players out on the court would prove to be the real thing although, to me, it appeared the promoters had some personal doubts.

When the game started, we soon found that we were up against a good team. The Railities had an exceptionally good defense, and one player in particular was outstanding. This man, their standing guard, was roaming in the vicinity of the free-throw line and causing us all kinds of trouble.

After a few minutes, Beckman called time, and we huddled around him. "We'll have to get that guy out of there," Johnny said. "He's breaking up our passing game."

"How about me playing in front of him and blocking him away from the passes?" Dehnert asked. "You can pass the ball to me and I'll pass back. That way he'll be busy guarding me and you guys can work your plays."

"Let's go," Johnny said.

Now, for the first time in the history of the game, the ball zipped in and out of the pivot. It worked beautifully, and after a few minutes Dutch called for a timeout. "This is great!" he said gleefully. "Let's adopt it as a regular play."

"Great" was the word for it. It's still great! Always a passing team, we had found the play which enabled us to pass the ball with blinding speed. We adopted the pivot right there and then, and before the game was over we were sold on it. We worked on the pivot play in the games which followed, and soon it became the hub of our entire offense.

The sportswriter who had been so worried about our ability before the game became our most enthusiastic booster. It was he who dubbed us "magicians" and ambassadors of the sport in his column the following day.

Defensive guards began to play Dutch on the side of the ball to prevent him from receiving a pass (just as we defense big men on the side and in front today) but our passing game took care of that. Now Dutch began to pivot away from the guards when they overplayed him and drove in for baskets. The pivot was not only a passing terminal but a potent scoring weapon.

The pivot (used as a high post) blended in beautifully with our give-and-go game, and our offense was really something to see. Dutch would stand on the free-throw line, and we would keep the ball "singing" on its way in and out of the pivot. Then we began to dribble and cut around and off of Dutch, to the utter confusion of our opponents. Later, Dutch found that he could use *our* cutting as a screen for a dribble and a shot, and this increased the effectiveness of the pivot to an even greater extent.

I liked the pivot play then, and I like it now! I have used the pivot (high and low post) from the first day I began to coach—even when not blessed with a player who could handle the job. In this case I used a player who could suffice merely as a feeder. I am not an advocate of the use of the pivot to such an extent that it overshadows all other parts of the offense. In my opinion, the pivot loses much of its effectiveness when it is regarded merely as a scoring weapon.

Dutch Dehnert utilized the pivot perfectly. He used it to feed the cutters, as an aid to hardpressed teammates, and to protect the ball until cutters could get free. Dutch attempted a score only when he felt it was necessary in order to keep his assigned opponent honest.

So, the pivot (high and low posts) has been considered an integral part of all of my front court offensive formations whether stationed in the high and low positions or as a "flash" type of weapon. Tied in with fast-passing, hard cutting, change of direction and our give-and-go type of play it gave us a fine straight-away offense. We also used the pivot in our control game and "weak side" offense. When used in our One-Three-One all-purpose offense it was the focal point in attacking zone and combination defenses.

THE WEAVE

The weave is a good pattern to use when you do not have a good big man but do possess fair over-all height. This formation or pattern requires good ball handlers and drivers. Its use forces the defense to move and pulls the opponents' big men away from the basket and into defensive areas to which they are unaccustomed. The weave permits a team to do some fast surgery on the defense. It will show up a head turner, lunger, and ball stealer. Putting a string on the ball will show him up.

As a rule, this is a good offense to use when you want to play control ball. The only shots you are looking for are either driving lay-ups or the short jumper. Short jump-shots are defined as those within 12 to 15 feet of the basket. The movement in the weave is quite flexible, and it is fairly easy to add maneuvers such as the come-around play, low pivot, and reverse.

The advantages of the weave are:

1. Players learn to move and screen without the ball.
2. They develop into good passers.
3. They learn to drive.
4. They get their jump shots off quickly.

All the maneuvers are made while moving, and this keeps the defense busy. They have little time to help out teammates or attempt interceptions.

The disadvantages of the weave are:

1. Defensive balance may not be maintained.
2. The players may commit charging fouls unless they have mastered the roll-screen and the screen-stop.
3. It is fairly easy to defense.
4. Defensive players are normally in good rebound positions.
5. Offensive rebounding opportunities are scarce.

Principles:

1. Spacing and balance must be maintained.
2. Passes must be made away from defensive opponents to protect the ball.
3. Players must keep their heads up and watch so they will not charge opponents.
4. They must know where the ball is at all times.
5. If defensive opponents overshift:
    (a.) Clear. Go to opposite side of court and reverse.
    (b.) Change. Buttonhook to the same side.
6. In changing direction, use sides of the court and limit passing to bounce passes.
7. Avoid passing down the middle.
8. If defensive opponents go behind, stop and take jump shots. If opponents guard closely, run them off the pivot or go off a screen.

9. If defensive opponents use the switch, split them and go for the basket (give-and-go).
10. Do not hurry shots. If there is insufficient time, start over.
11. Be patient.

Following a series of weaves, a smart back-court playmaker can often disconcert the defensive opponents by dribbling back to midcourt and starting over because he notices bad court balance or opponents' good defense.

Some coaches equip their players with numbered plays for each formation. Others establish a system whereby the location of the ball and/or players determines the action. I do not use set plays as such. However, I do believe in drilling my players in a number of possible plays for each formation to familiarize them with the possibilities.

DIAGRAM 10.1 Five-Man Weave. Player A dribbles a short distance, passes to teammate B, and continues on to the right corner to replace Player D. Player B dribbles to the left (left hand) and passes to teammate C. This rolling from corner to corner continues until a play develops. The dribble is combined with direct passing and plays an important part in this style of play. Its elimination would take away many opportunities to drive for the basket.

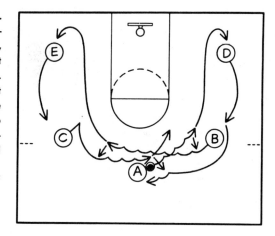

DIAGRAM 10.2 Come Around Play off the Weave. Instead of continuing the roll to replace teammate C, Player E reverses direction and sets a screen which enables teammate A to "come around" him, secure a shooting position, and receive a pass from teammate B.

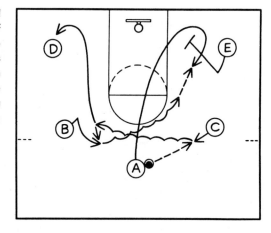

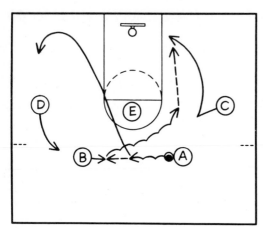

DIAGRAM 10.3 Four-Man Weave off the High Post. Player A dribbles left (left hand), passes to teammate B, and continues on to the corner. Player B dribbles right (right hand) and passes to teammate C, who has used the "back door" change to cut for the basket. (Used when C's opponent is applying defensive pressure or is attempting an interception.)

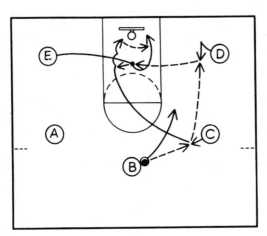

DIAGRAM 10.4   Bucket Play off the Weave. Player E times his cut to the "bucket" position when his teammates are in positions to recognize the play. The ball moves swiftly from Player B to teammates C and D in rapid order and to teammate E. Here, Player C receives the ball, dribbles a step or two, and returns the ball to bucket player E for a shot.

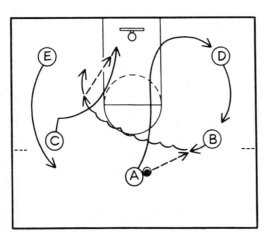

DIAGRAM 10.5   Dribble-Block Series (10.5, 10.6, 10.7, and 10.8). Player A initiates the Figure 8 and replaces teammate D. Player B dribbles left (left hand) and across the lane. Player C fakes a cut toward the baseline, changes direction, cuts behind teammate B's back, and receives a bounce pass in front of the basket for a shot.

DIAGRAM 10.6 Player B again dribbles left and across the lane. Now, when his (B's) guard switches to pick up teammate C, Player C returns the ball to teammate B.

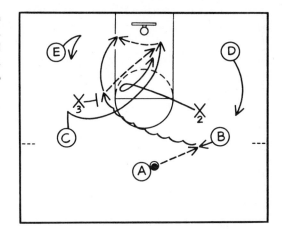

DIAGRAM 10.7 The "dribble" series continues with Player C cutting across the lane to a position behind D's opponent, where he sets a screen. Player B passes the ball to teammate D, who cuts around teammate C's screen.

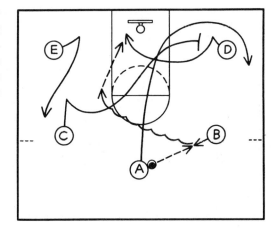

DIAGRAM 10.8 Quarterback A cuts left and sets a screen behind teammate E's opponent. Player C fakes in and retreats for defensive balance. Player B passes to teammate E cutting around A's screen.

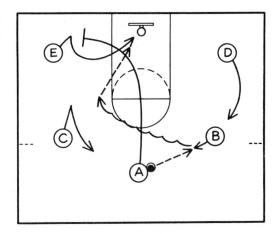

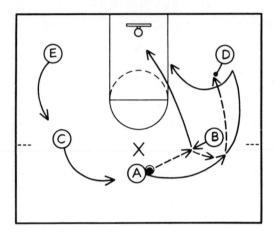

DIAGRAM 10.9   Overshoulder Play.   Quarterback A passes the ball to teammate B and cuts behind him for an over-shoulder pass. Player B cuts for the basket. If he does not break free, Player A passes the ball to teammate D breaking out from the corner. Player A then follows his pass, reverses, and cuts off D's back and to the basket, ready for a pass. Teammates C and E replace positions as shown, filling in the back-court spots for teammates A and B.

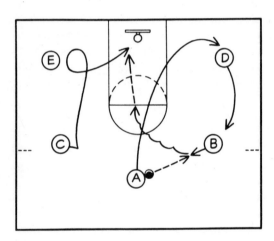

DIAGRAM 10.10   Exchanging Away from the Ball (Single).   Player A passes to teammate B. Player A cuts through as shown to replace teammate D, and teammate B dribbles behind the moving screen (A's) as shown. Teammate C moves behind teammate E's opponent and fakes a screen, cutting around and toward the basket in time to receive a pass from teammate B.

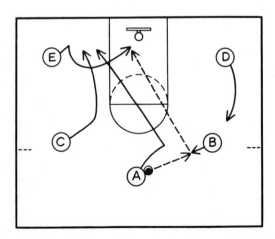

DIAGRAM 10.11   Exchanging Away from the Ball (Double).   Quarterback A passes to teammate B and angles away from the ball to team up with teammate C in setting a double screen behind teammate E's opponent. Player E cuts off the double screen and receives a pass from teammate B if he breaks free.

FIGURE 8 WITH VARIATIONS *

The Figure 8 is a basic formation. However, we use it in two ways —as a regular game offense and as a practice drill to teach passing, cutting, the lay-up, moving without the ball, and defensive balance. After the Figure 8 has been mastered, the variations may be added. The Figure 8 leads right into the Three-Two, and most of the plays will be found in this formation.

The variations include two- and three-man plays and utilize the give-and-go, the over-the-shoulder series, the dribble block, the pass-and-go-away, and the double screens. It is preferred that these plays be run spontaneously so that adjustments can be made according to the reactions of the defensive players.

The personnel requirements are as follows: The three outside players (back-court) should be the best ball handlers, smart and alert. It is important that they be good outside shooters so they may keep the defense honest. A good jump shot is a must, and the ability to drive and cut for the basket is vital. Back-court players who are not in on the play should try to set screens for teammates and take charge of the defensive balance. One of the three outside men should be the quarterback and take charge of the offense.

The corner men should be tall and tough off the boards since they will do most of the offensive and defensive rebounding. It is important that they be able to handle the ball well since they must feed teammates cutting to the ball or off screens. They should possess good, close-range jump shots and be able to fake and drive to the baseline.

The Figure 8 and the Three-Two are moving offenses. No player should be standing at any time; the players should be constantly moving so they can handle the ball or set up screens for teammates—particularly when the ball is on the "weak" side of the court. Keeping the opponents moving on the weak side prevents them from sagging or blocking up the middle of the court. It is important that the corner men be aware of the team's defensive balance or lack of it at all times.

Principles:

1. The middle must be kept open. Cutters who do not receive the ball keep going and fan out to the sides of the court.

---

* Dr. Harold C. Carlson, famous University of Pittsburgh athlete and coach, developed the Figure 8 offense. This offense, in some manner or form, is a part of every attack known to the game. Doc, as he was fondly called by his associates and contemporaries, hung up his shoes at the end of the 1952–53 season after 31 years of service to his alma mater. He died in 1965. Doc will long be remembered as one of the great contributors to the game.

2. Cutting is not restricted to "ball" plays but, preferably, to screening for teammates.
3. Players must move with a purpose and keep pressure on the opponents.
4. By passing and cutting away from the ball, teammates will know the cutter is going to screen on the weak side.
5. When a player passes and cuts behind the receiver, he should be ready for the "over-the-shoulder" series.
6. Dribbling to the "inside" means the man with the ball expects the respective teammate to cut around him and on to the basket.
7. When players cut deep to set up a double screen, the corner man must use this screen to cut to the ball.
8. The offense should be well spread to balance the court.
9. Passes should always be made to the "outside" of the receiver (eliminates interceptions and tie-ups).
10. Defensive balance is the responsibility of all players and must be maintained at all times.

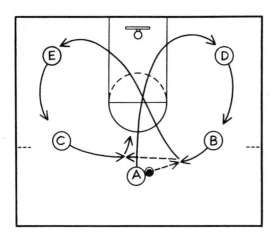

DIAGRAM 10.12 Basic Figure 8. The basic Figure 8 rotation is shown with players cutting and passing toward the basket with hand opposite the ball raised as a target for a pass and a possible shot. Player A replaces D, teammate B replaces teammate E, etc.

TWO-THREE OFFENSE

This is the standard professional-style offense. Most of the plays are limited to two or, at the most, three men who operate exclusively on a free-style basis. The give-and-go, give-and-go-away, give-and-go-around, and inside and outside screens blend in beautifully with a pivot-scoring attack.

In this offense the old Celtic slogan "Hit a green shirt!" is apropos.

In Shamrock hoop-language, "Hit a green shirt!" meant the players kept the ball off the floor and kept moving—cutting, screening, and hustling!

The Two-Three functions best when a big man is available. The pivot man here can operate as a scorer (turnaround jumpers, hooks, and drives). The corner men feed the big man and screen for him so they or a back-court operator can hit him with the ball when he comes off the "picks."

The guards initiate the plays by getting the ball to the corner men, cutting to the receivers for return passes, and feeding the forwards when they cut away from the ball or to it from the other side of the court. If it is impossible to get the ball to the corner men or to the big man, they can utilize personal one-on-one plays.

DIAGRAM 10.13 Two-three Formation (Basic Moves). Quarterback A passes the ball to teammate C and angle cuts toward the basket looking for a return pass. If he does not get the ball, he continues on and sets a screen behind pivot man E's opponent. Player C passes the ball to teammate E if he breaks free after cutting around A's screen.

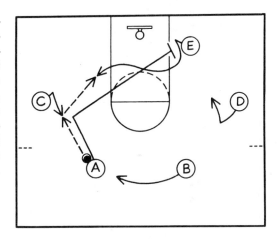

DIAGRAM 10.14 Quarterback A passes to teammate C and cuts behind him for a return pass. Player C hands off and clears for teammate A. Player A now has a one-on-one situation and may try to drive past his opponent. If Player A cannot get past his opponent, he looks for pivot teammate E, who may drive around the screen set by teammate C.

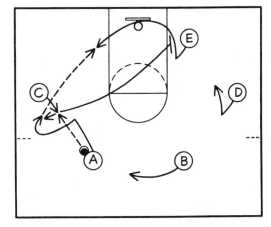

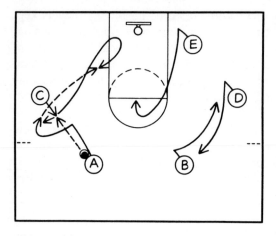

DIAGRAM 10.15   Turnaround Play. Quarterback A passes to teammate C and cuts behind him for a return pass. Player C returns the ball to teammate A and cuts for the basket for a return pass and a shot. However, when the pass does not come, he reverses around into a pivot position. Player A feeds the ball to teammate C. Pivot player E cuts out to the free-throw line to clear the under-basket area and to be in position for a pass if teammate C cannot get off a shot.

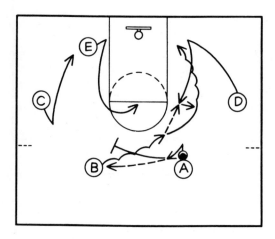

DIAGRAM 10.16   Weak Side Screen. Player A passes the ball to teammate B and sets a screen as shown. Player B dribbles past the screen and feeds teammate D, who had cut toward the basket and reversed to a post position. Player D returns the ball to teammate B, who dribbles in for a shot. Pivot man E breaks out to the free-throw line and teammate C follows in.

DIAGRAM 10.17 Corner-Man Drive. Player A feeds the ball to teammate C in a wing position. Player A follows his pass and receives the ball from teammate C. Player C now starts for the free-throw line and, at the same time, pivot man E breaks down the right side of the lane and sets a pick near the basket. Player C pivots around or simply changes direction at the free-throw line and cuts to the basket. A has dribbled to the corner after the return pass and now hits C on his way to the basket.

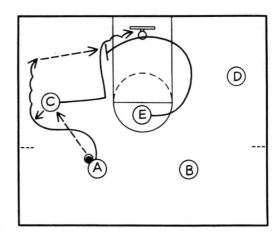

CHAPTER 11

TEAM DEFENSE —BASIC

MAN-TO-MAN DEFENSE has always been my forte. In coaching the St. John's University team and, naturally, the New York Knickerbockers, I used man-to-man defense with limited switching as the basic defense.

Many coaches equip their teams with several defenses. This practice, in my opinion, leads to weakness, because no team can master three defenses as efficiently as one. Despite the popularity of the various zone defenses and the zone presses which have followed the trend, I feel that man-to-man defense, thoroughly mastered, provides ample strength to contain any team and any offense. A man-to-man press applied full court, three-quarter, or half-court presents as many "trap" and "double-team" opportunities as any type of zone press. Man-to-man sloughing-off permits effective closing of the scoring areas, and, because of match-ups, boxing-out is easier to apply in the man-to-man than in the zone defenses.

Desire and the willingness to sacrifice personal glory for the good of the team are vital qualities in the development of a strong defense. When a team's offense goes badly or the opponents present a strong attack, the ability to counter with a strong, aggressive defense will provide players and coach with a sense of confidence. By playing good, aggressive defense the team can rest assured that the offense will take care of itself.

Use of the voice is important in building defensive teamwork. The coach should insist that his players use short, terse terms such as "stay," "slide," "switch," "pick left," "pick right," "hands up!" Desire, sacrifice, spirit, talking it up, keeping constant pressure on the man with the ball, and playing likely receivers closely will force opponents to take chances and invariably lead to costly misplays. For this reason I believe the man-to-man is better prepared to meet the various offenses than any other type of defense.

High-school players frequently come up to college ball without the faintest idea of the fundamentals of good man-to-man defense. The increasing popularity of the zone defense in our high schools is undoubtedly the contributing factor. In learning the mechanics of zone defense, the players never thoroughly absorb the fundamentals of defense. They leave their feet, turn their heads, and fall for simple feints and fakes. In a zone defense these mistakes may not get them into trouble since they are playing the ball and shifting positions on the floor. But in the man-to-man defense such errors can be disastrous.

Although team defense requires the coordinated efforts of all five players, individual responsibility is the key. Mastery of the mental qualities and proficiency in the physical moves discussed in Chapter 7 are necessary if a good team defense is to be developed.

I like a tight defense where all offensive moves can be quickly countered because of thorough mastery of all the facets of individual defense. This means the team is ready to meet post or pivot offenses by beating high-man opponents to their favorite spots, by playing in front of them or on the side, and through use of sagging and floating.

It means also that a team is ready to counter weaves, screens, and cutting attacks by means of good footwork, fighting through screens, and sticking with the opponents "over the top" and can apply the various man-to-man presses on a team basis because of proficiency on an individual basis. It means they are prepared to counter opponents' offensive follow-in tactics and control the defensive backboard through organized boxing-out and planned ball-recovery moves.

Against certain opponents (few, indeed) I like to be able to employ a zone defense as a change of pace (two-three or two-one-two) and have my team ready to defense the special game situations—held ball, out-of-bounds, free throw, and fast break. In our man-to-man defense I always try to keep switching within bounds. Too much switching is almost as bad as none at all. When a team places too much dependence on switching, you often find one player pulling a switch all by himself with the result that two men are defensing one opponent and the other opponent is unguarded.

The two-on-two drill described in Chapter 8 is used to firm up our switching principles. Two offensive players are given the ball and the two teammates are assigned to cover them. The offensive players work swiftly down the court, setting up as many screen and pick situations as possible. The defensive players must stick with their assigned opponents until one of them is screened away, at which time they are permitted to switch. I keep on top of the defensive players, calling "switch" whenever the set-up calls for it. If the defensive players over-switch, I immediately stop the drill and go over the situation so they can see how the switch could have been eliminated.

DEFENSIVE AREA CHARTS

The defensive area charts which follow have been prepared in order to aid young coaches in teaching defense. The basic defense chart illustrates the individual and team tactics and is divided into six main areas. In each area the defensive maneuver is shown—when to play the ball tight or loose; when to play in front or in back of the big man; when to switch or slide; where to play the shooters (one-hand set and jumper) and where and when to slough-off toward the ball.

BASIC DEFENSE CHART

In Area I we contest every pass and try to beat the "out" man to the ball. This move is important because once the big man gets the ball in this area, he is in good scoring position. We play the man with the ball very tight and try for the interception at every opportunity.

An important feature of our defensive play in this area is playing in front of the pivot man with our hands up. The opponent has us in close to the basket and can score easily once he gets the ball. We practice this defensive move by the hour in an attempt to prevent fouling him.

When contesting the dribbler, we converge on him and attempt the double-team in Area I. Here, sloughing-off by our front-line guards helps us to jam up the middle and prevents the dribbler from making damaging pass-offs.

In Area II we again concentrate on stealing the ball. We play the man without the ball loose and slough-off toward the ball. Here we play behind the pivot man since he is too far out to be a real scoring danger. It is important to give teammates room to slide through. When this is im-

AREA I

a. Contest every pass.
b. Switch to the ball.
c. Converge on dribbler.
d. Stop all shots.
e. Play in front of pivot man. Teammates must fight through screens.
f. Be aggressive.

AREA II

a. Play in back of pivot man. Teammates slide through.
b. Slough-off towards the ball.
c. Play semi-aggressive.
d. Switch to ball (if steal is possible).
e. Play the ball tight.
f. Play good shooter close.

AREA III

a. If offense weaves—slide.
b. Defense need not be too tight.
c. Men away from ball slough-off.
d. Do not switch to ball.
e. Some pressure on one-handers and two-hand sets (if any).
f. Disregard jump shots unless opponent is excellent shooter.

AREA IV

a. Sag-off and stop baseline drive.
b. Slough-off away from ball and clog the middle.
c. Let opponents use jump shot unless good shooters.
d. Little pressure on one-hand shots and two-handers (if any).
e. Force opponents into the middle.

AREA V

a. Let opponents weave—just slide.
b. Drop off drivers—clog middle.
c. "Give opponents outside shots."

AREA VI

a. "Help them shoot!"

DIAGRAM 11.1

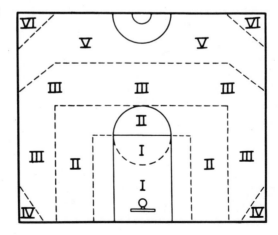

possible, it is vital that opponents who cut off the big man be picked up by means of the switch.

We try to be ready to switch to the ball, and if the opponents have a shooter who can score consistently in this area, we play him tight and try again to jam up the middle by sagging and floating.

In Area III we allow the offense to weave, sliding through without the use of the switch. In this area we let them shoot unless they are really good. Then, naturally, we have to go out and get them. We do use the slough-off and the slide in order to jam up the middle.

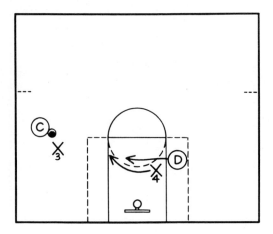

DIAGRAM 11.2 Defensive player X-4 beats offensive opponent D to the ball and contests every pass.

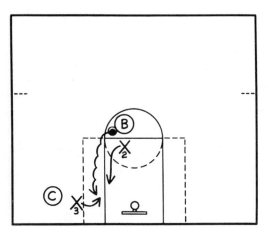

DIAGRAM 11.3 Defensive player X-3 converges on the dribbler (B).

In Area IV we slough-off the man in the corner and overplay him a little to stop his baseline drive and force him into the middle of the court, where teammates will be ready to pick him up if he gets loose. We let him jump shoot unless he is an exceptional shot.

In Area V we drop off and slough towards the ball. The only time we play opponents tight here is when we are pressing in the late stages of the game.

We play Area VI the same as Area V.

DIAGRAM 11.4 Defensive player X-1 switches to opponent who is dribbling past an opposing player's screen (switching to the ball).

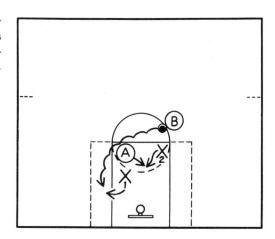

DIAGRAM 11.5 Defensive player X-4 drops back slightly to let teammate 3 slide through. No switch is necessary in this situation.

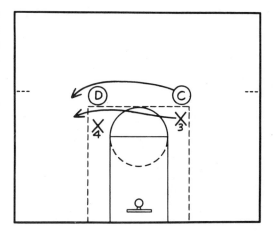

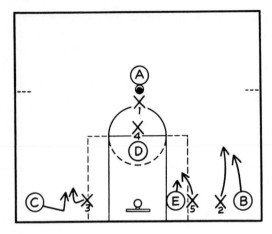

DIAGRAM 11.6 Playing in front of post and pivot (big men) opponents. Defensive player X-4 is playing in front of opponent D in the high post area. Defensive player X-5 is playing in front of opponent E in the low post (pivot) area. Teammate X-3 has shifted toward the lane to jam up the basket area but is prepared to play opponent C closely should he break out for the ball. Defensive player X-2 has moved out between his opponent (B) and the possible pass from opponent A.

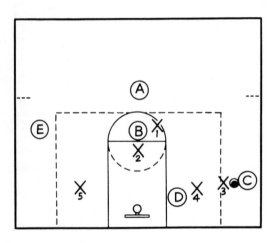

DIAGRAM 11.7 Defensive player X-2 plays behind opponent B in this area. Teammate X-1 has dropped back beside opponent B to shield him away from a pass or a move down the lane. Defensive player X-3 is playing the man with the ball tight. Defensive player X-4 is playing in front of opponent D, and teammate X-5 has dropped back in such fashion that he can see his opponent (E) and the ball.

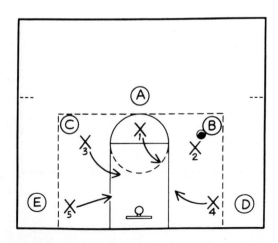

DIAGRAM 11.8 Defensive player X-2 plays the ball tight (Opponent B). His teammates slough-off to congest the "lane" area.

DIAGRAM 11.9 Defensive players all use the slide when the ball is in the center of the court. This enables them to "clog the middle."

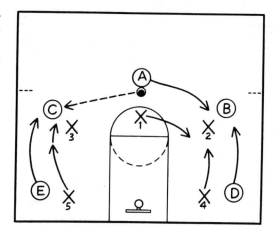

DIAGRAM 11.10 Area IV. With the ball in the right-hand corner, defensive player X-3 overplays toward the baseline to force opponent C toward the middle where teammates can help out.

Area V. Same as Area IV except when pressing in final stages of game.

Area VI. Same as Area V.

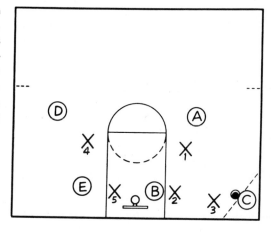

CHAPTER 12

SITUATION
PLAYS

S ITUATION PLAYS, with the exception of those from the center jump, were nonexistent in my early playing days. We had forward to forward and forward to guard plays from the center jump, but plays from out-of-bounds were more a matter of getting the ball safely in-court and in the hands of a teammate than of trying to score baskets. Then, too, most games were played on courts surrounded by a net or chicken wire. The fast break simply did not exist.

I recall the first time I saw a fast break. It was on a tiny court in Sandusky, Ohio, and I was playing with the Cleveland Rosenblooms, the World's Champions. The other team, a pick-up squad of college stars, was using a 2-1-2 zone. Every time we passed the ball inside, we wouldn't see it again until it went past us. The Sandusky boys would converge on the ball and take off for the races. And—they clobbered us!

I was impressed by the fast break and the zone, chiefly because it was the first time I had ever seen either one in operation. I was 30 years old and had been in basketball for over 15 years and these variations impressed me greatly. As the reader surely knows by this time, I was never what you would call a salesman for the zone defense. However, I realize that the zone defense has a place in basketball and certainly the fast break belongs in every team's repertory.

The fast break impressed the Rosenblooms so much that we sat up all the rest of the night trying to figure out how to beat it. The Sandusky combination, zone defense and fast break, is as effective today as it was that night so many years ago. Held-ball, out-of-bounds, and free-throw plays are common today and important in the general play of the game.

THE CENTER JUMP

Although the center jump is limited, due to the elimination of the tap following a score. I feel that it is important to try for the ball in any and all jump situations. Securing the ball from the initial center jump gives a team a decided advantage in providing each player with a chance to get the "feel" of the ball; this enables the team to probe the opponent's defense and find out what type is being used and how they are being matched. It also places the team in possession in control at the very outset of the game. Supporting this premise is my firm belief that every "turnover" in my team's favor adds to the chances of victory.

In tapping the ball (at the center circle and in held-ball situations) the player should bring his arm up straight at the top of his leap and tap the ball with the fingertips, using only his hand *from the wrist*. Too many players bring their arms into the act. A flip of the hand from the wrist is all that is needed.

I do not believe it is necessary to expose a team to a great number of formations to use at the center jump. At St. John's we used only three center jump formations. The standard "box" was used when we felt we controlled the tap or felt we had an even chance to obtain the ball, the one-three-one as a safety set-up when our opponents appeared to control the tap, and a formation we called the "pinch" when we intended to attempt a "steal" but wanted to make sure we had a strong defense set up.

Signals are important and may be the old "skin and cloth" type or other combinations. Nothing makes a team appear more foolish than to command the tap and lose the ball because a player fails to break to the right spot at the right time for the play.

DIAGRAM 12.1 **Box Formation. Old Guard Around Play.** This play is used when the tap is fairly sure. Player A taps the ball to teammate B. Player B passes to teammate D who breaks hard for the basket. Players C and E take care of defensive balance until possession is assured.

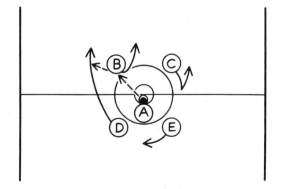

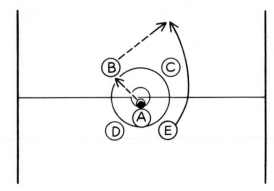

DIAGRAM 12.2 Box Formation. Guard Around Opposite Side. Same play as in preceding diagram with the exception that player B passes to teammate E coming down opposite side of court.

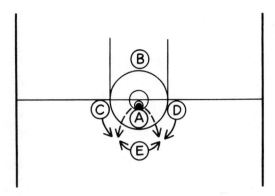

DIAGRAM 12.3 One-Three-One. We use this type of formation when opponents have the tap. Players C and D are trying to steal the tap. Should opponents get the tap, we have three players in good defensive positions.

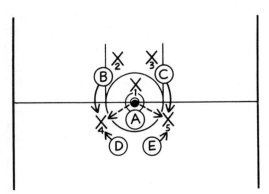

DIAGRAM 12.4 "Pinch." We use this formation when the opponents have the tap. Players D and E line up inside the opponents X-4 and X-5. As soon as the ball leaves the official's hand, teammates B and C put the pinch on opponents X-4 and X-5. If one can steal the ball, well and good. If not, we are in good defensive position.

JUMP BALL PLAYS

In our back court we use the box formation and try for possession only. We attempt certain plays in our front court and use the 1-3-1 formation.

DIAGRAM 12.5 Jump Ball Play. One-Three-One formation in front court. When we have the tap, we place our biggest man (B) in the lane. On the tap, C and D break toward the basket ready to receive another tap pass from B. Teammate E is responsible for defensive balance.

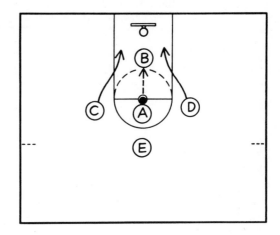

DIAGRAM 12.6 Jump Ball Play. One-Three-One formation. Ball is tapped to big man (B). Teammate E breaks around D and to the basket ready for a pass or tap from B. Teammate C drops back for defensive balance. Should the jumper (A) pick his opponent (opposing jumper) off on teammate B's pick, he may get the ball for a shot or dribble in for the lay-up.

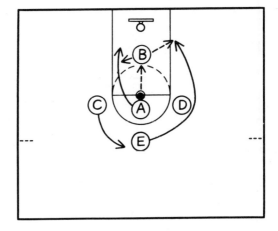

DIAGRAM 12.7 Jump Ball Play. Safety Box formation. Clair Bee's teams used this safety tap to perfection. It required control of the tap and good screening by players D and E. The jumper tapped the ball far back toward the 10-second line, and players B and C were responsible for obtaining the ball.

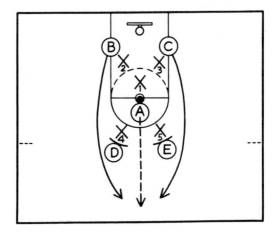

OUT-OF-BOUNDS PLAYS

Out-of-bounds plays are important not only because they score baskets but because they force players to move to secure the ball. This same philosophy governs jump ball plays. Rather than have players "stand and wait" for the ball, it is far better to have a play which requires movement and thereby increases possession chances.

Out-of-bounds plays executed with precision and speed stamp a team as being alert and well coached. Naturally, plays do not work as well against zones as they do against man-to-man defenses, but occasionally a clutch basket results against the best of defenses. The two or three baskets which work against tough opponents may very well prove the margin of victory and are worth all the time spent in perfecting them.

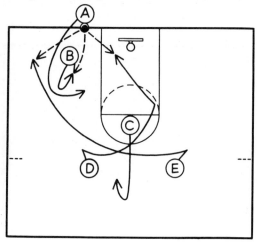

DIAGRAM 12.8   Out-of-Bounds Play. Triangle Formation. Players B and E move at the same time. Player D cuts as shown and is the number one target. Teammate C can retreat for the safety pass if A cannot hit D, B, or E in that order. A good take-off on this play is to fake a pass to B near the baseline and hit him with a bounce pass when he spins back toward the basket.

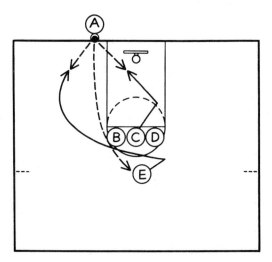

DIAGRAM 12.9   Out-of-Bounds Play. Free-Throw Line. Player E cuts around teammates B, C, and D as shown. This formation lends itself to a great number of variations. Player E can cut left or right, remain where he is, or tap a teammate on the back as a signal to cut to the basket. A direct pass from A to E behind the screen will provide time for a good set shot.

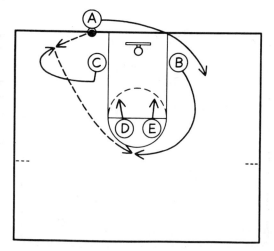

DIAGRAM 12.10 What few set plays we have are based on out-of-bounds and jump ball situations. We use the accompanying play when we have an out-of-bounds throw-in under our own basket. Player E is a decoy and starts the play with a drive around the pivot man. Teammate C crosses behind him and cuts to the basket. If defensive player X-2 switches to cover E, the ball may be passed to high post man B for a quick shot.

Player D is the team's best shot. If none of the preferred openings have materialized, the ball is passed out to him for a possible shot. On occasions he may drop into the spot occupied by teammate C, especially when defensive players X-3 and teammate X-5 drop back to keep everything in front of them. When this happens, player D (in the spot occupied by C above) fakes a cut around teammate B, drops back quickly, takes a pass from his out-of-bounds teammate, and shoots.

DIAGRAM 12.11 Player A passes the ball to teammate C. Player C fakes a shot to give teammate B time to cut around teammates D and E. Player C then passes the ball to teammate B for a shot. Players D and E hold and then follow in. The out-of-bounds player (A) continues on around for defensive balance.

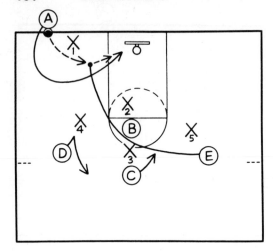

DIAGRAM 12.12 When the ball is taken out-of-bounds closer to the sideline, the players may try to do "business" with something like this. Player E races diagonally across the free-throw lane to a spot a few feet behind and on the inside of defensive player X-1. The out-of-bounds teammate (A) flips him a short pass and comes out immediately. Player A then swings around teammate E in a hook cut and takes a short pass for the "cripple" shot.

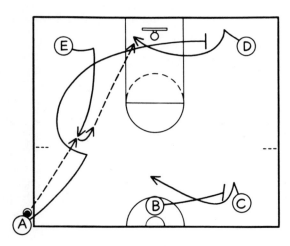

DIAGRAM 12.13   Player B changes with teammate C. Player E breaks out to receive a pass from out-of-bounds teammate A. As E gets the ball he turns and teammate A changes and cuts off his back. If he is free, player E passes to him. If player A is not free, he continues on and screens for teammate D.

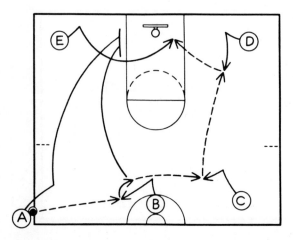

DIAGRAM 12.14 Player A passes to teammate B. Player B passes to teammate C. Following B's pass to C, players A and B set a double-screen under the basket for teammate E. Player C passes to teammate D, who hits E cutting around the double-screen.

DIAGRAM 12.15 Player A passes to teammate B and cuts for the basket. Teammate E moves slowly across the lane to screen for teammate D coming along the baseline. Player A also moves slowly toward the baseline to screen for teammate D. Player B (with the ball) dribbles to the left and passes to teammate D after he passes A's screen.

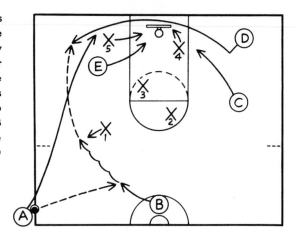

DIAGRAM 12.16 Out-of-bounds player A passes the ball to teammate B, who dribbles a short distance and returns the ball to teammate A. Player B then screens teammate C's opponent X-2. Player A times his dribble and then passes to teammate C after he clears B's screen. Player C takes a set or jump shot.

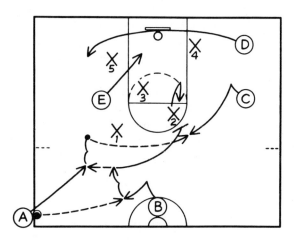

DIAGRAM 12.17 Out-of-bounds player A passes the ball to teammate B and cuts as shown. Player B returns the ball to teammate A. Player A dribbles a short distance and then passes the ball to teammate C, who has circled around teammates D and E. Player C may shoot or pass to A or E, who have cut to the basket. Teammate D drops back for defensive balance.

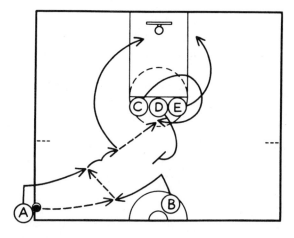

CHANGES IN THE GAME

The big change in basketball came in 1937 when the center jump was eliminated. Since I had played center all my life, it was hard for me to see it go, even though it eliminated most of the stalling and the foul trading which occurred in the waning moments of the games.

It seemed strange at the beginning to award the ball to the other team without a battle just because you had scored a basket against them. However, the value of the innovation in speeding up the game and increasing the scoring possibilities was adequate compensation and justified the change. Eastern basketball has always been based on passing. Years ago professional players would pass and pass and, in the end, perhaps take a shot farther away from the basket than the starting point. The Westerners had been playing a faster game and their scoring totals soared because they were using only four or five passes before attempting a shot.

Combined with the 10-second and the 3-second rules, the elimination of the center jump was expected to put a damper on the influence of the big man on the game. However, the changes merely served to accentuate the value of height, and today big men dominate the game in practically all positions. The players continue to get bigger and bigger, not only because there are more tall youngsters playing the game, but because the coaches have been searching for taller players. Elimination of the center jump also brought greater attention to the use of the pivot near the basket and to defensive goal tending.

So, along came the mighty George Mikan of De Paul, Bob Kurland of Oklahoma State, Mike Novak of Loyola, and Don Otten of Bowling Green (among others). These men became the game's first goal tenders. How well I remember them—particularly Mike Novak, whose goal tending had enabled Loyola (Chicago) to complete an undefeated season. Novak and Loyola eliminated my St. John's team in the semifinals of the 1939 tournament, but the Ramblers ran head-on into Clair Bee's undefeated LIU team. After watching our game, the Blackbirds won the championship by banking the ball high on the backboard where Novak could not reach.

The influence of the goal tenders brought another addition to the rules, which prohibited a player from batting or touching the ball in its downward flight above the basket. If this rule had not been put into the book, there is no way of telling what the result might have been. Certainly some enterprising coach would have come up with five seven-footers who could have surrounded the defensive basket and might possibly have held their opponents scoreless from the field.

THE FAST BREAK

Born of the changes in the game, the fast break has become standard equipment for all but a few teams and has brought color, excitement, and brilliant action to the sport.

In our use of the fast break we try to take advantage of the transition from defense to offense by striking quickly. We have no set pattern in attacking with this weapon, but we do set up lanes and try to get our players on their way with a fast outlet pass.

Our fast break starts with the opponent's shot at the basket. We box out our opponents and fight under the defensive board for the ball. Then, as soon as possession is sure, we break for our basket at full speed. The ball is worked down with a minimum of ball-handling, the pass going as quickly as possible to the free man up ahead.

No matter what type of offensive attack is being employed at the moment, the number one rule is to look up court and see if anyone is open under the basket. The same rule holds on defense. Our last retreating player always checks to see if an opponent has remained behind as a "sleeper" and is parked under *his* basket.

BASIC FAST-BREAK PRINCIPLES

1. The fast break begins by checking opponents, pounding the boards, and getting the rebounds.
2. Rebounders should use the following passes to pitch out to the wings:
   (a.) Baseball
   (b.) Shuffle
   (c.) Overhand hook
   (d.) Two-hand jump or one-hand jump pass
3. Once a pass is made to the wing, he must get the ball to the middle lane. The third man fills the open lane.
4. The ball is passed from middle to wing, back to middle, and so on. Do not throw cross-court passes. The best pass to use is the two-hand chest pass.
5. Middle-lane player stops at the free-throw line unless he can split the defense and drive in. The wings stay wide until they reach the free-throw line extended. Then they cut sharply to the basket.
6. Wing men return the ball to the middle if covered, since the trailer may be coming through.

FAST-BREAK REMINDERS

1. Always pass ahead—never back.
2. Keep the lanes well spread.
3. Make snappy and accurate passes.
4. Fill the open lanes. If there is no open lane, be a trailer.
5. Keep dribbling to a minimum. Use it only to escape the defense or to get the ball to the middle lane.
6. Wing players must cut sharply when driving to basket.
7. Player in middle lane does the feeding.
8. Do not force shots. Look for the trailer or wait for your set offense to form.
9. Clear boards quickly.
10. Yell "ball!" Don't bounce ball while waiting for help.
11. Look to the sides for the quick pass.

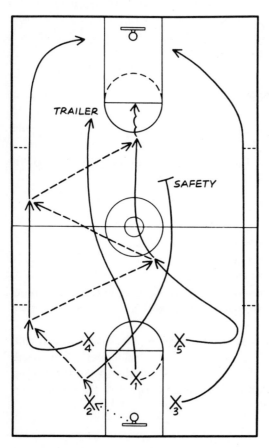

DIAGRAM 12.18 Rebounders X-1, X-2, and X-3 have formed the rebound triangle and teammates X-4 and X-5 are set near the free-throw line. The pitchout is made from X-2 to teammate X-4 on the left wing, back to X-5, again to X-4, who returns the pass to X-5. Player X-5 dribbles to the free-throw line. He may shoot, pass to X-4 or to X-3, or feed the trailer X-1. Teammate X-2 sets up defensive balance.

12. Wing players must meet the ball. Don't run so fast and far that you have to wait for the ball.
13. Keep break formation well spread.
14. If break does not develop after crossing ten-second line, slow down and set up regular offense.
15. If a defensive opponent is between you and a teammate breaking in for a lay-up, loop a pass to him.
16. Don't force the fast break. Hold ball and advance slowly.
17. Make passes short and snappy unless you have a sleeper down court.
18. A trailer must follow every break.
19. A teammate must always be "back" for defensive balance.

THE FREE THROW

At the very beginning of my professional career (Holyoke in the Western Massachusetts League) one man shot all the free throws for his team and was usually the high scorer for the team. And the high scorer was, naturally, the team's hero. Just before I arrived at Holyoke, they changed certain fouling rules to give the big man a bit of protection.

In my first game, I played against a center by the name of Noblock, who was known as the "Woodchopper." I found out *why* right away. He cut me to pieces. However, it was a blessing in disguise, because I shot eleven free throws and made them all. That was a good beginning for a newcomer and I made out just fine, all because of the "Woodchopper."

The free throw has always been an important "game-winning" factor, and with the advent of the "one-and-one" rule, its value skyrocketed. At the present time the majority of close games are won by the team with the best free-throw average. In checking the statistics of games which were lost by a close margin, I have often said to myself, "If we had only made more of our free throws . . ."

Most college teams are successful in no more than 60 to 65 per cent of their free-throw attempts. Professional team averages are not much better, hovering around 70 per cent. High-school averages are much lower, frequently below 50 per cent. It does not require the brains of a mathematical genius to recognize the potential which could turn a losing into a winning season.

In my opinion, an average professional team should score at least eight of ten free-throw attempts. A college team should hit on seven of ten, and high-school teams on six of ten.

The performance of Army's fine team under the coaching of a young-ster (26-year-old Bob Knight) in 1966 is worthy of citing here. Against archenemy Navy, the Army team scored 24 of a possible 25 free throws, 24 in a row. It was a noteworthy performance and enabled Army to win the game.

I have never tried to work plays in a free-throw situation but expect my team to be alert for fast-break opportunities. Here, as from a suc-cessful or unsuccessful shot from the field, the speed with which the ball can be brought into play after recovery is vital. In the first diagram the ball is put in play by the player who retrieves it from the board or, in the case of a successful try, by the player who retrieves the ball, steps quickly out of bounds, and initiates the first pass of the fast break.

In the second diagram, teamplay is brought into the action when the free throw is successful. This play gets the ball on its way more quickly and with more safety because the passer is facing up court and can make the in-court pass more accurately.

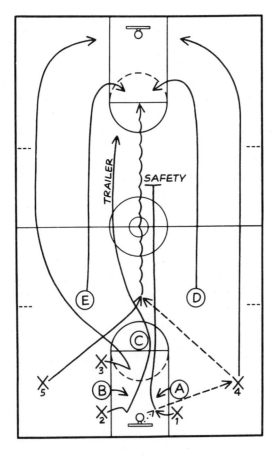

DIAGRAM 12.19 Fast Break from Unsuccessful Free Throw. Player X-1 got the rebound and pitched out to teammate X-4. Player X-5 (back-court playmaker) cut across the head of the circle and re-ceived the ball. He dribbled up court while teammates filled the lanes. Player X-4 continued up the right sideline lane, Player X-3 filled the left sideline lane, and teammate X-2 followed the drib-bler (X-5) as a trailer. Defensive rebounder X-1 took care of the defensive balance (safety).

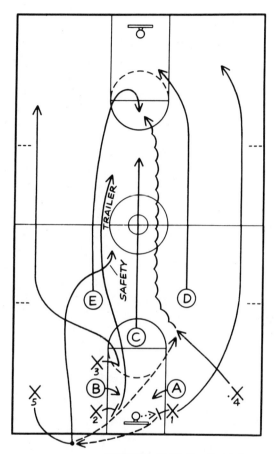

DIAGRAM 12.20 Fast Break from a Successful Free Throw. Big man X-1 tapped the ball to back-court teammate X-5 who hit teammate X-4 cutting across the head of the circle. Player X-4 dribbled up court to the free-throw line. Teammates cut as shown. In this situation, player X-5 plays safety.

PART FOUR

CHAPTER 13

OFFENSE
VARIATIONS

O FFENSE VARIATIONS and game tactics are determined to a great extent by the type of defense or defenses adopted by the opponents. In the few variations to our basic offense, the player is the essence. We employ certain principles and formations but avoid set plays and patterns. I prefer to leave attacking moves entirely up to the players in attacking zone defenses, meeting the man-to-man and zone presses, applying the deep freeze, the control freeze, and in executing the situation plays (one-shot, held-ball, out-of-bounds).

ATTACKING THE ZONES

The adoption of the 12-foot lane increased the popularity of the zone defenses. Many coaches feel that the big lane, with its 3-second restriction, strengthens the zone possibilities to such an extent that they would be foolish not to adopt the defense. They also feel that zone defenses are less costly with respect to player fouling. Players are more likely to foul when using the man-to-man defense than when using the zone. In attempting to stick with their assigned opponents, they are exposed to picks (charging possibilities) and may commit fouls when attempting to fight through screens.

Jump shooters have become so proficient that any type of defense which can force them to operate out of their range is desirable. Most zone defenses protect the area around the free-throw line since this area is the one in which jump shooters are particularly accurate. Most zone defenses force jump shooters farther away from the basket and this, naturally, lessens their accuracy.

OUTLINE OF ATTACK METHODS

1. Methods of Operation
   (a.) Fast break
   (b.) Outside shots
   (c.) Planned attack
2. Attacking Principles
3. Formations
   1-3-1 (All-Purpose)
   1-2-2 (Around the Horn)
4. Diagrams of Planned Attacks

ATTACKING PRINCIPLES

1. Determine defense used (send a man through the middle and/or exchange front men). If opponents do not pick up cutter, it is some sort of zone.
2. Establish type of zone. (Is it a 3-2, 2-3, 2-1-2, 1-3-1?)
3. Set up spots for passers, shooters, and rebounders according to type of zone.
4. All players must be facing basket ready to shoot or pass with exception of post players (high or low).
5. Shooting accuracy is a must. Shots must not be forced. The score will probably not be as high as against man-to-man defense and defense will probably eliminate "second" shots, so accuracy is important.
6. Passes must not be forced. They must reach their objective. Use short, snappy overhead and bounce passes preceded by fakes and feints.
7. Eliminate "banana" or cross-court passes.

8. Maintain defensive balance (two men back and three men rebounding).
9. Work for two-on-one and three-on-two situations.
10. Limit drives to quick opening situations. Screens will not be as effective against zone defensive players as against man-to-man.
11. Limit use of the dribble. (Use the dribble only to get away, to protect the ball, to create a play situation, or to score.)
12. Baseline teammates must break out from behind defense to meet the ball.
13. The attack must be controlled.
14. Slowly force the zone back so short shots may be obtained around the "key" area.
15. Study the defensive moves in order to attack weaknesses.

ZONE DEFICIENCY AREAS

The deficiency charts show the weak spots in the various zones. These spots (circles) are important in setting up attacking formations and in acquainting the players with the scoring areas. The locations of these weak defensive spots change according to the various zone formations.

Accompanying each deficiency chart are zone attack recommendations. It will be noted that in attacking all but one zone defense (1-3-1) the all-purpose 1-3-1 attack is recommended. In meeting the 1-3-1 zone defense we give our alternate zone attack (1-2-2) the preference.

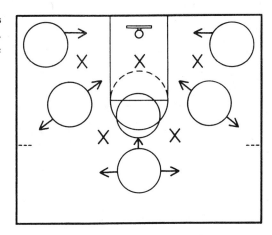

DIAGRAM 13.1 Deficiency areas (circles) in the 2-3 zone defense. Recommended attack formation: (1-3-1) or (1-2-2).

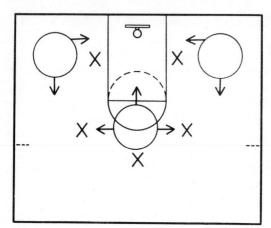

DIAGRAM 13.2 Deficiency areas (circles) in the 3-2 zone defense. Recommended attack formation: (1-3-1) or (2-3).

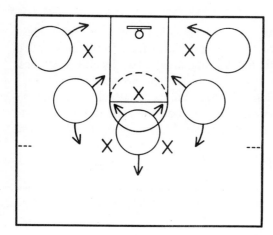

DIAGRAM 13.3 Deficiency areas (circles) in the 2-1-2 zone defense. Recommended attack formation: (1-3-1) or (1-2-2).

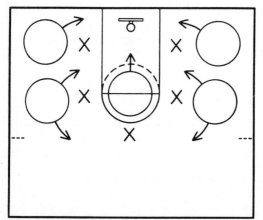

DIAGRAM 13.4 Deficiency areas (circles) in the 1-2-2 zone defense. Recommended attack formation: (1-3-1) or (2-2-1).

DIAGRAM 13.5 Deficiency areas (circles) in the 1-3-1 zone defense. Recommended attack formation: (1-2-2) or (2-1-2).

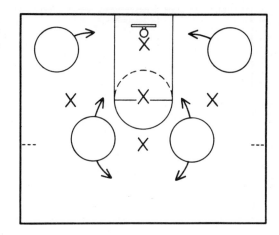

DIAGRAM 13.6 Deficiency areas (circles) in the 2-2-1 zone defense. Recommended attack formation: (1-3-1) or (1-2-2).

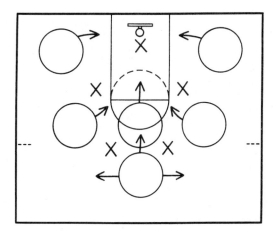

PLANNED ZONE ATTACKS

Our planned zone attack formations consist of the One-Three-One and the Two-Three. The charts which follow are examples of moves which the players make.

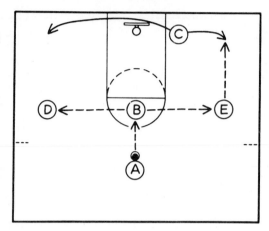

DIAGRAM 13.7 The 1-3-1 attack is excellent when employed to free the post player and side man against the 2-1-2 zone. Offensive player C (low post) moves to the side on which the first pass is made.

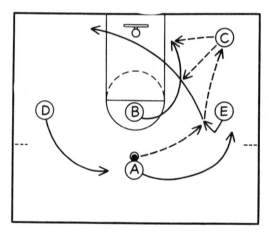

DIAGRAM 13.8 Each player moves after making a pass in this formation. The formation starts out as a 1-3-1 but changes alignment as the players move. The defensive players must worry constantly about the man breaking from the weak side and men cutting through on the give-and-go.

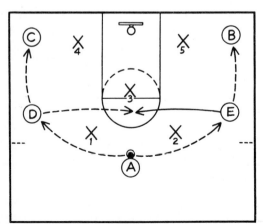

DIAGRAM 13.9 The 1-2-2 attack (around the horn) is designed to secure set shots and plays based on cuts across the lane.

DIAGRAM 13.10 In the 1-2-2 (overload), four players move to positions on one side of the court. One man remains on the other side (weak side). The ball is moved on the overloaded side until the defensive players overshift. Then a quick pass is made to the weak side. This play works on both sides of the court.

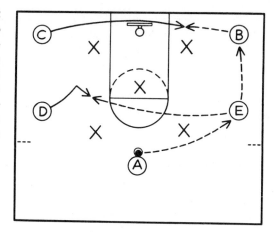

DIAGRAM 13.11 The double post is an excellent attack if two big men are available. The big men are placed on each side of the lane and the ball is whipped around the outside until a pass can be made to them. This formation concentrates the opponent's zone and provides a strong offensive rebounding attack.

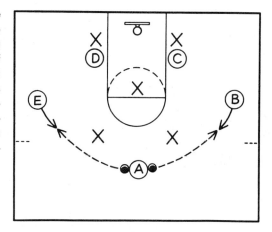

ATTACKING THE FULL-COURT MAN-TO-MAN PRESS

I feel that our back-court players can handle most traps or double-team situations in the man-to-man full court press. Therefore, the court is opened up so they can have room to operate.

If the dribblers have trouble, I like to turn immediately to the all-purpose 1-3-1 formation. In the 1-3-1 we try to get the ball (in-bounds) into the hands of our playmaker. He is usually the best dribbler and is accustomed to pressure. Our middle line (high post player, second back-court player, and one of our corner men) are stationed in line across the court and spaced as widely as possible. The fifth player, usually our center, heads for the area between the ten-second line and the head of the offensive circle. He is our "point" man.

The middle man (ball handler) and the low post man (center) are expected to be ready at all times to break out to the ball and leap high in the air to meet passes. Since they are hand-off men (feeders) in our set offense, we can count on them for protection should our back-court dribbler run into difficulty.

We also use the 1-2-2 formation (box) in attacking the full-court man-to-man press. In this formation we use the two men nearest the man out-of-bounds with the ball as blocking posts around which to run receivers. When the playmaker takes the ball out of bounds, the receiver attempts to get it back to him as quickly as possible. Occasionally the back-court teammate may take the ball out of bounds and pass directly to the playmaker, who then immediately advances up court.

We employ the free-wheeling style of play used in our basic offenses against the man-to-man and zone presses. We use our formations only as starting points. Thereafter, the players rely upon their resourcefulness and the reactions of opponents to determine their moves. In our practice sessions we set up situations and then apply our formations and let the players work out spur-of-the-moment plays. At no time do we use numbers or names to designate certain plays.

How often have we seen a taller, better team with a safe lead panic when suddenly confronted by a pressing defense. In preparing for pressing defenses, I found that I was able to stop players from pushing the panic button through the use of the following simple drill.

Placing my team as shown and opposing them with five good chasers who double-teamed the ball on every pass, I made the man with the ball hold it until I told him to pass it. That meant that the players who were double-teaming him were right on top of him.

After exposing him to the double-team action for a sufficient length of time, I would yell "Now!" and he was permitted to get rid of the ball by means of a pass to a teammate (who was also being pressed) or dribble through or away from his personal opponents.

My players picked this drill up quickly, and its practice day after day equipped them to cope with the press to such an extent that they never lost their poise in close games, nor did they commit many turnovers. (Scoring attempts were not permitted in this drill.)

DIAGRAM 13.12 Press Drill. Player A, with the ball, is being double-teamed by defensive opponents X-1 and X-2. Note that defensive player X-3 has left his opponent (C) and is screening offensive player B. Pressing players X-4 and X-5 have moved over to screen possible receivers. Player A may not pass the ball to a teammate or attempt to dribble through or away from the pressing players (X-2 and X-1) until the coach says "Now!"

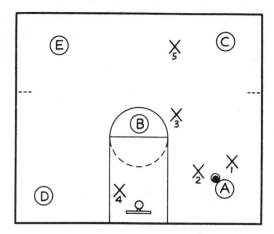

DIAGRAM 13.13 Attacking the Man-to-Man Press. Attacking player A passes to teammate B and cuts off him for a return pass. Player B fakes a return pass and dribbles up court.

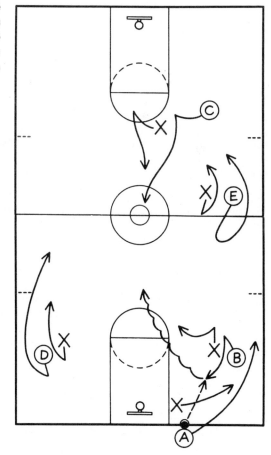

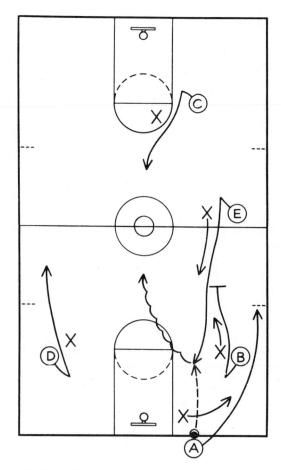

DIAGRAM 13.14 Attacking the Man-to-Man Press. Player B initiates the play by reversing direction and setting a screen for teammate E. Teammate E cuts off of B's screen to the ball. A passes the ball to teammate E, who dribbles up court.

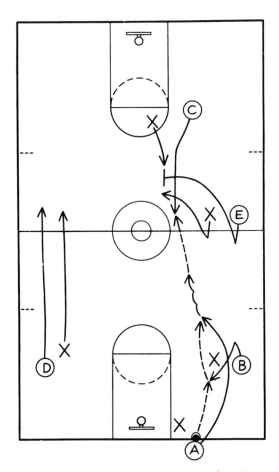

DIAGRAM 13.15 Attacking Man-to-Man Press. Player B fakes up court, reverses, and receives pass from teammate A. Player A cuts outside B, receives a pass as shown, dribbles several times, and passes to teammate C, who breaks to the ball around teammate E's screen.

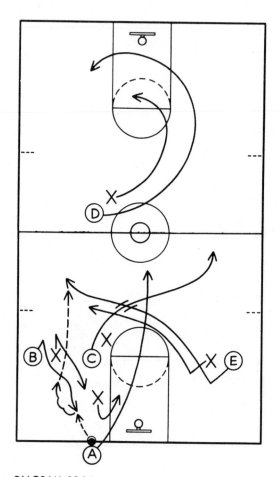

DIAGRAM 13.16 Attacking the Man-to-Man Press. Player A passes to teammate B, who has faked up court. Player B dribbles a short distance and hits teammate E, who has reversed his cut and gone behind Teammate C's screen to receive the ball.

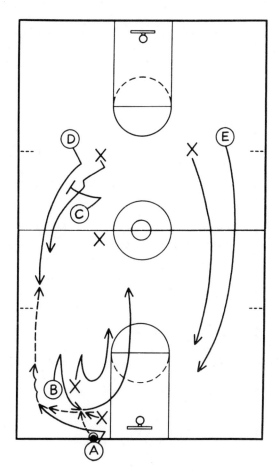

DIAGRAM 13.17 Attacking the Man-to-Man Press. Player A passes ball to B, follows his pass, and receives the ball back. He dribbles a short distance and passes forward to teammate D, who has cut back behind teammate C's screen.

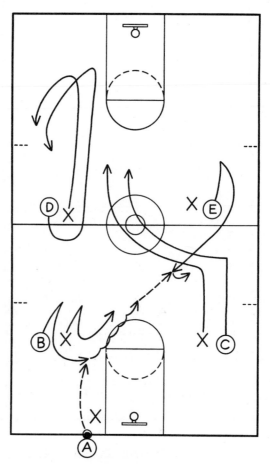

DIAGRAM 13.18 Attacking the Man-to-Man Press. Player B starts up court, reverses, and receives the ball from A. Player B dribbles a short distance and hits teammate E, who has faked up court, reversed behind C's screen, and received the ball.

DIAGRAM 13.19 Attacking the Man-to-Man Press.   Full-court press after a successful free throw. Defensive player X-1 takes ball out of bounds and passes quickly to teammate X-2. Following his pass, X-1 receives the ball from X-2 and dribbles up court. (Note set screen by X-3 so teammate X-4 can break free and cut up court at full speed.)

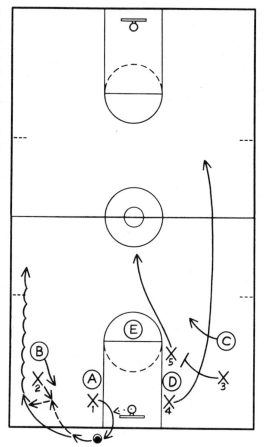

ATTACKING THE ZONE PRESS

The 1-3-1 (all-purpose offense) is also used in meeting the zone press. It is employed in much the same manner as in meeting the man-to-man press. I would like to reiterate once more that we have no set plays against any kind of defense. We do set up formations, but the plays are devised on the spur of the moment, according to the reactions of the opponents to moves made by our players. Possible plays are practiced, but no play or player-move is planned in advance for use during games.

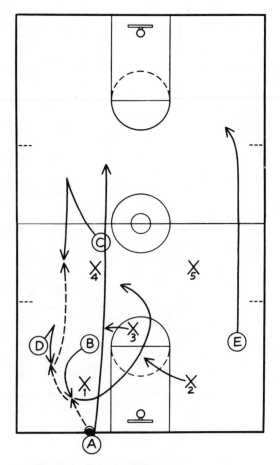

DIAGRAM 13.20 Attacking the 2-1-2 Zone Press. Player B breaks to the ball, fakes a return pass to A, and passes to D, who has reversed to the ball. Player D passes up court to teammate C. (Player B circles behind the pass and to the center of the court for a possible return pass.)

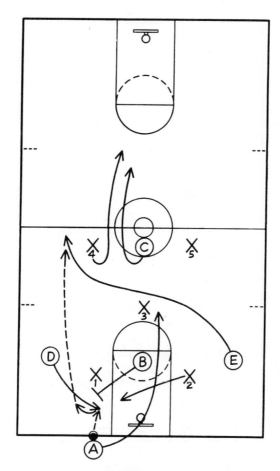

DIAGRAM 13.21 Attacking the 2-1-2 Zone Press. Player A takes the ball out of bounds and passes to teammate D who breaks around a screen set by teammate B. A cuts up court and player E breaks across court to receive pass from D. Note the trap attempt by defensive players X-1 and X-2.

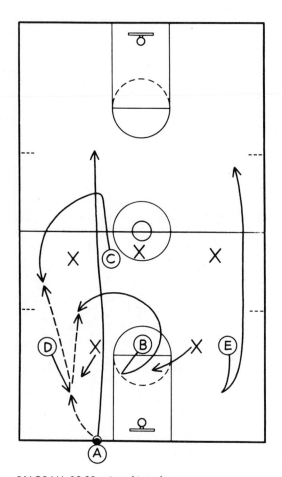

DIAGRAM 13.22 Attacking the 2-3 Zone Press. Player D breaks to the ball, receives it from A, fakes a return pass, and passes to B, who has circled back. The alternate pass is to teammate C, who has also circled back.

DIAGRAM 13.23 Attacking the 1-2-2 Zone Press. Player B angles to the ball, fakes a return pass to A, and passes to teammate D, who has also angled to the ball. Player D passes to C, who has cut across court behind E's screen.

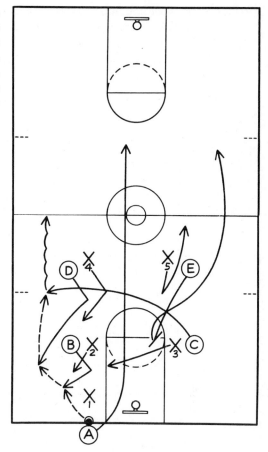

OFFENSE AGAINST HALF-COURT PRESS

1. Players must spread out and use as much of the court as possible.
2. Receivers must "meet" every pass.
3. Attacking players must not cross and must stay away from the "danger" spots (double-teaming and pinching areas).
4. The dribble is used sparingly.
5. Front court players attack from the rear of pressing players when possible.
6. Passers follow their passes at least one step. Keep alternate receivers in mind and note their positions.
7. Use of short, snappy passes is important. Lob passes are not used.
8. Front court players must be ready to break to post positions from their corner areas.

9. Players with ball must not turn backs to chasers (presents double-team and interception opportunities).

10. If pivot man is not contested when he receives the ball, he should turn immediately and use the jumper or drive to the basket for a close shot.

Offensively, I taught my players to invite the split. In other words, the player with the ball headed toward the two defensive opponents. As the defensive players closed in, the dribbler would pass to his teammate guard on the far side of the court.

The man without the ball would not cross the 10-second line until the dribbler was over. This man was the safety valve or "outlet" man. In attacking the half-court press, we usually set up in the 2-2-1 offense which follows.

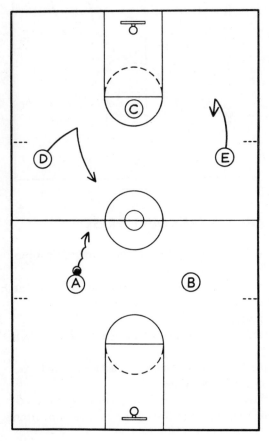

DIAGRAM 13.24 The wing men (D and E) were coached to alternate in filling the middle of the court at an angle. The angle provided a good receiving position should the dribbler find it necessary to pass in order to get the ball across the 10-second line.

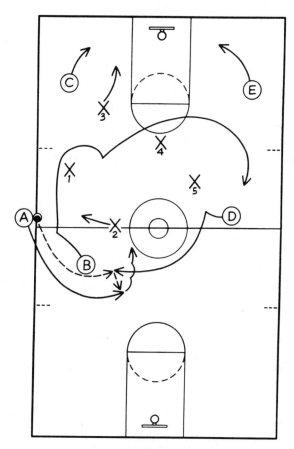

DIAGRAM 13.25 Player B moves to screen off opponent X-1. If opponent X-2 does not follow B, teammate A will pass to him (B). Player D comes over to replace teammate B. In the diagram above, Player A passes to D and cuts behind him for a return pass.

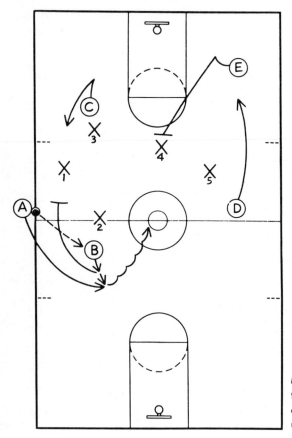

DIAGRAM 13.26 Player A passes to teammate B, goes behind for a return pass, then dribbles ball up middle of court.

FREEZING THE BALL

Freezing the ball has never been difficult for me to teach. The Celtics played possession ball, basing their entire offense on passing. As the Chattanooga *News* said in a 1933 story:

> The attack of the Celtics is one of the most baffling things in the realm of sports. To the first nighter it is all the more uncanny. There is no mad rush up the floor. The approach is slow although these smooth super-performers are moving much faster than they seem. Then, all at once, something happens! Suddenly what was a moment before five men now seems to be eight. And no one can guard eight men.
>
> With Dehnert as the key man the ball slips through the ozone invisible to the naked eye. Ordinary opponents have been known to go off Easter egg hunting unable for the life of them to find the leather. The Celtics employ the pivot play, short passes, control of the ball,

picks and blocks, the give-and-go and a slow-starting quick opening attack which features use of the bounce pass . . . not to mention a few of their weapons.

And from the Nashville *Tennesseean:*

Once the Celtics cut loose with their short-passing game they completely baffled the Peps. For 14 minutes they kept the Peps from making a point and for thirteen of those minutes they kept possession of the ball, making various kinds of short passes. They can whip those short passes around and they can drop the ball through the meshes.

POINTS TO REMEMBER

1. Be calm. Take your time.
2. Protect the ball. Meet all passes.
3. Make a big court. Keep players well spread.
4. Do not bounce the ball. Save the dribble.
5. Dribble only to get out of danger.
6. No dribble in the free-throw circle area.
7. Pass and go away from the ball.
8. Do not cross. Avoid bringing defense to the ball.
9. Keep out of corners.
10. Score only when a real "chippy" is possible. Possession is more important than the two points.
11. Do not throw lob or careless cross-court passes.
12. Use screens to free teammates eligible for passes.
13. Fishhook to lose opponent. (Go away and return quickly.)
14. Stay away from ten-second line.
15. If stuck and a tie-up is possible—call time!
16. And, above all, don't be afraid to bring the ball back toward the center line so you can start the offensive action all over again.

DIAGRAM 13.27 Pass and Go Away. Player A passes to teammate B and exchanges with teammate D in the corner. Player B passes the ball to teammate D and exchanges with corner man E. The pass-and-go-away series continues. Should opponents overplay, teammate C (high post) comes out as a release point.

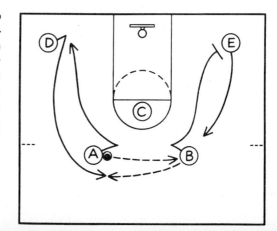

CONTROL FREEZE—KEEP AND GO AWAY

This maneuver is used to control the ball for long periods of time and keep it moving at the same time. The idea is not to score, but rather to keep possession of the ball. The only shots permitted in the control freeze are absolute lay-ups when no opponent is near or in a position to block the shot.

In the control freeze we use the Three-Two formation. The ball is kept moving from the sides of the court to the middle and vice-versa. Players must refrain from dribbling and crossing. Players must also avoid the corners and make certain the middle of the offensive zone is kept open.

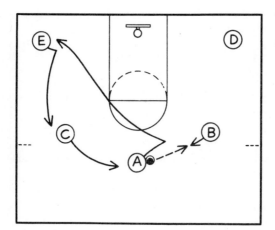

DIAGRAM 13.28 Player A passes to teammate B and cuts away. Player C replaces A, and teammate E replaces C.

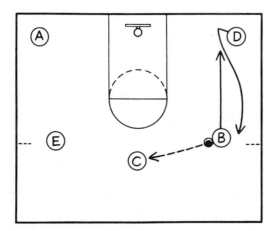

DIAGRAM 13.29 Player B passes to teammate C and goes away to replace teammate D. Player D (corner) replaces teammate B (position).

Rules to remember

1. Avoid the free-throw circle area.
2. No player interchanges. Keep away. Do not move close together.
3. No passes are to be made to corners.
4. Players must not move to corner positions from middle of court.
5. When opponents overplay, go away from pass and cut to the opposite side.
6. BASIC RULE: Always go away from the receiver of the pass!

DIAGRAM 13.30 Player C passes to teammate E and cuts to the corner, replacing teammate B. Player B replaces teammate D. Player D replaces teammate C (position).

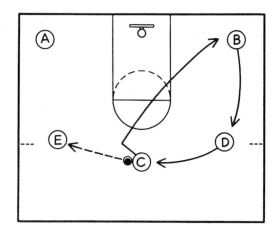

DIAGRAM 13.31 Player E passes to teammate D and replaces A in the corner. Player A replaces E (position).

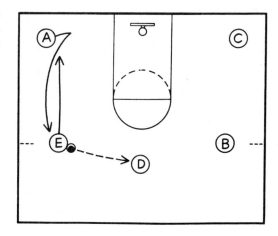

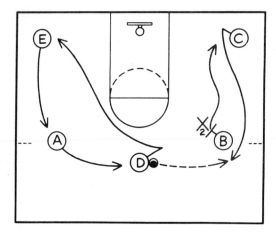

DIAGRAM 13.32 Player D passes to teammate C, who cuts around teammate B (who is being played tight by defensive opponent X-2). Following his pass, Player D cuts to left corner, replacing teammate E. Player E replaces A, and A replaces D (position).

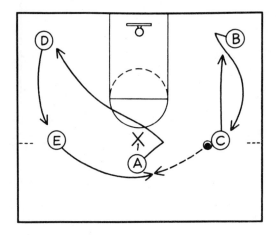

DIAGRAM 13.33 Player C passes the ball to teammate E, who cuts back of teammate A (who is being closely pressed by opponent X-1). Following the pass, Player A cuts to the left corner, replacing D. Player C replaces teammate B, and B replaces C (positions).

This completes the cycle of passes and cuts. The procedure is initiated once again by E, who is now in the center of the court and in possession of the ball.

SPECIAL TACTICS

My past experience as a professional player and coach has been of great help to me in my collegiate coaching. Needless to say, the pros are always looking for the edge. One example is the application of the mismatch (whether on a direct match-up or because of a switch).

When the opportunity presents itself, we like to take the low post position. This is not used as a steady diet but occurs as a result of movement. If the play does not result from movement, the defense will be able to gang up on the player in the pivot (low post) and spoil the execution of the play. Examples of the moves follow:

DIAGRAM 13.34 Mismatch (taking small opponent into low post position). Player A is opposed by a smaller opponent. He passes the ball to teammate C and cuts off the screen set by teammate B to gain a low post position. Player C passes the ball to A in the low post position, and the mismatch is complete. The high post player (B) clears out.

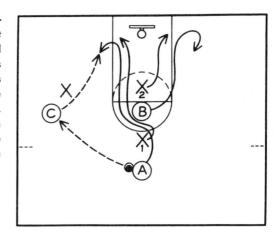

DIAGRAM 13.35 Mismatch on Switch Play. Player A's opponent is smaller or same size. Player A passes ball to tall post player (B) and cuts off him to receive a hand-off pass. A's opponent (X-1) is picked off. As soon as he has passed the ball to the cutter (A), the pivot man (B) cuts toward the basket. On the pick-off it is assumed that B's opponent (X-2) switched to cover A, leaving the smaller player (X-1) to cope with the big post player (B). Player A hooks the ball to B, who should have an easy shot against the small opponent (X-1).

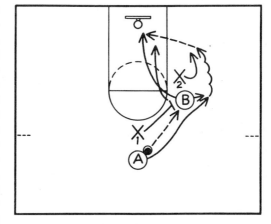

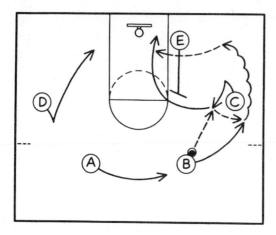

DIAGRAM 13.36 Bread and Butter Play. Player B passes to teammate C and follows his pass for a hand-off. Meanwhile, Player E cuts up the lane to a high post position. After passing to B, Player C cuts around the high post teammate (E) and down the lane to the basket.

Player B dribbles to the corner after receiving the ball. When teammate C clears teammate E, Player B passes the ball to him for a shot. The play runs from either side of the court.

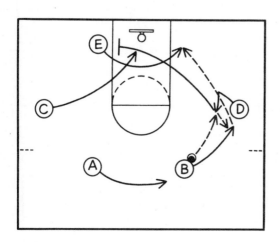

DIAGRAM 13.37 Bread and Butter Play (usually called after a time-out or a free throw). Player B passes the ball to teammate D and follows his pass. Player D returns the ball to teammate B and cuts across the lane to set a pick for teammate E. Player E cuts around the pick to a low post position and receives the ball from teammate B for the shot. Player C follows in from the weak side.

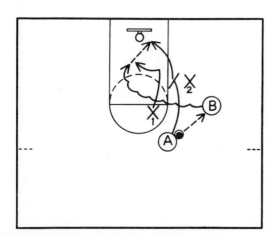

DIAGRAM 13.38 Roll-Off Play Against Switch. Player A passes the ball to teammate B and sets a pick (facing basket) as shown. When his opponent (X-1) switches as shown, player A hesitates until teammate B has dribbled past and then rolls to the basket. Player B passes to teammate A if he breaks free.

CHAPTER 14

DEFENSE VARIATIONS

I N MY EARLY DAYS as a player, there was only one defense. You played pure man-to-man and "nose to nose" on a match-up basis. Later the switch was added, but generally speaking the man-to-man defense was basic, and players and teams rose or fell depending upon their ability to defense match-up opponents.

When you lined up against an opponent at the start of the game, you stuck with him. If he went out for a drink of water when his team had the ball, you had better be on his heels. There was no such thing as a zone defense or the many variations which are so important in today's defensive strategy. We never heard of sagging, floating, overplaying, jamming the middle, or clearing out. There was no pivot play and your opponent never turned his back on his offensive basket, so it was easy for you to stick with him "nose to nose."

Every team had a standing guard. He was the "strong man" of the defense and played close to his team's defensive basket, almost as if playing goalie in a hockey game. Few, if any, teams used the fast break, and the only shot players took on the run was the lay-up following a number of passes made in a set formation. There *were* plays from the center jump. They were important at that time because the center tap followed every score.

Controlling the boards is vital to present-day team success. In the old days a fellow rebounded and fought to get the ball, but all he had to do was "get it." Now the rebounder must do a good job boxing-out big men up to seven feet or more in height, get the ball, and rush it safely into play so the fast break can function. In my days, you might get the ball all right, along with a punch in the nose, but you didn't have to hurry about getting rid of it. You got the ball and passed it to one of your team-mates. Then you advanced slowly toward your team's basket and watched the opponents hustle back on the defense.

Big men who have the ability to move and use the jump shot are common today. My contemporaries could move, but they were comparatively small. And if one of them had ever left his feet to try a shot, he would have amazed everyone in the place. In addition, he would probably have landed on his back, wondering what hit him. Before 1930 the big man could probably have matched today's high scorers if he had taken advantage of the pivot play under the basket. The free-throw lane was narrow (six feet), there was no 3-second rule to restrict his time near the basket, and there was considerably more freedom with respect to contact.

I've heard the argument that basketball in my salad days used a tough brand of defense. Actually, the defensive player had little to worry him. His man would either take a flat-footed set shot, pass off, or dribble in for a lay-up. About all you had to do was to follow the first rule of man-to-man defense and stay between your opponent and the basket.

The press or any of its variations is an important defensive weapon today and is used by practically all teams and at any level of basketball. It forces opponents to make mistakes and frequently demoralizes a better team. In the old days the press was of practically no value because the 10-second rule was not in effect and you could advance as slowly as you wished, take the ball forward and bring it back, or remain in the back court as long as you desired.

Defense on any basis is a tough grind and is the test of all players. To the casual observer, it may appear that the modern game eliminates defense and is interested only in offense. But there are sound reasons for the effectiveness of modern offenses. For example, how do you defend a player as tall as you are or taller who gets so much as a step on you and then goes up for a jump shot? About the only way the average defensive player can stop him is to pray. Naturally, fellows like Russell and Chamberlain and some of the other big men in the professional game who can leap higher and keep close enough can stop the shorter players. They are the exceptions. But even they have trouble with men near their own height and leaping ability.

There wasn't much opportunity for strategy in the old days, although we occasionally ran into a game ball in which the air pressure was too high or too low. Modern coaches, however, can take recourse to changing and combination defenses in their strategy plans. Today, when one type of defense cannot contain an opponent, most coaches have their teams prepared to change to another. When a team employs only one defense, the opponents can make specific plans to overcome it. However, planned attacks are vulnerable to changing defenses, and you can be sure the opponents will not overlook the opportunity of springing a surprise.

The high-scoring pace of offensive play in recent years has forced defensive-minded coaches to resort to a great many variations. If opponents employ a hard-driving type of offense, sagging and floating in the man-to-man defense may limit the effectiveness of the attack. Should the sag and float be inadequate, use of some type of zone or switching defense may be employed. If the opponents lack outside shooting accuracy, the middle can be strengthened by a zone or by sagging and floating.

The man-to-man variations include the switching defense, sagging, floating, overshifting (overplay), jamming the middle, and some form of the press. Zone use has increased and has developed its own variations. Multiple use of the man-to-man, zones, and the variations has resulted in all sorts of combinations, such as front line man-to-man and back line zone; one-man zone with four teammates using man-to-man tactics (and vice-versa) as well as any number of press variations.

MAN-TO-MAN VARIATIONS

The following diagrams illustrate some of the variations employed to add to the effectiveness of the man-to-man defense. Most of the variations are determined by the offensive positions assumed by the attacking players and the location of the ball. For example, a high post player who does not possess a good turn or jump shot might be guarded in orthodox position with the defensive player stationed between the opponent and the basket. He would be prepared to let defensive teammates slide through in order to keep up with their men or switch to the cutter himself should it be necessary.

In some situations, the point of the ball might be played loosely (when some distance from the basket) or attacked aggressively when it was in good passing or shooting distance. In other circumstances, the opponent with the ball and his teammates who are in good receiving positions may be played closely and aggressively.

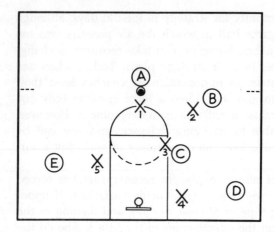

DIAGRAM 14.1 Defensive player X-1 is playing his opponent (point of the ball) closely and aggressively. Defensive teammate X-2 is overshifting to the left of attacking player B to screen him away from the ball and discourage a pass to him. Defensive player X-3 is playing between the big man (C) and the ball, and defensive teammates X-4 and X-5 have floated away from D and E. Defensive player X-5 could play opponent E close since he is in the best position to receive a pass. However, he may be playing "dummy" so that he can chance an interception unless E goes away from the basket when he would tighten up. Should X-5 try for an interception, X-4 is in position to cover under the basket and X-3 would move over to help in the under-basket area. A lob pass to D in the right corner would be a dangerous pass.

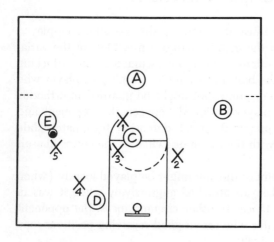

DIAGRAM 14.2 Defensive player X-5 is playing the point of the ball tight. Teammate X-1 has dropped back to screen the dangerous big man away from the ball, and teammate X-3 has shifted slightly toward the ball. Defensive player X-2 has sagged back in line with the basket to help clog the middle. Defensive X-4 is playing in front of D, who is playing the low post position.

FULL-COURT MAN-TO-MAN PRESS

The full-court press is designed to harass the offensive opponent. As soon as the opponents secure the ball (usually after a successful goal from the field or a free throw whether successful or not) the press players dog their opponents all over the court in an attempt to screen them away from a possible pass or to double-team them if an opportunity occurs. Although it can no longer be termed a surprise attack, it often disorganizes the opponents and not infrequently permits a weaker team to engineer an upset.

One of the weaknesses in the execution of the press with players who have been specifically coached *only to harass* the dribbler (to force a bad pass, fumble, discontinued dribble, or set up a double-team situation) is that they too often foul the opponent. This costly mistake means your team gains nothing. Conversely, the opponents gain everything—a free throw, possibly two free throws (one-and-one situation). Don't play the ball—*play the man!*

Summary of man-to-man press (full-court)

1. The score, the trend of the game, and the time left to play combine in determining the application of the press. The pressure may be used as a change of pace, as a surprise attack, or throughout the entire game.
2. The press must be an aggressive, all-out action to get the ball. The chief objective is to force opponents to make bad passes, fumble, or double-dribble. Maneuvering them into held-ball situations through pinches and traps is the second objective.
3. Every opponent must be covered. A free man may ruin the entire attack.
4. The opponent taking the ball out-of-bounds may be played aggressively to prevent good in-court passes, or the assigned player may drop away from him and help to apply the double-team on the receiver of the first pass.
5. The front men must be ready to switch on each cross made by opponents and attempt the double-team when the ball is exchanged.
6. Defensive players should try to force dribblers to the sideline and then apply the pinch.
7. Defensive players away from the ball should overplay their opponents.
8. The steal is attempted at every opportunity. We need the ball!

9. Defensive players must make every effort to maneuver opponents with the ball into double-team situations.
10. Be alert for lob and cross-court passes and try for the interception.
11. If an opposing dribbler gets past a teammate, the closest man must pick him up and call out the change.
12. The good dribbler and ball handler should be overplayed to discourage passes to them.
13. Use of the press does not mean freedom in fouling. We need the ball, not penalties.
14. When attempting a steal, the player should always slap up at the ball—not down.
15. Once the opponents cross the ten-second line and enter offensive scoring territory, drop back into the regular defensive formation unless trailing in the score or shifting from full-court to half-court press.

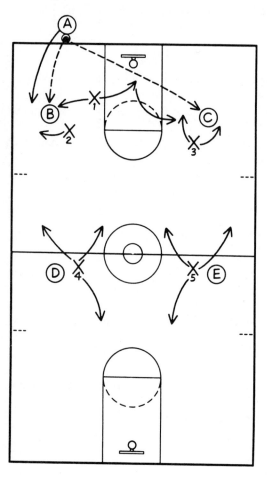

DIAGRAM 14.3 Defensive player X-1 has dropped away from the out-of-bounds opponent and will help teammates X-2 and X-3 attempt the double-team. Teammates X-4 and X-5 are playing in positions which will enable them to break in the direction of a pass or advance and double-team a dribbler who escapes from their frontline teammates. They must be ready for the long overhead pass.

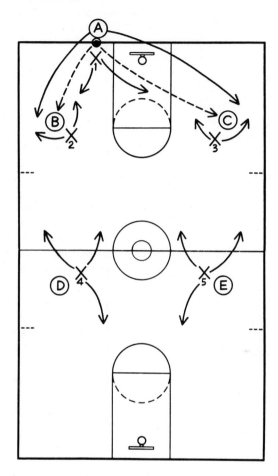

DIAGRAM 14.4 Defensive player X-1 is opposing the out-of-bounds opponent aggressively in an attempt to force a bad pass or delay him in making a pass. The assignment here is strict man-to-man with little switching. Defensive players X-4 and X-5 carry out the same maneuvers used when the out-of-bounds opponent is not opposed.

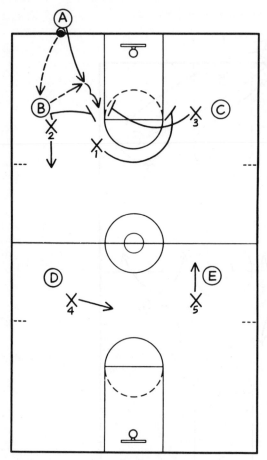

DIAGRAM 14.5 Defensive player X-1 has dropped away from the opponent out-of-bounds and screens attack player C away from a pass when teammates X-2 and X-3 apply the double-team. This maneuver may be changed on signal with X-1 joining X-2 or X-3 in applying the double-team. If X-1 joins teammate X-2 in applying the "second-pass" double-team, teammate X-3 will stick with his opponent (C). If X-1 joins X-3 in applying the "second pass" double-team, teammate X-5 may advance to cover opponent C, teammate X-4 may cross over to watch E, and X-2 may retreat to cover opponent D.

HALF-COURT COMBINATION PRESS

The half-court press which I used at St. John's was a combination defense; part man-to-man tactics and part zone. It is a defense of anticipation and interchanging of positions. Men are assigned lanes and areas and at the same time are prepared to pick up free opponents.

The purpose of the half-court press is to disorganize the opponent's offense before it can get set. This press is particularly effective against dribbling teams, clubs who like to screen, and teams who use a big pivot man. It forces the big man to come out and handle the ball instead of waiting underneath where he can do the real damage.

This type of press plays havoc with inferior ball handlers as it thrives on cross-court passes and "lob" heaves as well as long and loop passes.

These passes are easy to intercept and often lead to the fast break and an easy basket.

Although we always look for the interception, we are concerned more with delaying, harassing, and upsetting the offense. In other words, we like to throw the opponent's offense off balance rather than concentrate on stealing the ball. The opponents will usually step up their offense and make mistakes which they would not commit in their normal game.

The three front men should be fast, agile, alert, and always ready to switch, double-team (pinch), pick-up opponents and pounce upon loose balls and hurried passes. The front wing opposite the ball should be ready to drop back and protect the area around the key, block all passing lanes, and, most of all, challenge the offensive players as they approach the 10-second line.

The two back men should be tall, rangy, and mobile. They will have to "cheat" in defensing their opponents because they will often be forced to overshift or play in front in order to screen them away from the ball. Many times they must take chances in attempting to beat opponents to the high post position. They are also responsible for loose men coming down court following an attempted trap or double-team play.

We concentrated on this combination press at St. John's because Lou

Locker room between halves at the University of Kansas. We were leading and went on to win. Coach Carnesecca is in civies.

Carnesecca and I felt it was the simplest approach for maximum results. Perhaps the most gratifying victory achieved with this defense was against Michigan in the Holiday Invitational Festival in Madison Square Garden during the 1964–65 season. The Wolverines were the nation's number one team at the time. Behind 52 to 68 with nine minutes to go, we applied the 3-1-1, and it enabled us to catch up and emerge with a one-point victory, 75-74.

Principles (half-court press)

1. Meet opponents at midcourt. (Midcourt becomes a mental block to the opponents.)
2. Keep the ball in front of you at all times.
3. Force the dribbler into the middle, where all teammates can help out.
4. Double-team every time a dribbler stops with the ball. (He's dead!)
5. Switch on every cross.
6. Block all passing lanes.
7. Tie up the man with the ball at every opportunity.
8. A loose man is everybody's responsibility.
9. The defense thrives on hustle, aggressiveness, and stamina.
10. Foolish fouling is inexcusable.
11. Keep all opponents and the ball in view at all times (if possible).

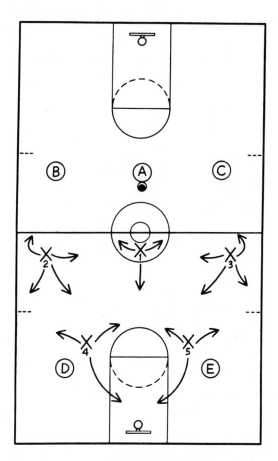

DIAGRAM 14.6 Position of the defense as the opposition is bringing the ball up court. The arrows point to the lanes and areas which particular defensive men cover. Defensive players X-2 and X-3 should place themselves in positions which will force opponents with the ball into the middle of the court.

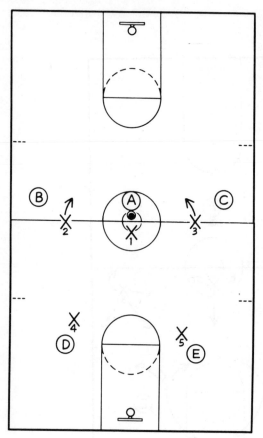

DIAGRAM 14.7 Position of the defensive players as the opponents approach the 10-second line. Defensive players X-2 and X-3 screen off opponents B and C. Teammates X-4 and X-5 play in front of their opponents.

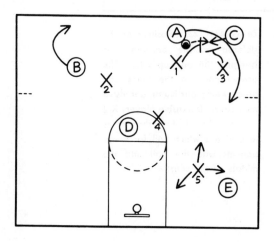

DIAGRAM 14.8 Defensive players X-1 and X-3 apply the pinch on receiver C. Teammates X-2, X-4, and X-5 are ready to close all passing lanes.

DIAGRAM 14.9 Should offensive player C manage to loop the ball across court to teammate B, defensive players X-1 and X-2 will attempt a trap play on the receiver (B). Defensive player X-3 will drop back to the middle, and players X-4 and X-5 will screen opponents away from a possible pass.

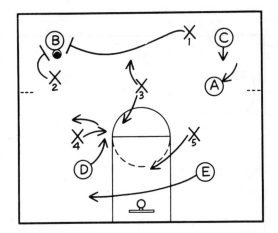

DIAGRAM 14.10 Attacking player B managed to pass the ball down the right sideline to his teammate E. Defensive players X-2 and X-4 double-team while teammates X-1, X-3, and X-5 block the middle and are prepared to help out in the free-throw circle area and in the lane.

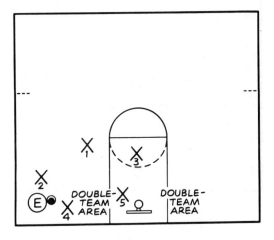

THE FULL-COURT ZONE PRESS

My greatest success in pressing opponents was achieved with the man-to-man and with the half-court combination press. However, there were times when the 3-1-1 full-court zone press was used. The front court setup resembled the man-to-man, with three players (X-1, X-2, and X-3) stationed across the opponents' back court while the first "deep" position was taken near the 10-second line by player X-4. The second "deep" position was taken by player X-5, who roamed near the opponents' free-throw line.

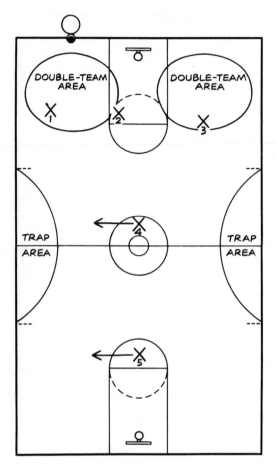

DIAGRAM 14.11 Player X-2 is the "point" man, with teammates X-1 and X-3 expected to assist him in setting up a double-team situation or forcing the receiver of the first pass toward the side-lines. The three front-line players, X-1, X-2, and X-3, are expected to be alert for "banana" passes to the middle of the court. Teammates X-4 and X-5 are alert for long up-court passes.

Should a double-team situation develop on the first or second pass in the opponents' back court, the point man will join either X-1 or X-3 in the double-up. The receiver of the first pass is encouraged to dribble up the nearest sideline if a double-up situation is not present. The point man usually initiates this move, but "wing" men are also expected to execute this maneuver. When one of the wing men picks up the dribbler, they play between the opponent and the center of the court and go with him.

As the opponent dribbles up to the 10-second line, help will come from defensive player X-4, who will join the wing man in applying the trap. The wing player on the opposite side of the court will retreat up court to replace teammate X-4 and to screen off a cross-court pass.

Pressing players X-4 and X-5 shift to the ball side when possible. Although they will attempt traps and double-teaming, under no circumstances will the under-basket area be left unguarded.

THE ZONE DEFENSE

Since the zone defense is banned in professional basketball, my knowledge concerning it has been limited to those very few times when we used it at St. John's University simply because we felt that our players could not cope with the speed of the particular opponent. Lou Carnesecca, who succeeded me as head coach at St. John's when I retired in 1965, took charge of our zone defense. Lou had used the zone to some extent in his coaching previous to coming to St. John's as my assistant, so I left the zone preparation up to him.

We restricted our use of the zone defense to the 2-1-2. The following principles, prepared by Lou, were applied in teaching the use of the 2-1-2 zone.

PRINCIPLES EMPLOYED IN USING THE ZONE DEFENSE

Two types of zone defense:
1. Active. Chasers pick opponents up high and go all out.
2. Passive. Chasers drop back and concede outside shots.

General principles:

1. Choose personnel carefully—chasers, middle men, rebounders.
2. Play the ball! All players *face* the ball.
   (a.) Always know position of ball.
   (b.) Know approximate positions of all opponents.
   (c.) Talking is a must. Back players (near defensive basket) must advise "front" teammates (chasers) of attack situations.
3. All passing lanes must be blocked by occupying them or by anticipating passes in the area. Hands up!
4. Harass and double-team shooters.
5. Rush passers (force bad passes).
6. Stop all drive-in shots by jamming the middle and the baseline.
7. Protect all vital scoring areas (overplay dribblers and force good shooters to operate from long range).
8. The rebound triangle follows every shot by opponents.
9. Go for the fast break when possible. One chaser can break in anticipation of a successful rebound following a shot by opponents.
10. Approach opponents swiftly with weight balanced. Hands up!
11. Float in front of opposing pivot men when possible.
12. Check area in back of zone for opposing "basket-hangers."
13. Hustle back to defense fast break. One lagging player can spoil an otherwise perfect defense.

14. All players must know the proper slides and the weaknesses and strong points of the zone in use (also counters for moves and formations).

Zone defense advantages

1. Checks most weaving, screening, and driving attacks.
2. Enables rebounders to secure good positions.
3. Zone defenses lend themselves to effective fast-break patterns.
4. The zone is effective in limiting the single pivot attack and shots from the vicinity of the "key."
5. The zone can be used to protect key players from fouling out of the game.
6. Proper placement in a zone defense can protect weak defensive players.
7. All zone defense players must be ball-hawks.
8. An efficient zone defense forces opponents to shoot from a distance and from difficult angles.
9. The zone defense slows down offense-minded teams.
10. The zone defense is easier to teach than man-to-man.
11. Zone play develops teamwork (coverage of special lanes and areas).
12. The zone may be used as a surprise maneuver.
13. Certain zones are effective in containing opposing star players (box-and-one, diamond-and-one).
14. Zone players are usually less tense and nervous.
15. The zone is particularly effective on narrow courts and when used in tournament play (changing from man-to-man to zone and vice-versa).
16. Tall and awkward players will be more effective in zone play than in man-to-man.

Zone defense disadvantages

1. Zone defenses are vulnerable to good passing and shooting.
2. Opposing shooters have more time to get set.
3. Use of zone defenses limits individual player responsibilities (no match-ups).
4. Zone defenses leave many scoring areas unguarded (sides, middle, free-throw circle, underneath).
5. Not all areas on large courts can be covered adequately by use of a zone.
6. Practically all zones are vulnerable to good outside shooting.

7. Zone defenses cannot be used when trailing (exception is zone press).

8. Front-line zone chasers foul more when forced to cover large areas.

9. Players often assume good man-to-man guarding principles are eliminated when playing zone defense and do not go all out in their personal defensive moves.

10. Spectator interest often lags when teams employ zone defenses.

DIAGRAM 14.12 Defensive players X-1 and X-2 are the chasers. They must possess quick hands and be able to move speedily. Good, strong legs are a must, since they must be able to go continuously. Defensive player X-3 is usually the "big man" and teammates X-4 and X-5 are the "wing" players. Rebounder X-5 should possibly be the better rebounder of the two (X-4 and X-5).

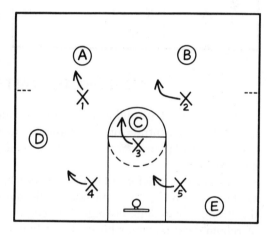

DIAGRAM 14.13 Zone Moves. Offensive player A passes the ball to his teammate D. Defensive chaser X-1 and wing player X-4 cover the receiver (D). Defensive player X-3 screens off the offensive pivot man (C) near the free-throw line. Defensive X-2 covers the weak side in the free-throw circle area. Wing player X-5 covers the lane area near the basket.

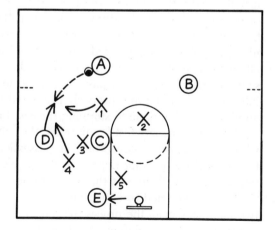

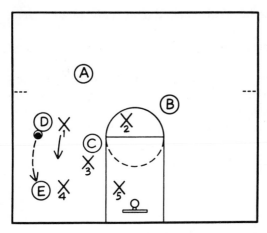

DIAGRAM 14.14 Zone Moves. Offensive player D passes the ball to his teammate in the corner (E). Defensive wing player X-4 drops back to cover and chaser X-1 starts back to screen off the opposing post player (C). Defensive X-3 now moves down the lane to help screen post player C away from the ball. Defensive zone players X-2 and X-5 protect the lane areas and the weak side.

STOPPING THE FAST BREAK

The fast break is used in some form by practically all teams. A number of coaches concentrate on developing it to a high degree of efficiency. These particular opponents require special preparation when planning game strategy.

In planning a defense for the fast break, I feel that the proper place to start is with the scouting notes. The notes will advise you regarding the strong rebounders; boxing-out strength; rebound alignment; efficiency of rebounders; players who lead in rebounding; the moves they make in getting position; the outlet passes; the side to which the pitchouts are usually made; the one-two receivers; the initial break formation; the use of passes or the dribble; the key player or players who advance the ball; the alignment in front-court scoring territory; the type of scoring technique (dribbler stopping at the free-throw line, continuing on in, passing off to cutters; and the area from which the scoring attempts are made—short jumpers, sets, or fast passes designed to provide lay-ups). With this information at hand and properly presented to the players, an intelligent approach can be made to stopping the fast break.

Against an expert fast-break team, the initial defensive strategy starts while the offensive players are in possession of the ball. Since all my teams used the passing approach, it was easy for them to maintain defensive balance. That was the number one starting point.

Second, we tried to adjust our offense so that we would always have two men back or in the process of getting back while the opponents were concerned with the defensive rebound.

Third, we concentrated on a strong follow-in attack. Our big men followed in all shots, their own as well as those of their teammates.

Fourth, we concentrated on the rebounders, our big men making every effort to beat them to favorite rebounding positions.

Fifth, when beating them to favorite rebound positions was impossible, the tactic was to "dog" them as soon as they got their hands on the ball. The purpose here, of course, was to prevent the outlet pass. We particularly stressed the importance of avoiding fouls and the necessity of active use of arms and feet in restricting rebounders' pitchouts.

Sixth, we concentrated on assembling our back-court defense with the guards calling out the open players and possible receivers.

Seventh, we tried to close the areas to which the first passes were usually made. Instead of falling back in a straight line toward the defensive basket from our offensive back-court positions, the guards in charge of defensive balance closed the outlet areas.

Eighth, we assembled our defense and retreated as a team, making sure all breakers were covered.

Ninth, since most fast-break teams use the dribble extensively, we made every effort to hamper the dribbler's progress by contesting his advance—feinting, faking, and attempting to maneuver him toward the sidelines. We were frequently able to steal the ball away from the dribblers.

Tenth, we always stopped the middle man at the head of the free-throw circle.

Eleventh, defensive players who were delayed in getting back headed first for the free-throw circle to prevent return passes to the dribbler.

Twelfth, we insisted that every player hustle back to help out. (The opponents might miss the first fast-break shot. We made sure they didn't get the second shot.)

STOP THE BIG MAN

Every coach in the game is looking for the tall man. A team without a big man can win, but the championships usually go to clubs with the giants. The high-school coach who takes the big boy and works with him through his gawky stage is sometimes rewarded with great seasons. However, it may turn out that all his efforts are fruitless simply because the boy hasn't yet arrived.

College coaches scout the country, looking for the big boys in the hopes of recruiting one or two of them for their schools. And, quite often, the big boy, the "diamond in the rough" who did not stand out in high school, comes into his own after reaching college.

With the influx of these skilled and well coordinated big men has come the problem of stopping them. Let's take a look at what has been done in the past to cope with the giants of basketball.

VARIOUS DEFENSES

Defenses have been designed by practically all coaches in an effort to stop the big man. Clair Bee has made two important contributions—the 3-second rule and the 1-3-1 zone. The 1-3-1 zone places a defensive man in front of the big man and another behind him with the purpose of limiting his moves and to prevent him from getting the ball.

Most teams using the man-to-man defense employ sagging and collapsing techniques to put added pressure on the big man. The zone defense was designed to move with the ball and go to it in the various areas. By using a zone, more than one player can cover the big man. The various types of zone defenses are: Three-Two (3-2); Two-Three (2-3); One-Two-Two (1-2-2); Two-One-Two (2-1-2); Box-and-One, and the Diamond-and-One.

The man-to-man and zone presses (full and half-court) are designed to put added pressure and constant harassment on the opponents and as a result keep the big man from securing the ball in his favorite scoring position.

Playing the opponent with the ball aggressively and using "team" efforts (sagging, floating, jamming the passing lane) to surround the big man are effective.

If the big man is weak defensively, it is possible to eliminate him through fouling. This means creating situations which may lead him to commit fouls in order to make the necessary defensive play. Sometimes it pays to sacrifice an extra player and, in some cases, even two extra players in order to control him.

In professional basketball most teams let the big fellows make their points and apply a tight defense to the big man's teammates. In this situation it is important that you have a big man of your own who can equal the dangerous opponent in scoring.

CHANGES IN THE RULES

Along with the various defenses designed by coaches to check the big man, great strides have been made through the years by the basketball rules committees. Some of the rules are: The 3-second rule; widening of the lane to 12 feet; the 19-foot baseline (International rules); awarding of free throws only when a shot is attempted; and awarding the ball to opponents out-of-bounds on other infractions.

In 1961, Abe Saperstein (owner of the famed Globetrotters) sponsored a nationwide professional cage circuit (The American Basketball Association). Saperstein wanted more defense in the game, and he realized the 6–5 player was considered of medium height in professional basketball.

Incorporating some of the Olympic rules, Saperstein widened the lane to 19 feet, as mentioned above; increased the value of a shot from a distance of more than 25 feet to three points; eliminated free throws except for fouls occurring on field goal attempts; eliminated the 10-second line; and awarded two free throws on all fouls occurring in the last two minutes of the game. The league did not last, but some of Saperstein's ideas still remain a part of the international rules of the game.

In addition to the above methods of containing the big man, the baskets could be raised from ten to twelve feet; players could be required to rotate positions during the course of a game; and height limits could be placed on players in the various positions (centers—unlimited; forwards—six-six; guards—six-three).

It must be remembered that any changes aimed at the big man will also affect the small player. There is a place for the smaller man in basketball. His quickness, agility, and ball-handling abilities are great assets and should never be overlooked. Whatever is done to limit the tall man will make it that much more difficult for the small man, and the big man will still have the advantage.

St. John's star center, Leroy Ellis, shooting a hook shot over Paul Hogue of Cincinnati University. Paul Hogue was the Knickerbocker's No. 1 draft choice in the NBA professional players selection meeting. Today, Leroy Ellis is a fixture with Los Angeles in the NBA and Loughrey is playing with the Baltimore Bullets. No. 25, Leroy Ellis, St. John's; No. 22, Paul Hogue, Cincinnati; No. 33, Kevin Loughrey.

It will be up to the coaches to develop big men, recruit them, or concentrate on shorter men and develop a precision ball club like the UCLA team which won the 1964 NCAA championship.

Basketball has given the big man an opportunity to exploit his talents, and he is in the game to stay. They are working more and more on their own to master the skills necessary to play the game. The Chamberlains, Russells, and Bellamys are teams within themselves. These men are a breed of their own. The desire to excel was great when they were on the way up, and they made many sacrifices of time and energy to become great.

Where are the other big man "greats"? Few come out of the college ranks today. Perhaps they aren't hungry anymore, are too easily satisfied, too quick to accept mediocrity. I hope this is not true and that the big fellows who are not geared to other sports will pay the price, accept the challenge. As for the smaller player, I hope he gets help from the rules or some other source, because he still has an important role to play in basketball.

CHAPTER 15

GAME
PREPARATIONS

"**N**O MAN can make it big until he has learned to shake hands with disappointment." This little axiom has been one of my favorites, but I am always quick to add, "And a man deserves his disappointments unless he has done everything in his power to eliminate them."

Another favorite is the following: "The tinsel of fame is a cloud of smoke. What you did yesterday becomes unimportant. What you do today and tomorrow is vital."

Why do I start this particular chapter with those little sayings? Because they express my philosophy with respect to game preparation. I feel that I must plan several days ahead for each game, taking into consideration the following items.

HOME COURT OR OPPONENT'S COURT

Is the game to be played at home or on the road? I fully realize that I have a home court advantage when the game is to be played on our floor. And I also realize that when I play on an opponent's court, I am at a disadvantage. The following quote from the *New York World Tele-gram,* written by Bob Stewart, summarizes my belief in the advantage of the home court:

"St. Joseph's got caught at St. John's the other night in one of basket-ball's unalterable rules, 'thou shall have trouble away from home.'" Certainly the Redmen turned in a great performance against the supposedly No. 3 team in the nation, but I have to wonder what would have been the outcome in Philadelphia. In no other sport does a home team have a greater advantage.

It has always been that way in basketball. In my early playing days it was worse because you "had" to win the home games. On the road you seldom won. The exception was, of course, the Celtics. The wearers of the Shamrocks won, with rare exceptions, whenever and wherever they played. Everyone was against you in those days—officials, opposing players, and the crowd. If you won three or four games a season on the road, you won the pennant. And when you won a game on the road, you had to stay in the building until the crowd had gone home.

So, in preparing for a game, I begin with the court. On my own court I know the advantages. So do my players. I know the enthusiasm of the crowd will keep my players on their toes mentally and physically, so it is unnecessary for me to even think about getting them "up" for the game. However, if I am not to be disappointed, I must work hard to prepare my team to use these advantages to the fullest extent. And I must be wary of overconfidence.

If the game is to be played on the opponent's court, I must prepare my team to *contend* with the very same advantages we have going for us on our home court. Familiarity with the opponent's home court is im-portant, and I must familiarize my players with all the factors, perhaps through a special practice, scrimmage, or shooting session as well as a long warmup prior to the game.

If we have shaken hands with disappointment, then we are fortified with team spirit, primed with the urge to make a comeback, dedicated to an uphill fight, hungrily seeking an upset and determined to show everyone that we *are* a great team.

RIDING FOR A FALL

The second saying is also important in my game preparations. Per-haps the team and I are riding high because of a string of victories. We are, therefore, vulnerable to overconfidence and may forget that the games we won in the past have little or no bearing on the game to come.

Because of our successes, we may tend to let up a little, rest on our laurels, so to speak, and begin to believe our clippings (we always cherish the headlines).

If so, we must forget yesterday and our past successes and prepare diligently for the game to come. Our game plan must be rehearsed as carefully for a weak opponent as for a strong one. We must realize that all teams come into a game against a successful team with their sights set on an upset and keyed up for a great performance.

OFFICIALS

Coaches know officials just about as well as they know their players. Perhaps a little better, because an official usually runs true to form whereas players vacillate because of studies, girls, indigestion, emotional problems, or just plain staleness.

Coaches usually observe officials from an objective point of view and exchange observations and evaluations with other coaches until they know about how the official in question will "work" in given situations involving crowd pressure, coach personalities, and player demonstrations.

Warning the players ahead of time with respect to certain peculiarities of the official may exert some influence on a decision which might change the trend and results of a game. I have found it valuable to discuss officials with my players from time to time, and I have always made it clear that it was my job to discuss rules, plays, and penalties with the arbiters. All I expect from the players is that they come prepared to play the game.

Some of the officials whom I consider leaders in the field were Dave Walsh, Chick Murray, Chuck Solodare, Pat Kennedy, Jocko Collins, and Sid Borgia. Dave and Chick were pioneers, Pat had great talent and personality and called the plays as he saw them. Sid Borgia made his own rules and had the guts of a burglar, and Chuck could fight with any group of fans and still hold their respect.

THE SCOUTING REPORT

The scouting report is the key to thorough preparation for an opponent. At St. John's I was fortunate to have Lou Carnesecca as my assistant. Lou was, and is, a student of the game. He had coached high school (St. Ann's, later Bishop Molloy High School) basketball successfully, and had turned out some fine college players in the process. He was a hard worker and an excellent scout.

Lou scouted opponents and also set up the second string players to present their offense, defense, and situation plays. In addition to scouting our opponents, Lou also came up with the answers to some of our game problems. For example, during the 1965 Madison Square Garden Holiday Festival, we upset Michigan, then the nation's number one team, to win the tournament. Lou had studied the zone press in a clinic, and he suggested that we might use it as a surprise at some stage of the Michigan game, since everyone knew I was a disciple of the man-to-man defense. Lou had the right answer, and we were able to win the game and the championship. (See Chapter 14—The Full-Court Zone Press.)

The form which follows was designed by Lou. He used it to secure the information we needed to prepare our game plan and familiarize our players with the opponent's players as well as their team offense and defense.

Game movies of opponents are an important source of information even though they may be a year or more old. They were studied in order to acquaint ourselves with the opponent's style of play even if the individual players were no longer around. Sometimes we were able to borrow films from coaches whose teams had played some of our opponents.

I believe in scouting only the offensive and defensive strengths of the opponent. The players will discover quickly enough the weaknesses.

A CHECK AND CIRCLE SCOUTING CHART

Lou's "check and circle" chart was used to provide basic opponent information. In addition to the chart, Lou was able to grasp much more information than shown by his circles and checkmarks. He would come back with a mental picture of the type of floor, baskets, lighting, closeness of the crowd, work of officials, location of scoring table, game clock, scoreboard, height of ceiling, basket background.

He would also come up with far more individual personnel information than is shown on the chart. He would report on each player's physical condition; follow-in strength; height; weight; aggressiveness; rebounding; fast break; headhunters; scorers; ball handlers; whether players were big, small, fast, or slow.

From the point of view of the team, Lou would have all the answers—big or small team; slow or fast; ball handling in general; team dribbling ability; variety of offenses and variations; defense variations; special situation plays; freeze; press; stall.

FIRST QUARTER	Opponent's Name	No.	Ht.	Rh	Lh	ST	SM	Pts.
SECOND QUARTER								

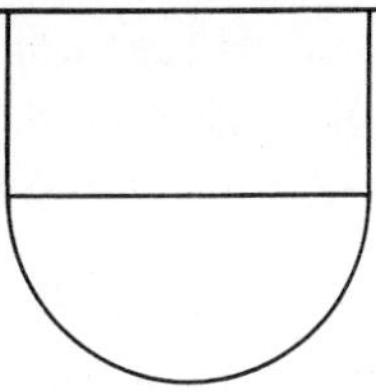

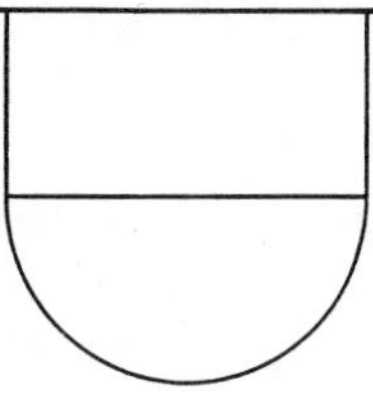

THIRD QUARTER

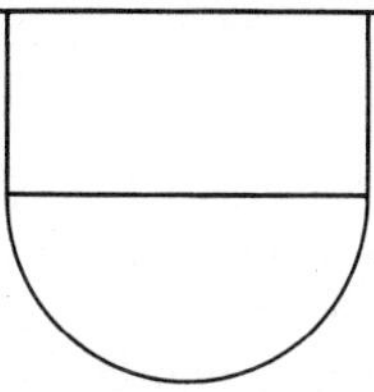

FOURTH QUARTER

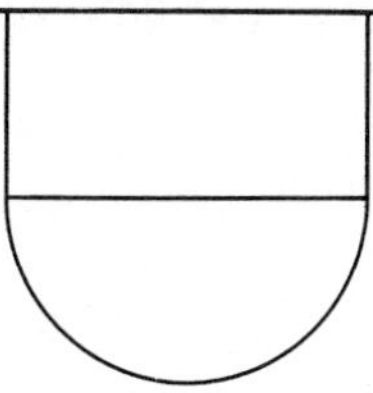

Opponents' Offense - weave; high post; free lance; 3 out and 2 in; 2 out and 3 in; double post.
Shooting: outside; inside; off a screen.
Use Fast Break: , after fouls   , from a zone   . Crash offensive boards   , and defensive boards   . How many men stay back   , Do they sag   , Do they press   , full court   , half court   , after fouls   .
Defense - M-T-M   , zone   . If Zone - 2-1-2; 2-3; 3-2; 1-2-2; 1-3-1; aggressive   , passive   .
Zone Attack - 1-3-1; circulating 1-3-1; overload; 2-2-1. Depend on outside shots   , corners   , sides   , key under   . Drive - vs. M-T-M   , vs. Zone   . Is their M-T-M aggressive   .
Their Best Drivers #   , Set shot #   , Jump shot #   , Rebounder #   , Ball hawk #   . Who is their poorest foul shooter #   , are their substitutes strong   , do they tire in 4th quarter   .

LEGEND:
If shot is made circle No.; J means Jump; S means Set; T means Tap; D means Drive; G means Garbage. If shot is missed, plain number.

DIAGRAM 15.1

PERSONAL STUDY OF SCOUTING REPORT

The report would be the basis of homework for the entire staff. We would study it and get a mental picture of our opponents, plan our match-ups, analyze our opponent's offense and defense, possible surprises, and special tactics.

Next, we would prepare our game plan. If they played a tight defense, we would screen. If they used the zone, we would attack its weaknesses. If it was a driving team, we would float. We would play their scorers tight, hawk the star, play to the strength of the individuals, and plan our substitutions.

TEAM MEETING

In the team meeting we would use the blackboard to discuss the opponents individually and as a team. Then we would outline our game plan—our individual and team offense and defense. Next, our special strategy. Here we might discuss some mistakes made previously against similar teams and make sure we did not repeat them in this game. We might beat ourselves once—never twice!

COURT WORK

We would start with half-court and slow motion application of opponent's players and our planned match-ups. Lou would review and show the moves, strengths, and weaknesses of the individual opponents.

A question and answer period would follow, and Lou would demonstrate through slow motion moves the match-ups in operation.

The opponent's team offense and defense (half-court) would follow in the same manner with slow motion action. Then we would speed it up. Finally, we would go full-court, first in slow motion and finishing up with full speed.

DAY BEFORE THE GAME

We would review once more the opponent's offense and defense, then discuss our game plan, conduct a question and answer period, and finish with a light workout.

DAY OF GAME

Reporting time was at least an hour and a half before the time to go out on the court for our warmup. Here we would conduct a last-minute review and briefly detail once more our game plan. Then, just before time to go out on the court, we would back off and let everyone do a little thinking on their own. We never went for pep talks. We felt that our game preparations sufficed to bring our players up to the game in the proper frame of mind.

THE COACH'S PERSONAL PREPARATIONS

Not all game preparations are directed toward the players. The coach should prepare for *his* part in the game, and it should not be restricted to worrying about the outcome. He should plan his personal action and decisions on the bench—game plan and possible changes; special strategy (use of the stall or freeze with the clock running out when ahead or behind in the score, one-shot plays, etc.); player or game situations that may require changes in substitutions; personal decisions regarding player fouls; team fouls; time-outs (own team as well as opponents), and all the ramifications of bench coaching.

CHAPTER 16

WIN
THE TOURNAMENTS

G AME PREPARATIONS as discussed in Chapter 15 are related to a specific and scheduled opponent. Preparing for tournament opponents is not quite as simple. The scheduled opponent is usually known a year in advance. Not so with respect to tournament opponents. The preparations discussed in the previous chapter would certainly apply after the teams had been invited or qualified, but that would be too late to get ready for tournment play. I like to think and get my players to thinking about the tournaments before the season even begins. I hope the checklist which follows will be of help in preparing the reading coach's team to win the tournament.

THE BIG GOAL

Although we prepare for our opponents "one at a time," I want my players to know we are pointing for a postseason tournament as well as a holiday festival along the way. This setting of our sights on a tournament is naturally more psychological than physical, but I make sure to plant the seed.

Mob scene following 1965 National Invitational championship victory. Coach Joe Lapchick in middle of "mob" of cheering fans and students. Final step of 1964–1965 "second" Grand Slam (Holiday Festival and National Invitational).

Joe Lapchick holds the National Invitational Tournament trophy after his St. John's Redmen defeated Bradley for the championship March 21, 1959. Left to right: Dickengert, Trainer; Players Gus Alfieri; Lou Roethel; Coach Joe Lapchick; Assistant Coach, Lou Carnesecca. Al Seiden (No. 33) was high scorer with 22 points. Gus Alfieri, No. 11, wrapped up the game on a three-point play with 30 seconds to go in the overtime period. (UPI Photo)

Coach Joe Lapchick on bench with three of the victorious Redman stars after St. John's won the Holiday Festival tournament in 1964. Left to right: Ken McIntyre, Coach Joe Lapchick, Sonny Dove, Bob McIntyre. (UPI Photo)

Coach Joe Lapchick on shoulders of players following victory over Michigan in 1965 Holiday Invitational tournament to win championship. Left to right: Ass't. Coach Lou Carnesecca, Bob McIntyre, Billy Jones, Ken Wirrel, Coach Joe Lapchick, Ken McIntyre, Hank Cluess. (UPI Photo)

In thinking of the psychological approach, I well remember the 1945 National Invitational Tournament when a bit of psychology may have helped us to put together two tourney championships back to back. We had won the 1944 tournament but had lost three great stars to the armed forces—Harry Boykoff, a 6-9 center; Fuzzy Levane, a great leader and rebounder; and Larry Baxter, an outstanding back-court operator.

The 1945 tournament was unusual in that there were three great All-America "big men" on the rosters of the contenders. Oklahoma A & M (now Oklahoma State) had 7-foot Bob Kurland; Bowling Green featured 6-11 Don Otten; and De Paul boasted of big George Mikan, who was 6-9!

As defending champions, we weren't given much of a chance and were seeded seventh in the eight-team field. We held our last practice before the tournament in the Garden. After the workout I figured I would give the players something to think about. Calling them over to the sideline, I said, "The winner of this tournament is going to play the winner of the NCAA Tournament in a Red Cross benefit game. As you know, Ned Irish gives local college players little jobs helping out around the Garden that night and he wanted to know how many of you fellows he could count on."

There was a dead silence. Then one of the players said, "What do you mean, *work*, Coach? We're going to be right out here *playing* that night!"

"Right!" another player said.

"Say that again!" someone added.

"And how!" the rest chorused.

That was the reaction before the tournament, and that was the way the kids played in going on to beat De Paul and big George Mikan in the finals to win it all.

That championship game was the one in which I conked out with five minutes of the second half gone. Mikan had just fouled out of the game and we were ahead by five. Suddenly I realized that St. John's was going to win it all. Win it all with a new bunch of kids who, with the exception of Gotkin, were playing in the tournament for the first time.

That's when the lights went out on me, and when I came out of it, there were only five minutes left to play in the game, and our guys were 12 points ahead. We won the game, and during the dressing room celebration, Garry Schumacher, our public relations man, said, "Joe, you dealt strategy a hell of a blow tonight!"

IMPORTANCE OF SCHEDULE

Competition should become increasingly strong as the season draws to a close, in order to bring the team up to a peak.

CATALOGUING THE STRONG TEAMS

On the college level it is a good idea to keep a folder on the strong teams met during the season as well as those not on the schedule. The national press services rate the leading college teams (usually the first 20 teams) and many papers in the various states do likewise with respect to high school teams.

Keeping files on these teams and including scouting notes, newspaper clippings, previous season's films, consulting enthusiastic graduates, coaches, estimating strength of their opponents, and checking the box scores will be important when tournament time rolls around. Several of these teams *may* be included in the tournament selections.

TRIP AND TOURNAMENT ORGANIZATION

A standard trip organization should be developed so that coaches, managers, players, and the press may be aware of the procedure. This organization of the trip and tournament procedures should be put into effect during the in-season trips so players, managers, coaches, and members of the press may become acquainted with them.

DEVELOPING RESERVES

There will be many opportunities during the season to develop the reserves. The experience gained by these players can be invaluable in the tournament should illness, accidents, or game fouling sideline one or more of the regulars.

REVIEWING FUNDAMENTALS

A championship team gets that way by being offensively and defensively sound. Work on the basic skills should be a part of every practice, from the first day to the last.

UNUSUAL TECHNIQUES

During the season the team should be drilled to meet offenses and defenses not normally encountered during the regular course of the season. Working out "counters" is part of the coach's job, and trying them out during regular games is important, because the players will recognize that they work during the process of a game.

When tournament time arrives, it is too late to get ready for the freeze, stall, zones, and the various presses. Make sure they are practiced offensively and defensively and give them a try from time to time in the regular season games.

MENTAL LETDOWN

As the season draws to an end, the coach and the trainer should be on the lookout for mental or physical letdown. It is good to keep in mind that staleness is a matter of the mind and that mental tiredness leads to physical letdown. A rest or a change of interests for a day or two will usually provide the pick-up needed.

PRE-TOURNAMENT PRACTICE

While waiting for a tournament bid or for the tournament to begin, the team should continue regular practices. After the last game, provided a week or ten days remains before the first game of the tournament, the players may be given a day or two off from all basketball. I have found that my players are eager to practice and usually find time on their own for a workout. There should be no long vacation in the workouts. It may be wise to shorten the practices, but the players should be kept going at top speed.

At the end of the season there is a natural inclination to relax. However, I feel it is foolish to let the high level of condition the players have reached go by the boards. As a professional player who averaged over a hundred games a season interspersed with long, grueling hours of travel between stops, I know how quickly the body bounces back.

TYPE OF OFFICIATING

When the site of the tournament is known, it is wise to check on the officials who are usually called upon to work the games. A skull session regarding their interpretations of the rules and their strictness or leniency in making calls is desirable.

GAME STRATEGY

The game plan and probable strategy should be discussed and practiced at this time. Such important tactics as use of zones, presses, the freeze, stall, fouling to get the ball when behind, trying to steal the ball, double-teaming and the importance of the bonus rule in winning the close ones can be stressed.

CHECKING CONTESTANTS

When invitations have been concluded, the coach and his staff should immediately attempt to determine the seedings, the brackets, and possible opponents. Then, all the material in regard to each of the opponents to be met should be assembled, along with available scouting notes, so that a game plan can be prepared. Now is the time to set up the offensive and defensive counterattacks and practice them, as well as review the freeze, stall, situation plays, and the press.

During the interim before departing for the tournament site, there should be a regular practice schedule. Now that the team has been assured a spot in the tournament, everyone should be looking ahead and getting ready for the first game.

ARRIVAL AT TOURNAMENT SITE

I feel that an early arrival is important. Getting settled before the mad rush of the tournament gets under way and setting up a regular daily schedule is important. Hotel arrangements should be made well in advance and preferably at a hotel some distance removed from the playing site.

An early arrival will provide the players with a chance to get their bearings and escape the excitement, noise, and rushing about which is present when the tournament games are about to get under way. Definite rules must be established with respect to visits from friends, well-wishers, students, fans, and parents. A reunion can be held at home and after the tournament. The team came to play!

TIME SCHEDULE

A time schedule which will establish regularity in the daily routine is important. The players are under tremendous emotional stress and an irregular time schedule will add to the pressure. Placing them on a regular time schedule will tone down much of the excitement to which they would otherwise be exposed. The schedule should include the following:

(a) Rising
(b) Meals
(c) Rest Periods

(d) Relaxation
 Walks
 Entertainment
(e) Attendance at Tournament Games
(f) Practices
(g) Physical Check-ups and Injury Treatments
(h) Bedtime

THE BIG GAME

Now I invite all of the readers of this book to join me "on the bench" in Madison Square Garden and live with me through my last game as a coach. To those readers who have never coached, who have never suffered through the long, never-ending minutes of a close or championship game, the following abbreviated recording of my thoughts and feelings may seem to be pure fiction. Not so! It is pure truth and reflects my thinking, emotions, and reactions to the game.

Hundreds of coaches go through the same excruciating pressure experience in game after game each season. The big difference is that this is a record of my thinking, actions, and feelings in my final game as a coach.

Well, here we are again. Just like last year. Everyone said we were just another team at the beginning of the year and the tournament committee seeded us next to last only a week ago. But here we are in the championship game against top-seeded Villanova.

I can feel the tension building up in my chest, but I don't know how there can possibly be room for anything more. The tension is building up in the crowd, too . . .

This is it, Joe Lapchick. This is your last game and it hurts. But I'm standing out here in front of the bench in Madison Square Garden and my insides are clawing like a couple of wildcats in a fight and I don't know whether or not I'll ever get another deep breath but I'd rather be right here than any other place in the world.

Oh, oh, here comes the National Anthem and in a minute or two the kids will be out there battling for the works. The kids have all the information. We practiced two hours yesterday against Villanova's zone and combination defense and we have our game plan down pat. We're going to move the ball and keep moving it until we get what we want— a good shot underneath or over a good screen. Our "game word" today, as it has been every game this season, is *patience* . . .

No one can say much of anything but good about this bunch of kids, no matter what happens today. They've come a long, long way. Mostly on hustle. Now, I've got one more thing to do today and that's to be alive on the bench so my kids will be alive out there on the court. They say a coach's biggest job is to motivate his players. Well, I didn't have to motivate or "get them up" for this game. Fact is, I tried to keep them down . . .

The officials are moving out to the center of the court and the kids are huddled and they're waiting for me to join in the team clasp but I'm holding back. Don't think for a second, Joe Lapchick, that the kids aren't thinking the same thing you are. It's the last game for some of them but they *all* know as well as you do that it's *your* last time to send a team out on the floor. This is more than a championship game to them— it's a crusade.

I never felt game pressure like I'm feeling it today. Well, Joe, get on with it . . .

"O. K., gang—let's go!"

My eyes are closed and I'm saying a little prayer for the kids but I can feel them closing in. Now I'm clasping hands with the starters and some of the other kids can't make it but they're leaning over me and gripping my arms and crowding together and we're going to fall down as sure as . . . They break, just in time, too, and there goes the starting team out on the floor and— Listen to that crowd!

Lou and the rest of the kids are lined up beside me and I wonder if any coach ever thought about the huddle the way I'm thinking about it right now. For the life of me I can't think of any action in life that's more expressive of the closeness of a gang and their dedication to a cause than when a bunch of players huddle on a sideline. It's been a long road with enough action along the way to fill a couple of lifetimes and for the life of me I don't know where the years have gone . . .

They're jockeying for positions now and the only thing left for me to do is help them win this last game, the biggest victory of my life, my last chance for a grand slam . . .

The ball is up and Sonny leaps but Washington got the tap. Villanova has the ball and I'll get a look at their offense. As if I didn't know what they're going to do. They're going to give the ball to Melchionni and he's going to shoot. O.K., let him shoot. It's their defense that I'm worried about. Huh! Kraft and his combination defenses . . .

One thing is for sure. I don't have to worry about our defense. My kids always play good defense.

Our ball. Now we'll see what kind of a defense they're going to use. It's the combination, all right. Move the ball, gang, and be patient. Make them come to you. Now you're working. Good shot, Sonny. We're out in front.

Things are looking up. We're playing our game and we're moving steadily ahead. You've got the better team, Joe Lapchick. You've got to believe that. The kids have sure earned your respect. You keep that in mind . . .

We're still going. Kenny is looking great on his screen shots and Sonny and Bob are hitting underneath. This is too good to be true. Less than five minutes to go in the half and we're out in front by twelve. No! Fourteen! Hmmm, Melchionni must really be sick. He's only got two points so far.

Fourteen points ahead. Not enough!

There goes Washington. Two in a row! Another. And another. Eight straight points. We gotta get on him.

Keep moving the ball, gang. Make 'em come to you. Hmmm, out in front by eight points and fifteen seconds to go. Our ball.

"One shot, gang!"

Move it, now. Seven seconds.

"Shoot!"

No good. There goes the buzzer. First half. Thirty-six to twenty-eight.

Guess I'd better hustle into the dressing room. Wish it was all over. No, I don't mean that. This is my last game. I've got to enjoy every second of it because this game has to last a long, long time. All the time I've got left, I guess.

What am I going to say to the kids? What can you say when a team is hustling like they are and following the game plan to the letter? Gotta put pressure on that Washington, though. Hmmm . . .

Quiet in here. The kids know me as well as I know them and they know I'm pleased. Well, I am. I won't say much. Just let everyone rest out the minutes and pat a couple of them on the head. Heck! I'm not going to say anything! They know what we have to do . . .

There's one thing I can do. I can say a little prayer for the kids and their fight for glory. And I'll thank the good Lord for the opportunity he gave me to work with them.

Out we go. Pandemonium! This crowd cheered every move we made in the first half, and now they're at it again. They want this one for the kids. For Joe Lapchick, too, I guess . . .

We got the tap. Good! Villanova is in a man-to-man defense. That's different. They're playing it tight and good. Real good. Too good! Washington is taking the play away from Sonny. Bad shot, Bob!

Villanova ball. They hit! They're closing up on us!

"Time! Time-out."

The kids are coming slowly and confidently to the bench. There is no sign of panic or even worry on their faces. This gang thrives on pressure.

Wish I could. I've got to snap Sonny out of it. Good boy, Sonny. But he's only a youngster and a sophomore and he's tired . . .

Sonny reminds me of Boykoff. Same nice kind of kid.

Jerry and Kenny and Bob—those kids have ice water in their veins. For all the emotion that shows in their faces, they could be birdwatching.

"Keep moving the ball, gang, and be patient. Sonny! Box out Washington and start beating him to his spot. Another thing—move on him.

"Jerry, Kenny, good shots now. Only good ones. All right, keep going, gang!"

I put out my hand and they clasp it and walk back out on the court as calmly as if they were sauntering down a country lane. Never will understand it.

I need a drink of water. I remember how I used to kick the water bucket when I rode the bench right here in the Garden with the Knickerbockers. Things are different now. Not like the old days. If a guy takes a deep breath when he's on the bench, he insults an official. Huh! Bench rules!

Villanova is still pushing us but my kids are playing good defense. The score is getting closer and there's only a little more than a minute left. We're only leading by two and we're into the last minute. The kids are doing a good job freezing the old apple.

"No cross-court passes, Jerry!"

I better take another time-out . . .

"Time-out!"

I watch them closely as they come over to the huddle and they all look as if it's all pie and ice cream. How do they get that way? I'm dying . . .

"Now, listen, Jerry, Ken, Bob. Move the ball and play for a driving shot. No cross-court passes now. Everyone comes to the ball, right? Clear out of there, Sonny. Try to get Washington out of there too."

The Garden is a bedlam. I'm yelling too! The kids look as fresh as daisies. Look at Lou. He's yelling and jumping up and down but there's no way of knowing what he's yelling about. Everyone's yelling as the clock ticks out the last seconds. Boy, a minute can be a long time . . .

Great guy, this kid Lou. Gonna be a great coach too. If it had to be anyone to take over when I retire, I'm glad it's going to be Lou Carnesecca.

Villanova isn't giving up! They're pressing now. Melchionni has been out of this game a long time but you would never know it the way the rest of them are playing.

Two-point lead and if they get the ball, anything can happen . . .

Zzz! That was close!

We gotta drive pretty soon. Gosh, I feel just like I did in the championship game back in '44 when we were playing De Paul and Mikan. I really conked out in *that* game.

Boy, I feel terrible. This stomach of mine is for the birds. *"Give the ball to Jerry!"*

"No! Kenny, no!"

I remember the fifth foul on Mikan. I can still see him walking off the court, but I sure didn't see the kids score those thirteen straight points during the time I was out . . .

Is this game ever going to end? Two-point lead and only seconds to go. Must be something wrong with the clock . . .

There goes Jerry. "Lou! He's gonna drive!"

"FOUL! FOULED HIM! Sure he did! Everyone in the place saw it. Two shots! Good call!"

"Sink 'em, Jerry. Sink 'em both!"

Ten seconds left.

If he makes one of 'em, they'll have to drive in for a three-point play. We're not going to foul if they do. Let them have the two points. I can't look at this.

"Drop it in, Jerry! Good. That makes it three points."

"One more, Jerry. One more, boy. Two of 'em, Jerry!"

Good! He made 'em both . . .

You don't suppose they could . . . Maybe! It's been done . . .

No! They can't. It's impossible— There's the buzzer! That's it! We win, we win, we WIN!

"What a way to go! WHAT A WAY TO GO!"

This crowd is crazy and I'm crazy too and I'm dying and I'll never go through this again and I couldn't if I wanted to but it's great and even if it is the last, it's great . . .

"Yes, yes, yes. And thanks! Sure, just great! The kids did it just like I knew they would."

It's the end, all right . . .

"Hey! Sonny, Bob, Jerry, Bob, Ken— You guys *did* it! YOU WON IT ALL! Do you know *that?*"

"I know, I know. I know you did. You're the greatest."

What a team and what a way to go . . .

"What a way to go . . ."

This brings me to the end of the book, and I am glad it ends on a championship note. It's great to stand in the winner's circle with the kids, but it's out of this world to do it twice in the same year.

Coach Joe Lapchick receiving the National Invitational trophy after St. John's beat DePaul March 26, 1944. Jack Coffey, Athletic Director at Fordham University, made the presentation. Left to right: Ivy Summer; Bill Kotsores; Ray Wertis; Norm Major; Coach Joe Lapchick; Murray Robinson; Don Wier; Tom Larkin; Jack Coffey; Ed Hurley; Hy Gotkin— Captain; Wade Duym and Trainer Joe Scotland. Coach Joe Lapchick appears solemn here for good reason. This is the game in which Joe "dealt strategy a great blow" by collapsing during the game. (UPI Photo)

Commander James W. Liebertz, United States Merchant Marine Academy, presents 1958 Holiday Festival trophy to Coach Joe Lapchick. This was the first step in the 1958–1959 grand slam because Joe's team won the National Invitational championship three months later on March 21, 1959. (See next picture)

When St. John's University entrusted their coaching job to me, I possessed one extremely valuable asset. I could put myself in the shoes of the players. I knew how they felt and how to treat them. I knew when to push and when to pull. I have made many mistakes, and all of them were because I was satisfied with the team. When you are satisfied, you are settling for mediocrity. With this thought in mind, I periodically took stock of myself. And I did the same with my teams.

Championships came again and again. The greatest of all was to win the National Invitational Tournament as my coaching career came to a close. That was NIT Championship number four. No other coach has done that! And no other coach has won a Holiday Festival Tournament and the NIT championship in the same year.

The tournament victories convinced me that I belonged, that I had won a place with the great coaches of the game. This idea was accentuated by the fact that I was offered several college jobs as well as a professional coaching position following my retirement at St. John's. Today I am a businessman, active in the basketball shoe business, and there is no longer a pressure cooker to activate my thinking and living. I am at peace.

I was thrilled when I entered the Hall of Fame as a member of the great Celtic team. Then, to top it off, I was inducted into the Hall of Fame as a professional player. The race is won and the trials and tribulations, ups and downs, losses and victories all add up to fifty glorious and wonderful years of basketball.

INDEX